REIMAGINII.

CULTURE
AND
ECONOMIC
LIFE

REIMAGINING MONEY

Kenya in the Digital Finance Revolution

SIBEL KUSIMBA

STANFORD UNIVERSITY PRESS
STANFORD, CALIFORNIA

Stanford University Press
Stanford, California

Printed in the United States of America on acid-free, archival-quality paper
Library of Congress Cataloging-in-Publication Data

Names: Kusimba, Sibel Barut, 1966- author.
Title: Reimagining money : Kenya in the digital finance revolution / Sibel
    Kusimba.
Other titles: Culture and economic life.
Description: Stanford, California : Stanford University Press, 2021.
Series: Culture and economic life | Includes bibliographical references
    and index.
Identifiers: LCCN 2020020346 (print) | LCCN 2020020347 (ebook) |
    ISBN 9781503613515 (cloth) | ISBN 9781503614413 (paperback) |
    ISBN 9781503614420 (ebook)
Subjects: LCSH: Digital currency—Kenya. | Digital currency—Social
    aspects—Kenya.
Classification: LCC HG1710 .K877 2021 (print) | LCC HG1710 (ebook) |
    DDC 332.4—dc23
LC record available at https://lccn.loc.gov/2020020346

LC ebook record available at https://lccn.loc.gov/2020020347

Cover illustration: A drawing of a digital microloan network

Cover design: Rob Ehle

Typeset by Newgen in 10/14 Minion Pro

Contents

Figures and Tables

FIGURES

TABLES

Acknowledgments

Any research project is a collective effort. There are so many people who made this book possible and without whom the project never would have been realized. I would like to thank the funders, research participants, hosts, friends, colleagues, supporters, and interlocutors who made it all happen. Many of my interlocutors cannot be named, but I express to all of them my gratitude. The research reported here was conducted based on anthropological fieldwork in Kenya beginning in 2009 when I was a Fulbright Scholar teaching at Egerton University in Kenya. Thank you to the U.S. Department of State, and to Simiyu Wandibba of the Institute for African Studies at the University of Nairobi, who has been a mentor for me for many years. I would like to also thank Egerton University and its Department of History for hosting my stay. Bernadette Wambui Kusimba, along with Julie, Jordan, Alan, and Ivy, shared their loving and generous home with me. It was a hive of activity and full of relatives. My brother-in-law also helped me arrive in style and make a splash with the U.S. Embassy. Bernadette, thank you for teaching me what an African household is and for showing what a loving Kenyan family is all about. At Egerton, I would also like to thank Susan, Liz, and Albert Lagat and their children for their support and friendship. I would like to thank Lillian Musombi, Joyner Nanjulula, and Stephanie Luti for being amazing roommates, nieces, research participants and team members, and fashion stylists.

I would also like to thank Elizabeth Gross and John Terrell for teaching me social network analysis through an excellent class that John Terrell offered at the University of Illinois at Chicago and the Field Museum. My many supportive colleagues at the Field Museum, the University of Illinois, Lawrence University, the Smithsonian Institution, and Northern Illinois University have provided me with the best examples and advice anyone could ever follow, including R. Barry Lewis, Winifred Creamer, Fred Smith, Carla Daughtry, Peter Peregrine, Natasha Gray, Jonathan Haas, Michael Kolb, Andrea Molnar, Leila Porter, Bennet Bronson, Deborah Stokes, Kendall Thu, Judy Ledgerwood, Sue Russell, John Terrell, Chuimei Ho, Alaka Wali, Dan Gebo, and Mark Schuller. I would also like to thank the University of South Florida Department of Anthropology for their welcome and their support.

The Institute for Money, Technology, and Financial Inclusion (IMTFI) at the University of California, Irvine, supported the fieldwork in Kenya described in this book in 2012, 2014, 2015, and 2016. IMTFI also provided travel support to attend the Mobile Money Research Day Conference, held by Professor Susan Johnson at the University of Bath in 2016, and the Society for American Ethnology Conference in San Diego, California, in 2015. IMTFI conferences brought together many experts from different disciplines to exchange ideas. The conferences, website, and digital network, including a blog, helped create a community of practice around the complex issues of financial inclusion. Without this support, community, and access to specialized knowledge through IMTFI, this book would never have happened. I would like to thank Jenny Fan, lead administrator of IMTFI, and the board members of IMTFI, along with all of the postdoctoral scholars and the many scholars and researchers associated with the institute who have shared ideas with me, including but not limited to Ivan Small, Smoki Musaraj, Mrinalini Tankha, Ursula Dalinghaus, Solène Morvant-Roux, Milcah Mulu-Mutuku, Ndungu Kiiti, Maria Elisa Balen, Magdalena Villareal, Vivian Dzokoto, Simiyu Wandibba, Jenna Burrell, Isabelle Guérin, Taylor Nelms, and Stephen Rea, for their Bill and Melinda comments and for sharing their knowledge and interest in the topic. I would especially like to thank IMTFI director Bill Maurer for being an example through his enthusiasm and scholarship for what an anthropological view might contribute and for his incisive comments on journal articles and reports. I would like to thank Dave Kim of the Bill and Melinda Gates Foundation, Kyai Mullei, Dr. Andrew Mullei, and Dave Mark of M-Changa, and the people at Busara, Inc., and ThinkPlace for involving me in the M-Changa fundraising project. My many hosts, participants, friends, field team members and collaborators, and interlocutors were generous with their hospitality, knowledge, and friendship.

For assistance in the field I would like to express my gratitude to Andrew Nakhisa and Simon Nabie, and to our team, Gabriel Kunyu, Harpieth Chaggar, Joyner Nanjulula Musombi, Alex Wanyama, Cristabel Waluse, and Chap Kusimba. I could not have done the research without them. Thank you also to those known in this book as Dorcas, Marianne, Violet, Praxides, Consolata, Mary, Emmanuel, and the many other participants. A special thanks goes to Gabriel Kunyu, whom I first met as a student at Egerton University. Gabriel has worked with me on each of the three IMTFI grants and on the M-Changa project. He was a crucial link to communities and research participants around Bungoma. I have seen his skills as an ethnographer develop. He is a deep listener. The drawing exercise was born through his example of patience and presence. Chap Kusimba made sure the team always had food, transportation, and safety and brought an intimate familiarity with the community and its concerns to the project. He was very careful to document our activities with excellent photographic skills. We have shared this home of Western Kenya, which has become my home, over many years. Thank you, Chap. And at my other home, I would like to thank Suzan and Jonathan Filley and their family, and my parents, A. O. Barut and Pierrette Barut, for the footsteps to walk in, and Jesse Kusimba and Eve Kusimba for all the joy of these past twenty-five years.

I want to extend my gratitude to Susan Johnson of the University of Bath, an authority on the social dimensions of finance in Kenya, for sharing her work and perspectives on finance inclusion landscapes. She generously provided comments on my articles and papers and during a Nairobi conference call also helped the M-Changa team think about how the project should be positioned. She invited me to an important event that she organized, the University of Bath Mobile Money Research Day, and her comments on that paper, which was eventually published in the *African Studies Review*, greatly improved the work. At Bath, I was able to meet Maia Green, of the University of Manchester, whose work in Tanzania has been an important guide for me as well.

The Society for Economic Anthropology (SEA) is an active research group that made possible the Wealth in People Conference, which I chaired together with Ty Matejowsky at the University of Central Florida. I would like to thank Ty Matejowsky, Bram Tucker, Dolores Koenig, Nora Haenn, Brandon Lundy, Daniel Souleles, Dawn Rivers, Caela O'Connell, Anya Bonanno, Andrew Bonanno, Maia Green, Aaron Pitluck, Cynthia Isenhour, Dillon Mahoney, Courtney Lewis, and the many other SEA members and participants. Aaron Pitluck, Daniel Souleles, and Fabio Mattioli chaired an excellent SEA conference on financialization. In working with me to develop my paper, Aaron Pitluck pointed me in a crucial turn toward the Zelizer view of relational work and media of exchange.

I would like to thank Nina Bandelj, whose writings on relational work and cultural wealth have also enriched my understanding of Kenya and for organizing an exciting Society for the Advancement of Socio-Economics panel on relational work with Smitha Radhakrishnan, Cheris Shun-Ching Chan, Fred Wherry, and Alya Guseva. I would also like to thank Erik Bähre for his scholarship on South Africa and for inviting me to the conference Moralizing Misfortune at the University of Leiden. This excellent event, especially through comments from Susanna Narotzky, helped me position this book to unite anthropological and sociological perspectives. Erik also got involved in the SEA conference Wealth in People and provided a thought-provoking keynote address. I would like to thank John Sharp, Dare Okoudjou, Sean Maliehe, Riaan de Villiers, Stephen Nduati, Nnamdi Oranye, Jeremy Leach, Ross McEwan, Peter Vale, and especially Lena Gronbach for organizing Digital Finance in Africa's Future at the beautiful setting of the Johannesburg Institute for Advanced Study. This interdisciplinary conference helped me understand the dilemmas of entrepreneurs and regulators. I hope I have done them justice. A special thanks to John Sharp for his perspectives on the relationship between Kenya and South Africa, for his helpful comments on Chapter 2, and for a successful collaboration at the University of Pretoria in spite of a pandemic.

I would also like to thank Susan Johnson again, who recommended me to attend a stimulating conference on Dignity and Debt at Princeton University. This book would not have been written without the conference organizer Fred Wherry, editor of the Culture and Economic Life Series, who took an interest in this work and also took the time to Skype with me about the manuscript twice. These sessions were invaluable. Thank you, Fred. Both of the anonymous reviewers devoted enormous time and care to an earlier version of this manuscript. I paid great attention to their detailed comments and their pointed questions, which helped resolve a lot of the problems I was having with the manuscript. Finally, thank you to Marcela Maxfield of Stanford University Press for all her time, expertise, and support, and all of the editors and copyeditors for their help with the manuscript.

REIMAGINING MONEY

A Central Banker Talks Money

"Now we have digital money," economist Dr. Andrew Mullei, former governor of the Central Bank of Kenya, explained. "This money can be seen. With this technology you can see the fund and how it is developing. You can log on to the computer to see who has contributed." Dr. Mullei went on to contrast digital money with earlier forms. "Previously we had cash money, which came to us from British colonialism. Cash money can be hidden in the pocket. You do not see it. You do not know where it is. This hidden money brought corruption." Ironically, the money of colonial modernity had not brought Africans a more rational society, but instead had made possible mistrust, secrecy, and the pursuit of personal gain.

An economist by training, Dr. Mullei had spent a career reimagining money. As Central Bank Governor, he had set up Kenya's first interbank real-time gross settlement (RTGS) system in 2005, which ushered in the subsequent digital payments revolution.[1] He was well known for his tough stance on corruption and for going after banks involved in money laundering. At the time of our July 2016 interview he was in his seventies, semiretired and advising his son, who was CEO of a crowdfunding software platform, one of many new technology companies in Nairobi's emerging start-up scene. I had been hired as a consultant to help the company, named M-Changa (*kuchanga* means "to collect" in Swahili), to design a product as a financial tool for low-income people. Through mobile phones, they could use the M-Changa platform to conduct family and community fund-raisers, a long-standing local practice.

"In the traditional African setting, for example in my [WaKamba] community, our money was goats. You might give one to your nephew . . . you could take a stroll to your brother-in-law's compound and just pass by and see how the goat is doing. Is my brother-in-law taking good care of [the goat]? Has it reproduced?" Back in the day, Dr. Mullei explained, one of a man's duties was to maintain ties with his sister and her children after her marriage into her husband's lineage. A brother-in-law, an uncle, was a bridge across a social divide. Gifts to his nephew allowed a man to demonstrate generosity and continued involvement in his sister's welfare, and also to assess whether her husband was taking good care of the family. The goat was a gesture of trust, notwithstanding the different patrilines involved.

Dr. Mullei's story compared three kinds of money. The original money, the goat of his WaKamba community, was circulated through public gift giving. Later during colonialism, cash money replaced the goat. Colonial currency was a source of deceit and corruption because it could be individuated and hidden in pockets or bank accounts. Dr. Mullei explained that now, new forms of digital money could return Africans to their roots in shared money with value that, like the goat, can be seen. "And now with computers we have digital money . . . everyone in the fund can see the fund on their computer. You can trace the performance of each member of the kitty. How is each person contributing? How is the fund performing?" In digital money, Dr. Mullei sees a return to the original sociality of African money, a public and shared currency where visible contributions produce a group fund.

Digital payment technology is rapidly changing the use of money across the globe.[2] Although mobile payments have been slow to take off in the United States and many other countries, they are rapidly displacing cash in settings as diverse as China, Kenya, and Sweden. The Global South has been a leader in money innovation. Some readers may think of Venmo or PayPal. Actually, M-Pesa achieved popularity several years before Venmo. It does not require a smartphone, bank account, credit card, or Internet connection, but works through a network of human agents where users can cash in and out. In 2007, Kenya became the first country to use the mobile phones as a payment channel on a broad scale when the mobile phone company Safaricom launched the M-Pesa money transfer service to paying customers. Kenyans use M-Pesa to send money to friends and relatives via text messaging and to store money on a phone-based mobile wallet. Marketed as a remittance service for urban migrants under the slogan "Send Money Home," the M-Pesa mobile money transfer service soon became part of daily life.

For Dr. Mullei, most important properties of money either make money hidden or make money visible. Many others in banking and finance are similarly inspired to consider how money's material form changes its work in society. Scholars, investors, and everyday money users are following suit. For them, Kenya offers a window into the future of money as reimagined by new communicative and digital technologies. As a laboratory of design and policy innovations, this country is producing new experiments in digital money and digital financial services (DFS), including banking, credit, insurance, crowdfunding, fundraising, peer-to-peer lending, sports betting, e-commerce, government payments to and from citizens, treasury bonds, and paying for utility services such as electricity, water, and solar power. Kenya is a laboratory of innovation[3] and one of the few market success stories for mobile money. It is a site for reimagining money within an emerging consumer financial system and based on a mobile payment channel. Over the past ten years these innovations have produced a new commercial space for digital entrepreneurial innovation called the Silicon Savanna.[4]

Digital Money in Kenya: What's at Stake?

Amartya Sen wrote in a 2010 essay, "The Mobile and the World," that the mobile phone was the greatest development tool ever invented.[5] It forged a link to reach billions of people at the speed of light with information, communication, and new kinds of services. New monetary technologies promising to reach customers at the last mile have brought a flock of interests and billions of dollars to the project of financially including the unbanked. M-Pesa's success has captivated observers, investors, academics, and policymakers who envision an investment space and a development opportunity to spur poverty reduction, women's empowerment, and financial inclusion. Mobile network providers, technology start-ups, payments companies, and, increasingly, major Internet platforms like Facebook are developing their own monies. The rapidly evolving world of financial technology, or fintech, is now considering the roles of blockchain, cryptocurrencies, and super platform (Google and other Internet giants) monies. Especially for technology entrepreneurs, one microfinance expert wrote, "there is so much energy, creative thinking and money going into this space, it is breathtaking."[6]

Swept up by all this innovation, the field of development is getting involved, and embracing the promise of digital finance to reduce poverty—notwithstanding the finance and microfinance crises of the last decade.[7] As a World Bank economist wrote, "To eradicate poverty, achieve gender equality, provide quality education, or meet any of the United Nation[s'] Sustainable Development Goals (SDGs), we must begin by creating a financially inclusive world."[8] Socially minded investors in the West are supporting products for the developing world like digital credit via mobile phone.[9] Studies purporting to provide evidence that mobile money reduces poverty are widely touted.

On the one hand, claims of financial inclusion and poverty reduction are supported by household economic studies showing that remittances help poor households maintain consumption levels in the face of sudden emergency events—shoring up their resilience—and invest more in farming needs.[10] A widely cited study[11] claimed that access to mobile money agents lifted 194,000 households out of poverty and enabled them to drop farming for other income activities like small businesses (why farming is undesirable is unclear). The numbers make an appealing headline. However, the study does not explain why these households held more money. The study measured only proximity to a mobile money agent. The authors suggest an array of possible causes for the households' increased receipts, such as more wage work or income, money transfers, value storage, use of digital microloans, change in occupation or investment, shifts away from farming, or internal migration—not all of which imply less poverty in either the short term or the long term. Like many studies, this one does not provide enough context, and does not explain the change.

On the other hand, other work is questioning any direct relationship between digital finance and desirable outcomes like poverty reduction and financial inclusion. Although digital payments are proliferating globally, they are not leading to use of formal banking; an analysis of survey data in six countries found that the financial inclusion effort had stalled—accounts often lie empty.[12] Another review found that financial interventions have small and variable effects on income, assets, and health.[13] Beyond the hype, many are asking deeper questions about digital money as they weigh what is at stake for the poor. The enthusiasm is waning as problems with new money technologies mount and providers fail to glean profit.[14] People in rural areas struggle with poor mobile networks, understanding how to use technology, and the high costs of phones and services.[15] Taxes are allowing governments to extract more value from users. Hacking, fraud, and customer data surveillance and breaches have taken people's money. Widespread use of digital small loans is miring poor people in debt.[16] All of these problems raise the prospect that new monies will leave the poor, illiterate, digitally invisible, or disabled excluded or even harmed, while fintech innovations, ranging from cryptocurrency investment funds to mobile banking, to low-cost consumer credit, to e-commerce, to data-based products and marketing become the domain of wealthy investors, and consumers and companies. In fact, financial experts and everyday people all over the world have misgivings about a new cashless future and its potential to create barriers, exploit or steal data and personal information, and obscure forms of extraction.[17]

Is money on a phone bringing banking inclusion, and is this inclusion a benefit? Is digital finance reducing poverty or is it creating new divides? With billions of dollars of investment at stake, these questions need answers. A lot of reports are being written and a lot of data are being generated by academics and industry researchers to measure impact. Trawling through the abundant studies fails to yield a clear evaluation of how digital finance affects poverty, if at all. There is no consistent story on whether these innovations actually work and, when they do, why.

The Value of Context and Ethnography

Much of the data generated to evaluate or support financial inclusion are based on surveys that try to measure growth in bank or mobile accounts, the frequency of usage, gender gaps, or the percentage of non-performing digital loans. Studies called rigorous use experiments to show effects for a study group as compared to those for a similar control group. Fewer studies still use a financial diary approach that models the household as a firm and tracks income and expenditures—these provide incredible detail, down to daily spending, but without rigorous attention to why financial and consumer choices are made. All of these kinds of studies have an important role to play. They all prioritize measurement. They say less about the context and the specific kinds of people involved, and even less about why and how different kinds of people are doing what they are doing and why change might be happening. Measurements abound, but far less attention is being paid to what is being measured—the problems of context and definition, the intentions and desires of different users, how to operationalize concepts, and how to recognize definitions of success across very different settings and kinds of people. What are we actually measuring?

Finally, researchers in financial inclusion by and large do not think very much about money and its varying ends and uses. They often take for granted its function as economic agency, asking few of the broader questions that Dr. Mullei pointed me toward. Mobile phone money is often viewed as a delivery mechanism to a last-mile customer, and not as an agent of change in itself.

What is missing is context, observation, and a user perspective. This book tries to correct the balance. Instead of testing hypotheses and measuring detail, I have used a more inductive approach that asks what money is, what it does, and what it means, and that tries to get at local understandings of wealth, relationships, and well-being.[18] My goal has been to focus on context and on people's intentions with money. I describe unique people and their different degrees of access, their strategies and goals, and the outcomes they achieve. Through these ethnographic studies, I will show that mobile money has created new divides and barriers that are social and technological. Furthermore, having access to digital finance does not benefit people in the straightforward ways that one might expect. In some cases, people are even being harmed, economically and socially, by these technologies.

The findings in this book are based on fieldwork conducted from 2009 to 2018 in Western Kenya, including the towns and hamlets of Kimilili, Bungoma, and Naitiri, and in Nairobi, Kenya. This research has been funded by the Fulbright Senior Scholar Program of the U.S. Department of State, which sponsored me as a lecturer at Egerton University from 2009 to 2010. In 2012, 2014–2015, and 2016–2017, this research was funded by three grants from the Institute for Money, Technology, and Financial Inclusion (IMTFI) at the University of California, Irvine. Also in 2016 and 2017, I served as a consultant to Changa Labs, where I worked with the crowdfunding platform M-Changa, the human-centered design firm ThinkPlace, and the behavioral economics consultancy Busara Center for Behavioral Economics. Above all, I rely on my understandings based on "deep hanging out" during several decades as an anthropologist working in Kenya and as an in-law to a Western Kenya family (I apologize for abusing the privilege).[19]

The research involved multiple methods, including semi-structured interviews, unstructured interviews, social network analysis, coproduced drawings, questionnaires, focus groups, human-centered design, and analysis of customer data from the M-Changa company. In 2009 I began interviews with Egerton University students and staff members. Work for IMTFI in Kimilili was a team effort of myself and Gabriel Kunyu, Harpieth Chaggar, Nanjulula Musombi, and Alex Wanyama. We began with 47 intercept interviews in Kimilili town about the use of M-Pesa. Using a snowball method, we then broadened and deepened the engagement with the community, conducting semi-structured interviews with 35 women around Kitale town about land access, marriage, and M-Pesa. Twenty-two women answered questionnaires about M-Pesa usage in savings groups. We also began the social networks study of family remittances, which in 2012, 2013, and 2014 collected information from more than 200 people about money transfer in order to draw 12 sociograms depicting money transfer networks of up to 70 people. In 2014 we conducted a study of coming-of-age rituals with multiple visits to 46 families in the Bungoma and Kimilili region. In 2016, we conducted a study of women's use of digital financial tools including digital microcredit, where we worked with eight women who provided diary information to us and participated in semi-structured and unstructured interviews. Also in 2016 and 2017, we involved 61 people—31 in Nairobi and 30 in Bungoma, Kitale, and Kimilili—in semi-structured interviews on their use of digital financial tools.

A Theory of Money: Wealth-in-People

We are so used to thinking of money in its mathematical character, in its ability to help us compare and measure disparate goods and services as we budget. Through money accounting, we can weigh our many acts of spending, saving, and earning against a single scale—and see how much money might be left. Money helps us make rational decisions about price, quantity, and time, and it helps us make plans for the future. But if all money is the same, then it might set up a conflict between economic rationality and everything else we do with it, whether that is to have fun, meet needs or wants, take a few risks, or help others. It might make us dispassionate and calculating.

Viviana Zelizer posits a quite different view in *The Social Meaning of Money*. In practice, we create different kinds of money all the time, using words like "gift," "allowance," "inheritance," "dividend," "fun money," and so on. We direct different streams of money toward sustaining and symbolizing distinct relationships.[20] An example comes from Zelizer's study of middle-class American women at the turn of the century, who lobbied for more status in their marriages and more control over their husbands' wages by insisting on an "allowance," which implies an entitlement, rather than merely a "gift," which implies dependence.[21] These marked forms of money or, more broadly, "media of exchange," draw the boundaries of relationships, and the power asymmetry or moral obligation they may imply.[22] Zelizer's theory of the social meaning of money does not deny money accounting but gives money decisions context and takes into account intention, relationships, emotions, and meaning— dimensions which are often undertheorized in economics.[23]

In Dr. Mullei's story, for example, an uncle's gift of a goat maintains a relationship with his married sister. He can look after her interests across the social divide that separates in-laws. Historically, anthropologists working in East Africa noted the importance of these animal gifts such as bridewealth, which sealed the deal at public events like weddings and funerals and served as a history of social alliances. Over time, such economic transfers build up a web of relationships.[24] As participants in these economic networks, people seek to accumulate ties, influence and mobilize people, and lay claim to their affection, support, resources, labor, or loyalty: wealth-in-people. These networks and communities offer inclusion to people with diverse embodied skills and knowledge; giving them both belonging "to" and belonging "in."[25] Wealth-in-people explains the popularity of digital money and how it is used in an array of practices to build relationships that channel material value. These relationships are more than just social capital; I avoid that concept because wealth-in-people is equally about both economic value and social value, and about collective and individual value, and also because the kind of value people are seeking is not just capital. Throughout this book I will unfold the idea that the use of digital money is aimed at accessing, building, distributing, accumulating, preserving, and protecting wealth-in-people.

Digital Money as Wealth-in-People

Before M-Pesa there was an even earlier mobile phone currency, airtime money. I first encountered airtime money in 2009, a form of social gifting in intimate circuits of close friends, relatives, and romantic partners. In Chapter 2, I describe how I entered into its connections and networks. Its circuits of gifting are the original wealth-in-people of digital finance. I also describe what cash-in/cash-out agents are and how agent, mobile phone, and banking networks built on airtime networks to create mobile money.

Innovators and investors are captivated by the promise of leapfrogging African money and shunting Africa ahead of the West. But the leapfrogging development narrative, as I discuss in Chapter 3, reinforces an evolutionary view, leading to an assumption that innovation in Africa is somehow surprising. Important players in the innovation story are African entrepreneurs, a local wealth-in-people. The technological path here is deviating sharply from that followed by the digital money of other regions, particularly because of the continued importance of agent networks—charting a unique future for African moneys.

For Kenyans, M-Pesa is their own money, not an imposition from the West. They lay claim to their own invention through enthusiastic storytelling, adding symbolic value to their invention and rejecting the leapfrogging trope. Their narratives, recounted in Chapter 4, emphasize local creativity and cultural wealth, pointing to informal inventions with airtime, Kenya's innovation hubs and entrepreneurial spaces, and the regulatory experts at Kenya's Central Bank as important examples of Global South innovation. Unfortunately, the attention paid to the M-Pesa miracle has been far greater than that given to the subsequent failures of digital finance. These failures include digital inequality and digital divides; the rise of indebtedness to digital microloans; and questionable uses of consumer data. Furthermore, e-money deployments across Africa have become ensnared in political conflicts over excessive taxation and fees and political patronage, and in Kenya M-Pesa provider Safaricom was the target of a consumer boycott over charges of election rigging. These dramas are challenging the value of cultural wealth. Instead, an increasingly urgent distributive politics besets digital money—who owns, regulates, and profits from the value channel?

In Chapter 5, I describe the practices and ideas of the wealth-in-people theory of value that underlies the use of digital money. What kinds of money and value have been long-standing in this area, and what strategies of wealth-in-people? How have new kinds of money been incorporated into the web of wealth-in-people? I use anthropological theory and a coming-of-age ritual as it played out in Western Kenya in 2014 and 2016 to answer these questions.

Using digital money transfer, new collectives and groups of wealth-in-people are forming. In Chapter 6, I use maps of money transfer pathways to reveal the interconnections of money transfer and show how they are embedded in social network positions and roles. Money-sending networks in families reveal important social norms around generosity and obligation relating to age, generation, and gender. I also ask my informants to draw their networks. I call their drawings "network self-portraiture." Their drawings represent different kinds of money or media through visual metaphors. Drawings of hearts, buses, and boats describe the moral and symbolic qualities of money. Self-portrait drawings can reveal the process behind social networks—the relational work[26] around money exchange. The money networks are an important means of distribution in family groups and friendship groups.

In Chapter 7, I use ethnographic information to explain how people form digital money networks. Landlessness, unemployment, inequality, and the increasing importance of cash money weigh heavily on the families I describe. Fathers fundraise for life-cycle rituals, bridewealth, and other ritual gifts with brothers, sons, and male age mates who support one another in building and bequeathing durable assets. Women use their central positions in networks of siblings, mothers, and mothers' families to help fund schooling, medical care, and everyday needs. These networks are ways of generating, circulating, distributing, and accumulating wealth-in-people: they are ways of surviving, ways of belonging, and ways of getting ahead.

As wealth-in-people circulates, people experience far more requests for money than their resources can support. They frequently work to lessen the social pressure to support others and withdraw from their networks. By disconnecting from technology, they deflect responsibility to address needs in their networks, instead adopting a liminal position of strategic ignorance.[27] These disconnections, described in Chapter 8, are not an assertion of self-interest, as might be assumed. I see these strategies of non-use as a way to protect wealth-in-people when powerful social norms that value helping, caring, and generosity collide with the scarcity of money.[28] Changeable strategies reveal the fragility of wealth-in-people, the dilemmas of responsibility, and distributive politics of informal financial practices. In this chapter I draw attention to practices of deliberate self-exclusion from financial networks.

Digital microcredit—small loans offered over the mobile phone—have been a focus of African fintech. Numerous industry-side reports justify these loans as empowering women to support their enterprises. In Chapter 9, I use a network perspective to show how these digital debts become a part of women's social and financial relationships. Women attend to weighty social obligations as they struggle to build businesses using microloans as capital. The stigma of private digital debt presents risks to their reputations. Furthermore, I show how one research participant juggles loans across her social networks, and how the hidden labor of cash-in/cash-out agents assists users in accessing and paying for loan services.

Nairobi's Silicon Savanna is an emerging fintech hub and entrepreneurial space seeking to scale innovative finance for the bottom of the pyramid. Here, a crowdfunding platform called M-Changa enables people to raise money online from across their family and friend networks. The M-Changa case study in Chapter 10 explores how wealth-in-people can be reimagined as a solution for poverty. I describe how our design team used human-centered design and behavioral economics (BE) interventions aimed at scaling the company. The lessons learned from this project throw into relief the obstacles facing Kenya's fintech scene: digital divides and inequalities of technology access, social inequalities, and deliberate self-exclusion: strategic ignorance. In Chapter 11, I summarize some design principles based on my findings.

Evaluating the impact of digital money depends on knowing what users actually do with it. This study follows money flowing through the web of relationships. As members of networks, people can help and care for others; pursue aspirations for a better life in financial clubs aimed at saving and investing; express belonging by sending gifts and contributions; find prestige and recognition by mobilizing others and solving problems; and secure assets for their communities and their heirs. But being a member of these networks also requires access to technology, social connections, collateral, and skills. People without these means may be left out or risk shame. As a result, they may through their own strategies of non-use find the margins and liminal spaces of wealth-in-people. Money networks are thus creating new divides, barriers, and inequalities, which need to be addressed if digital finance is to fulfill the promise of inclusion.

Airtime Money

2

Millions of people use various forms of mobile banking, including bank-to-phone apps, mobile payment, and phone-to-phone money transfer. Few know that the digital money revolution actually began in Africa. In 2007 the mobile network operator Safaricom rolled out its M-Pesa money transfer service. Following Safaricom's success, Kenya became among the first countries to adopt the mobile phone network as a payment system.

New monies and payment channels using digital and communication technologies actually constitute a variety of technical systems and are basically of two kinds. Many people are familiar with smartphone payment apps like ApplePay, Venmo, and WeChat Pay. These apps access existing credit card and bank payment setups.[1] M-Pesa is by contrast a different setup and actually an earlier invention. As an example of mobile money, it does not require a smartphone, bank account, credit card, or Internet connection. Rather, mobile money is a money transfer system that uses mobile phones and a network of human agents who cash in and cash out for customers, exchanging e-money as text messages for currency money. This version of mobile phone money is common in Africa, Cambodia, and Bangladesh.

To discover the origins of M-Pesa and really understand how it works, one has to dig even deeper into the story, going back to the first decades of the 2000s, and Africa's first mobile phone users. In fact, the first mobile phone currency was not mobile money, but airtime money. This invention of mobile phone users eventually inspired the money transfer system that followed. To understand everything that came afterward, one needs to understand airtime money, and the relationships, networks, and distributions it created.

The spread of the mobile phone in Africa was one of the most rapid technological diffusions in history. I began doing anthropological research in Kenya in the mid-1990s and got to see the mobile revolution firsthand. Before mobile phones, phone connectivity was rare for most people in Kenya, as in many other countries. Landlines were too expensive and limited largely to government offices, the homes of wealthier and urban residents, and some businesses. In the capital city of Nairobi, it was common to see people queued up by the hundreds to make calls outside of phone booths covered in peeling red paint. I was told that these red call boxes were London castoffs, a legacy of the colonial relationship with Great Britain. The people queuing were calling government offices or other authorities or relaying urgent news to relatives in the rural areas. Young people were selling sweets and biscuits, and more importantly, making the precious change the phones required. Social life in Kenya at that time was still face-to-face or through letters or telegrams to relatives. A group of friends would stuff into a *matatu* (minibus) and travel to the other side of town, just to see if a friend was home. You might see that person a few days later and tell them, "We came to see you, but we bounced." As late as the 1990s, phone service was also famously unreliable; one of my professors sarcastically described my repeated screaming into a faulty landline as playing "the Great East African Hello Game."

Beginning in the late 1990s, mobile phones changed all of this. By the early 2000s prepaid airtime was widely available on a "pay-as-you-go" basis via a scratch card. This accessibility for low-income users kindled the spread of mobile technology. By 2010, about one-third of sub-Saharan Africans (close to 400 million people) had purchased at least one SIM card.[2] During this decade, I had returned to Kenya frequently to conduct archaeological and anthropological research. I had married an anthropologist and had two children, so my frequent travels to Kenya for research inevitably included communication with and visits to my in-laws in Nairobi and in the rural countryside in Western Kenya. By 2009, when I accepted a yearlong Fulbright professorship at Egerton University, close to 70% of Kenya's 40 million people had access to a mobile phone—*simu ya mkono* (phone of the hand). Kiosks dubbed *simu ya wanainchi* (citizen's phones) were now in every marketplace—they rented out phones or charged your battery for a fee. Kenya's last red British call box was removed in 2010 amid nostalgia for the long lines and the surly operators. Mobile phones had brought both connectivity and mobility, creating a direct line from person to person that could shift across space. Waiting in line at the kiosk and bouncing at a friend's house were in the past. One now operated on the assumption that one's contacts were always available through a mobile phone. Staying in touch throughout the day was the new normal for many people.

The Start of Airtime Money

One of the first things to know about using a phone in Kenya is the importance of airtime. Prepaid airtime is still purchased on a scratch card, or nowadays frequently from one's handset. It is hard to walk a few steps without seeing airtime for sale, and even in the rural areas scratch card sellers crowd every local market. Airtime cards are sold in denominations as small as 10 Kenya shillings ($0.10) and as large as 2,000 shillings (about $20).[3] Most people, however, buy airtime cards of 50, 100, or 250 shillings. In 2009, one could call for around 8 shillings per minute within the country to another Safaricom subscriber, but over time, with more customers and more phone companies, these costs have diminished drastically to less than one shilling. Nevertheless, airtime is used with great economy, and people always seem to be running out of it. People who call and text frequently nevertheless keep very little airtime on their phones, grudgingly "topping up" in tiny amounts of 20 to 50 cents. Topping up often involves dispatching the nearest young person to a kiosk for a scratch card. Conserving airtime is also accomplished through short conversations of abrupt hellos and no good-byes.

Besides the scratch cards, there is another way to get airtime. In 2009 my sister-in-law Bernadette showed me how to send and receive airtime. Bernadette is a Nairobi civil servant and mother whose home is always full of relatives and visitors, and she graciously included me. The first step was to select *sambaza* on the phone menu. *Sambaza*, which is a Swahili word meaning "to distribute," is a way to send your stored airtime to other registered Safaricom numbers. Bernadette told me that she had "too much" airtime on her phone and asked if she could she send me some. The best way to get airtime is to receive it from someone else through *sambaza*—usually someone who is assumed to have enough to spare.

Several weeks later, settling into the Fulbright lectureship at Egerton University, I ran out of water and asked the upstairs neighbor, Susan—a fast-moving, busy lady who turned out to be the school's athletic coach—to lend me some from her storage tank. We exchanged numbers, a meeting ritual now as common as the ubiquitous East African handshake. As she recorded my incoming call and typed in my name, she noted her lack of airtime. I decided to ask her why it was that Kenyans never had enough airtime.

"Well, I'm waiting for you to send me some!" she replied with a laugh. Because Bernadette had prepared me, I selected the *sambaza* menu item and sent Susan eight cents' worth of airtime. She was delighted and surprised that I already knew about *sambaza*. So began a close friendship, and a bridge of rapport and entrée into the research setting.

Phones and airtime are a significant expense and strain on the weekly budget. While buying airtime is a chore, sending it to others through *sambaza* is fun and a social connection in itself—and invests in the value of friendship at no extra cost. Airtime sharing is a widespread practice and can rekindle a connection with just a few shillings. Sharing and sending airtime have a variety of social purposes, from gifting, to repaying a debt arising from a past interaction, to flirting.

Among the college students at Egerton, texting was very popular and served as an informal, casual, or even intimate channel. The gender roles were apparent. Male students at Egerton blamed women for starting flirtations with airtime requests: "Women start it. They start it with airtime. When she starts asking for airtime, be careful." Women said men were at fault for making advances (considered little more than a bluff) by offering to *sambaza* them airtime! These same students were fond of purchasing 10-shilling airtime bundles—what Safaricom calls *bonga*—and other promotions. Text messaging had become cheap enough that students confessed to me that they could spend entire nights texting a romantic partner through to morning. When I asked them about airtime-saving strategies, some mentioned *bonga* promotions, but an equal number cited the 90-kilogram bags of maize or beans they hauled to school from rural areas to feed themselves for an entire semester and, more importantly, to keep them in airtime.

Airtime users recognize many media, or ways of getting their message through—text messaging, talk, and flashing. These media vary in airtime cost; for example, in flashing, the caller hangs up after a few rings, which signals "Call me," without using airtime.[4] Flashing is used to contact someone of greater status or means and press them to return the call—a boss, an older sibling, or a provider in the family. A wife in a polygynous marriage may simply sniff when flashed. "He can call me if he wants to talk to me." Such messages can spur others—those who hold the expected social role—to pay for the call-back whenever possible. A text message is cheaper than talk and should be used with caution, possibly never with people to whom, according to social rules, you must show avoidance, such as a mother- or father-in law.[5] Recently free "Please call me" messages have become more common than flashing—but they are still known to be free.

Airtime is the currency of information and emotions at the heart of mobile phone use. It is a medium through which people create, calculate, and represent the value of their relationships.[6] As such, airtime is a kind of money, defined as "an idea . . . of a measure of value."[7] Like money objects, airtime money has a material dimension when it is purchased on a card. Users create a record and a memory of who owes what to whom, a record that people will access on their handset or remember for the next call.[8] In this way airtime money can reinforce an existing obligation or perhaps realign a new connection.

Some may believe that money can depersonalize relationships. They prefer to keep the personal and intimate spheres separate from those of money exchange.[9] For this reason money requests and money gifts can be a dilemma for anthropologists attempting to gain the trust of research participants.[10] But in this setting, material exchange defines who owes what to whom and has long expressed the value of people and social ties. Early anthropologists noted: "The African is frankly and directly concerned with the material transfer itself as indicative of the quality of the relationship."[11] Gift giving reminds people of what they owe to others, but also gives relationships an open-endedness: an exchange can rekindle or reestablish a friendship after a long absence without any cynicism.

Similarly, airtime heightens the obligation to reciprocate. I came to experience the sense of obligation that Bernadette called having "too much" airtime, which often emerged from my interactions because of my position as "prof," foreigner, and white person, well-off aunt to nieces and nephews, and in-law. My nieces and nephews texted me requests for airtime top-ups. In time, I learned who I could count on to answer my questions about young people's use of phones. Like many anthropologists before me, I was using money to establish rapport.[12] Participating in *sambaza*, the circuits of airtime, enabled me to enter the social worlds of my Kenyan friends and informants. I once sent Susan an airtime gift; coincidentally, she had just heard that a friend was stranded without bus fare. She forwarded my 50 cents to her stranded friend almost immediately. "God had been working through us," she explained later, adding that soon I must meet her friend—which I did.

From Airtime Money to Mobile Money

Airtime sending became widespread in Africa beginning in the early 2000s. In several countries, mobile network operators established airtime sharing services. MTN's Me2U service, for example, is still one of the provider's most popular features. People began using it as a substitute for money transfer: Those without phones could use the public mobile phone found in many marketplaces to receive airtime money. The public callbox operators would buy the airtime at a discount from the receivers, and then resend it. MTN noted that by the late 2000s these public mobile phones accounted for 35% of its market— and that a good deal of its business was in airtime transfer.[13] Airtime money can work several ways: Friends and relatives can send airtime codes, and the recipients can get cash from phone airtime agents in exchange for passing the airtime codes on. Airtime sending is also a way of moving money as exchange value to friends and relatives far away. One can also use airtime as a means of exchange to purchase goods.

Airtime money was "the world's first genuinely valuable digital commodity."[14] *The Economist*, in 2013, reported that airtime was still a commonly used currency in many parts of Africa, redeemed for money or goods, sometimes with a small commission for the agent willing to convert a scratch code back into cash. Airtime money is a good example of users' rescripting—repurposing intended usages to new ends.[15] The anthropologist Bill Maurer has written that airtime has a "creative instability. . . . [I]t can be a commodity in one instance, an actualized, technologically mediated relationship in another (through talk and text) and a method of payment, means of exchange and store of value in a third moment (when used as alternative currency). It can continuously pass into and out of each of these moments—it is unstable, and reversible."[16]

The creative instability of airtime inspired the birth of mobile money as a collaboration of private and development interests that eventually deployed a fee-based money transfer service, M-Pesa.[17] The effort involved the United Kingdom's Department for International Development and the mobile network operator Vodafone through its Kenya subsidiary, Safaricom. The service allows people to use text messages to send not airtime but Kenyan currency money to friends and relatives. This e-money can then be exchanged for cash through an agent. Agents are humans, often shopkeepers, whose ubiquitous stalls fill rural markets and urban malls alike. Agents buy cash from local banks and exchange it for e-money with mobile money users.

M-Pesa captured the "creative instability" of airtime, fixing it into a digital representation of the Kenya shilling. Money transfer services provided a means to save and transfer money value. Built on the cash-in/cash-out service of agents, who buy cash at banks, the service also allows an easier flow of cash to rural areas. The technology of money transfer, conceived of as a development intervention for people without bank access, was now a new infrastructure of people, banks, and mobile phone networks, a means toward financial inclusion for people who were at too great a distance from physical bank branches. Since 2007 and because of M-Pesa's success, development and industry interests have put billions of investment dollars into developing similar systems.

When M-Pesa launched in 2007, 80% of Kenyans did not use formal banking. In the early days of M-Pesa, the experiment was uncertain; customers were few and several banks challenged Safaricom's ability to provide financial services. But M-Pesa became popular quickly. After one year a million customers had been added. In 2008, after just fourteen months, M-Pesa had 2.5 million subscribers.[18] After two and a half years 8.5 million had subscribed.[19] By 2012, the Government of Kenya reported more than 30 million mobile phones in a country of 40 million people and almost 20 million mobile money accounts—more than the adult population. In 2018 more than 90% have used the service and 60% of Kenyan adults use money transfer at least once a month.

Agents have been at the root of M-Pesa's success. You can sign up for a mobile money account if you have a national ID or passport and a SIM card from a mobile phone company. A basic phone or "feature phone" with no or limited Internet capability will do; no smartphone or Internet connection is required. Then, a mobile money/airtime agent (working out of a stall or storefront easily located in marketplaces and stores) can exchange your cash into e-money. You hand the agent your cash, and they will send you a text message confirming that the amount has been added to your account balance. You can then keep the money in this wallet account or send money to another phone number with a text message. Other services initially offered included checking account balances, making deposits and withdrawals, paying bills, and purchasing airtime.[20]

In 2009 I signed up for M-Pesa by visiting an agent and shopkeeper at a small market near the entrance gate to Egerton University. With a blunt pencil he wrote down every customer transaction in a thick, frayed book, including amounts, names, and phone and ID numbers. From that point on, I kept money on the M-Pesa account, since I regularly sent money and airtime from my handset, especially to my mother-in-law and nieces. "My" agent sealed my customer loyalty early on. By my third visit he knew my passport number by heart and greeted me by reciting it. I knew I would not have to risk carrying the passport anymore. Unfortunately, like many agents in those early days, he had trouble keeping the reserve stores of cash "float" used to stay balanced against electronic deposits. The agent must buy cash from a local bank. When he was out of float, I was out of luck. In these moments when I was unable to cash out, I realized that the mobile money network is far more than just digital. It is also a material network that includes human agents, banks, and cash money, which still moves from bank to bank the old-fashioned way, by armored transport van.

In Safaricom's well-known "Send Money Home" advertisement, an urban worker in suit and tie sends 1,000 shillings ($10) to his grateful rural parents via mobile phone. Money flies into his mother's phone, and she receives the text message with a smile; then she and her husband pay a visit to the agent to retrieve the remittance. The service provides a solution to the tremendous need for urban Kenyans to send money to rural family members.[21] Existing services—such as Western Union, bus and *matatu* (minivan) companies, and sending cash through a letter carried by a relative—were risky and expensive.

Banks in this former settler colony were mainly frequented by Europeans. A title deed or similar asset was, and often still is, needed as collateral for loans, effectively excluding most people. Fear of pickpockets also encourages value storage on the mobile money wallet. Maintaining the network of agents and cash floats is an ongoing expense for Safaricom, but the service is profitable for the company because it brought customer loyalty, the sought-after "stickiness." This stickiness was fostered by an exclusivity policy whereby transfers to customers outside the Safaricom network paid significantly more—a policy that built Safaricom a near monopoly on money transfers.

By the time of my 2009 visit, the M-Pesa service was already in wide use. Airtime was still circulating in very small amounts—often not more than 50 shillings ($0.50). One young man explained his monthly budget to me, earmarking several 50-shilling transfers for *mabibi* (girlfriends). The *sambaza* service is free, so the circulations are frequent. Mobile money remittances, on the other hand, are at least ten times larger, and users consider the amounts they send carefully, given that the service costs money both to send and to cash out. However, the use of mobile money still bears the stamp of its genesis in airtime gifting. E-money can be sent "to appreciate" a parent, to demonstrate caring and providing for a partner, to "condole" the bereaved, or to represent the sender "because I cannot be there."

Money sending is also commonly associated with specific crises, emergencies, purposes, and needs. A friend or relative is stranded without transport, needs medical care, or must pay a fine or bribe; a family has no food; the farm requires planting or weeding; a child has been sent home for lack of fees. One might even know a friend in need and begin soliciting donations from other friends and relatives—"finding money" on her behalf. One might send money to someone who is embarrassed to be caught without biscuits and juice when friends drop by. Interestingly, in common etiquette the cash-out fee that providers charge to the recipient is almost always paid by the sender—who when asked for money can be politely reminded to "ongeza ya kutoa" (add on the cash-out fee). Just as in airtime sending, the relationship between sender and receiver reflects the asymmetries around obligation and social inequality. Fees increase incrementally with the amount sent, and users often send the maximum amount allowed for a given fee.

Sambaza and its cousin, mobile money sending, form two circuits of exchange[22] or thresholds.[23] Mobile money sending moves parallel to airtime, but with larger money amounts and with an added sense of instrumental purpose. One circuit can merge into another—when a young man asks a female friend for "airtime" and she surmises that he is broke—and sends him enough money for "at least a few items for the week." Both practices interlace with mobile phone use as ways of maintaining connections and intimacies with family, partners, and friends. In later chapters, I will describe these circuits and networks in more detail, using the idea of wealth-in-people.

Since the 2007 M-Pesa launch, digital Kenya has expanded. Submarine fiber-optic cables laid down beginning in 2009 made the Internet widely available at reduced cost. Over the next decade the public "citizen's phone" became common but then more rare, as mobile phone registrations increased, by 2018 nearly exceeding the population.[24] During that same period, the number of Kenyan households with electricity went from 22% to more than 70%.

These improvements in electricity and Internet have laid the groundwork for building out digital financial technologies. A variety of parties, including banks, financial and other providers, government agencies, and numerous local and international NGO organizations make transactions easier and faster and offer other services through this channel. Using digital money, people can connect to banks, take out digital microloans, buy insurance, pay fees, send money to other countries, hail rides, and purchase utilities like energy and water. Startups offer crowdfunding and peer-to-peer lending. Some products may be key to preserving lifeways threatened by climate change: index-based livestock insurance (IBLI) products use phones to collect premiums and deliver cattle insurance to herders in arid lands, and algorithms are now bringing credit to smallholders and farming cooperatives. The sports-betting craze blurs the lines separating finance, entertainment, and social media. In Kenya you can buy shares in a government bond or invest in a mutual fund using mobile money. Government cash transfers can help needy citizens using mobile technology and the agent network. Finally, for those who have asked why poverty can't be solved by just giving people money,[25] the charity GiveDirectly uses M-Pesa to send beneficiaries unconditional monthly payments. People are also linking their financial and social relationships on M-Pesa to Facebook, M-Changa (an online fundraising platform), and other emerging fintech platforms. Use of WhatsApp, a free cross-platform instant messaging software used for group texting, e-commerce, and fundraising, is ubiquitous. The mobile money network now connects to many other networks—networks for banking, mobile telephony, ride hailing on motorcycles, and so on. It is an infrastructure that "facilitates the flow of goods, people, or ideas and allows for their exchange over space."[26] Its boundaries are fuzzy as its functions and connections grow.

In many parts of the world, the rise of digital money is threatening to replace cash, both for everyday transactions and even at the level of central banks. But in much of the Global South terms like "cash-lite" or "cashless" are misleading. Mobile money is not an alternative to cash money. Rather, one could say that it is a better form of cash—a way of using human agents to move cash where it is needed.[27] As of 2018, there were 156,000 mobile money agents in Kenya and 4.2 million mobile money agents all over Africa. Human agents transform cash to e-money and bring the mobile network, banks, senders, and receivers together. Agents purchase cash and e-money reserve, or float, from banks or super-agents, who regularly balance these reserves. Through their services, the agents have distributed cash money to rural areas where it was scarce. The agents are the connectors—they make possible the "transportation of agencies over great distance."[28]

And airtime money, too, still endures. Merchants in Egypt give small change as airtime cards called Fakka. After the 2008 earthquake Rwandans sent airtime as emergency support.[29] Some companies reward users for reading their ads or credit them with airtime for responding or sending texts; others have experimented with accepting airtime payments or converting airtime into money in a bank account. Kenya's digital financial system is still grounded in the everyday experience of money gifts and money messages—*sambaza*. In Chapter 3, we will see where the story leads.

Money Leapfroggers

3

> People love cash because they are conditioned to use it. They used to love cowrie shells and dogs' teeth too, but their preferences evolved as new forms of payment came along. They can do so again. Cash must be excised from the system as much as possible.
>
> Mas and Sullivan, "Mobile Money as Information Utility," 24–25

Based on the success of M-Pesa, innovators, entrepreneurs, and development thinkers from both Africa and the West are reimagining African moneys. Given the history of poverty and underdevelopment in this region, many innovators are captivated by the promise of leapfrogging, the idea of using innovation to spur development that will put underdeveloped Africa ahead of the West. Leapfrogging brings together interests in development, engineering, finance, investment capital, and industry to create positive innovations and interventions in poorer countries. It seeks to lift the non-industrialized world ahead, into the service and digital economies of the present and near future.

The pressure for leapfrogging is putting the agent network at risk. These agents are the network of humans who exchange e-money for cash and back again. Payment networks in other parts of the world are rapidly creating cashless ecosystems using smartphone apps and platforms, such as China's WeChatPay. Much of the world has left the agent network behind, along with the cowrie shells and the dogs' teeth. After all, agents are expensive—even a business loss—and may be source of fraud and theft. To leapfroggers, the agent network is a barrier to innovation that cuts African fintech off from the platforms and smartphone apps proliferating in other settings. The agent network creates inclusion for large numbers of customers who lack access to smartphone and Internet, who receive remittances on feature and basic phones, and whose immediate lives are largely cash-based. They are the link to the informal cash economy that enabled the digital network to first expand.[1] But now this network is hindering the big tech giants such as Google and Facebook, who are eyeing Africa as the last frontier to further scale up a data-based economy. As of 2019, Google and Facebook planned to lay down undersea data cables to encircle Africa. Facebook's is called Simba.

Concern is growing that providers will pull back the agent network, isolating the poor. Or the agent network could end up focused on peer-to-peer money transfer, separating the poor and digitally invisible from more-sophisticated money innovations such as blockchain or cryptocurrencies. South Africa's former minister of finance Trevor Manuel[2] and microfinance expert Greta Bull have both warned that "the risk of a digital divide is very real."[3]

Africa's Leapfroggers

Prominent leapfrogging advocate and development academic Calestous Juma wrote: "The mobile handset in the hands of an ordinary African has become the symbol of leapfrogging."[4] The late Professor Juma celebrated the potential of mobile technologies to address previous failures of development in his native Kenya. With the advent of the mobile phone, the possibilities to reach remote beneficiaries of development were multiplied. The mobile phone became not merely a means of communication, but a delivery vehicle for products and services ranging from information to finance to water.[5] The leapfrogging story emphasized economic growth, optimism, resourcefulness, and innovation. The commercial success of M-Pesa put it at the center of the narrative. Headlines proclaimed that M-Pesa had transformed Africa "from a scar on the conscience of the world to the most exciting continent on the planet."[6]

Soon after a submarine fiber-optic cable reached East Africa in 2009, Internet access improved dramatically, and countries developed ambitious plans to attract foreign investment to techno-cities and innovation hubs. Nairobi's Silicon Savanna is a collective of start-ups and technology incubators such as iHub, an innovation collective. These are do-good start-ups, innovators designing with careful attention to everyday issues and challenges, such as access to services, utilities and water, mapping, and improving governance, health, and security. Technology inspires imaginings around varied futures and ideas, such as global connection or transparent governance.[7]

A planned technology project south of Nairobi called Konza Technology City hopes to employ large numbers in low-end outsourcing for the technology industry, known as BPO (business process outsourcing).[8] Such visions of information and communication technology (ICT) development involve connection to a global economy. At the same time, other visions make local solutions the priority. Kenya's entrepreneurship and innovation incubators are seeking not just connection but "innovation for Africans by Africans": applying digital technology to Africa's most pressing problems with an emphasis on local needs.[9] At iHub, developers imagine locally driven innovation and problem solving, "customizing a complex technology to local environments . . . to make it . . . simpler and more relevant."[10] These innovations include index-based insurance, digital microcredit, QR code payments, and pay-as-you-go water and power. BRCK is a wireless WiFi device designed for use in emerging markets whose slogan is "Designed in Kenya and Made in the USA."[11] Ushahidi (Kiswahili for "evidence") is an information-gathering and interactive map that first collected eyewitness reports of violence during 2007–08 political unrest. Beyond these better-known products and apps, building a market infrastructure is another goal—the mobile and digital connection between buyers and sellers.[12] Filling the voids means creating relationships and institutions that endorse credibility, analyze information, aggregate and distribute supply and demand, and make payments. Some examples: Weza Tele has digitized supply chains for consumer goods at small shops; BitPesa is a digital foreign exchange and payment platform that leverages blockchain settlement; Sendy is an Uber-style motorbike delivery service; Kuhustle matches freelancers to jobs. Cellulant[13] is a company that has scaled dramatically from its beginnings selling ringtones around Nairobi into one of Africa's largest multi-country payments aggregators.

The Struggle for the Digital Ecosystem

In leapfroggers' cashless vision, the peer-to-peer (P2P), agent-based transfer network will eventually close its loops and seams, freeing money to circulate digitally and voiding the expense and risk of moving cash through agents. Various new services, platforms, and business models for mobile money are being developed in the name of cash-light ecosystems. Person-to-person transfers should, in this view, shift toward connecting people to financial and other institutions. The reasoning is as follows: If I am in the habit of paying for things using mobile money, I am likely to keep e-value stored on my phone, rather than cashing it out. This would eventually lead to consumer habits built around using the value on the wallet. Safaricom's retail payment service is called Lipa na M-Pesa (Pay with M-Pesa). With it one can pay digitally for water, solar power, electricity, and satellite television via SMS. In 2015, use of these services was relatively rare and they entail merchant fees. Among a low-income sample in 2014, only 1% of such purchases were made via mobile, and by 2015 only 4%–5% of Kenya's cash purchases had been replaced by Lipa na M-Pesa.[14]

Internet and smartphones are also key to the digital ecosystem. A new advertising push from Safaricom began in 2014 to showcase smartphone and Internet payments. In these ads, a jet-setting businessman pays school fees from his airplane seat, and a family views a soccer game on a tablet. An ecosystem of bank connectivity, microcredit, and bill payment is touted as the developing world's first "cash-light" economy.[15]

When supported by adequate Internet speed and breadth and electricity for charging, the Internet and smartphones can expand the options for financial services to include visual applications, or better communication for people with disabilities. Anticipating such a migration, M-Visa in May 2017 announced it would offer free money transfers to Kenyan smartphone customers who used its app. In this way, transnational and international companies, like the payments giant, are strategizing their initial foothold in an emerging fintech market that has airtime money and *sambaza* at its root. Many of them do a sizable portion of their customer connectivity through Internet websites, or they may, like M-Visa, encourage the customer to have a smartphone. Is money transfer through agents set to be disrupted?

The Digital Divide

Digital inequality describes the uneven distribution of connectivity and access to digital infrastructures. Often these inequalities are assumed to be a natural problem of rural areas, one that broadening the agent network or switching to smartphones will remedy. The way these networks themselves produce and amplify inequalities is less rarely considered. Maintaining a phone over time, replacing and fixing it, purchasing airtime, and paying for money transfer (including cash-in/cash-out fees) displace significant costs onto the users, with the result that inequalities based on social class, gender, and disability affect the ability to securely access mobile technology.[16] Users in Western Kenya frequently access the phones of others or keep a SIM card that they insert into a borrowed handset. Accessing phones or handsets through social relationships may be more likely among women and can create social dilemmas and risks ranging from compromising one's PIN number to jeopardizing one's physical safety.[17] Literacy and numeracy are also barriers: at least one billion people cannot read digital displays of money amounts accurately; yet people in Myanmar, Ethiopia, and Tanzania are quite competent in using colors and symbols on cash money to denominate, earmark, and plan money use.[18] Accessing services often requires local knowledge—for example, which hill is the one to climb to find mobile network service? People who are more than a short walk from a mobile money agent may see no reason to keep e-money on a mobile wallet when they will need cash for their daily use, which they can keep at home. Most rural areas—including rural Western Kenya, the setting of much of the field research for this book—still experience regular interruptions in electricity, and smartphones are largely nonexistent. According to FSD Kenya, in 2016 only 16% of Kenyans owned a smartphone—a fact frequently forgotten in the race to become a fintech hub.[19]

In Kenya's urban settings, smartphone and Internet access are more common. Here, the mobile money channel is increasingly used together with social connections on platforms such as Facebook. WhatsApp, the cross-platform instant messaging and voice over IP service offers text and media messaging, voice and video calls, and user location sharing. WhatsApp, I learned, was the main reason why the Nairobi dweller wanted a smartphone. It can be an achievable status marker: Chinese Huawei smartphones were widely advertised for around $60–$80 in 2016. By this time, the feature phone I had fondly kept since 2009 provoked concern, as it hardly connoted sufficient status. When visiting the doctor's office in Rwanda in 2016, I was told, "Such a person as yourself should not have a phone like this." The handy feature phones were now called *kabambe* (roughly, "little cute thing") or *mulika mwizi* ("to shine light on a thief"). They were sold for as little as $20—and still used.

I discovered the importance of *kabambe* when living with my sister-in-law Lillian in 2016 and 2017 in Kawangware, an area in the west of Nairobi. A high school teacher with two daughters in college, Lillian's husband had died suddenly a few years earlier. Her Samsung smartphone stayed in a locked bedroom cabinet during the day, while she rose at four a.m. to commute across town to her school by public transportation, returning at close to nine every night.

After dinner she unlocked the phone and connected to her WhatsApp groups and to Facebook on its generous screen.

Twice during my stays, Lillian's *kabambe*—which she used during the day on her commute—was stolen at a crowded bus stop. I also was once on the city bus with several thieves, one of whom posed as a ticket collector. As they left in a rush, my seatmate discovered that his money and *kabambe* were missing. Although smartphones are widely advertised and sought after, they are rarely in view outside of upscale restaurants and spaces. Hopeful international start-ups with Internet-based products have not considered the contingencies of daily life in the city nicknamed "Nai-robbery."

Instead of following an approach based on creating and installing apps on expensive smartphones, designers can use another medium—universal applications. Universal apps can reach people on any phone, including basic phones, and are particularly important for development initiatives. Universal apps include voice, SMS (Short Message Service), and USSD (Unstructured Supplementary Service Data), which has the most design flexibility. M-Pesa and Safaricom's group messaging service, Semeni, use USSD programming. Safaricom users have memorized many sets of star codes that allow them to query balances or perform other functions. However, USSD communication sessions have a set time duration, and many designers consider them limited. Regardless of which design approach they choose, digital commerce and finance start-ups are flocking to Nairobi's growing fintech sector. Aside from digital microloans (see Chapter 4), digitizing agriculture is a big focus. I attended a reverse hackathon (technology redesign event) in Nairobi in 2017 as an anthropologist to crowdfunding start-up M-Changa (see Chapter 10). Here I met representatives from local companies who had come to help farmers get comfortable using digital financial products. The start-ups included iShamba (*shamba* means "farm")—an information service for farmers; Cowsoko (*soko* means "market")—for livestock e-commerce; Chomoka ("unleashed")—record keeping for savings groups; and Maano, another virtual farmers' market. Timiza digitizes microfinance group savings programs; Digicow enables farmers to make data-driven decisions about dairy production; AcreAfrica links them to insurance; Farmdrive, Digifarm, and many others provide them with loans. Data-driven agriculture could make credit and insurance much cheaper and more available and make a precarious and risky way of life more predictable. Many platforms such as Digifarm, a Safaricom partner, bundle end-to-end services, offering credit, inputs like seeds and fertilizer and pricing and weather information, and improved access to a market through its Digisoko partner. For example, some platforms are managed by the buyers of, say, green beans meant for export to Europe; they sell the seeds, offer credit, and buy the finished product, and they work with individual farmers or with farming cooperatives. These platforms also bring together and control as much data as possible about clients, including social media use and financial behavior, along with farm productivity, weather, and geospatial data, all of which are used for credit scoring. Observers worry that this kind of pervasive data control could embed inequalities and disadvantage farmers who experience drought or those who lack other sources of income to repay loans.[20] Over a buffet lunch, company representatives at the hackathon shared an extensive array of quite different concerns: their difficulties in advertising for, finding, and retaining customers. They bemoaned what they saw as the communicative limitations of SMS and USSD protocols: once customers have memorized star codes to interact with a mobile operator, they don't like changing or learning new ones. Other problems they mentioned included, the inability to advertise, and problems with network connectivity. Digifarm, by far the largest of these agricultural digital finance platforms, has about one million users already subscribed and aims to enroll five million subscribers by 2022.[21]

The hackathon event itself provides clues as to why such platforms fail to find customers. The gathering was held at a posh hotel in the upscale Westlands neighborhood of Nairobi. The farmers I met included a member of parliament, college students interested in commercial farming, and representatives of farming cooperatives. One farmer told me he had paid to take a 60-kilometer bus ride early that morning. Developers and farmers were paired up or put in small groups that tested apps or SMS scripts for opening accounts and communicating with providers. Little else of the experience or needs of farmers, particularly rural smallholders, was probed, such as the ongoing rural crises of landlessness, low productivity, climate change and food insecurity. The event focused on the Nairobi area and on commercial markets, especially international ones, and exemplified the reasons why so many apps and platforms fail to give target customers a reason to use them.

The most successful approach builds on what people are already doing. As the lessons of *sambaza* showed, remittances are the key, along with using the agent network to reach customers. Equity Bank became the largest bank in Kenya by scaling rapidly through its agent network and through mobile phone loans. And the agent network is indeed very capable of scaling across the continent. Consider the case of MFS Africa, which has grown one of the largest payment networks in Africa by building on the agent network. Dare Okoudjou is CEO of MFS Africa. Originally from the Ivory Coast, he began his career with MTN, the South African mobile network operator (MNO). Early on he realized that the problem of scaling African fintech would be interoperability. Interoperability refers to the fact that mobile money systems operated by different companies and in different countries were unable to communicate with each other. Interoperability severely limits people's ability to send and receive money.

Okoudjou's company, founded in 2015, gradually built a cross-border remittance product to connect the patchwork of MNOs across national boundaries. MFS Africa designed an application programming interface (API) that had the capacity to act as a messenger between the mobile money systems operated by different companies, thereby making it possible for MFS to draw more and more mobile service providers over time into the interoperable network provided by its API. Beginning in East Africa, where MFS Africa first applied their API to integrate MTN and M-Pesa transfers, the company has gradually integrated more and more MNOs and countries into its network. In 2020 MFS Africa's partners included 22 MNOs in 27 African countries, and together this network can reach 180 million mobile money customers through 2 million cash-in/cash-out agents. The network also includes money transfer operators like World Remit, as well as banks, fintechs and companies that want to pay commissions or salaries.[22]

Okoudjou's goal is to eventually connect all mobile money agents in Africa and to provide the interoperability that can lower costs. He works with "the reality . . . that the vast majority of people across sub-Saharan Africa are still using feature phones, or even more basic phones."[23] He explained that many innovators don't want to work with the USSD communication language of these phones:

> North of the Limpopo, people use USSD, which is a very rudimentary channel to try to do any type of service. The ability to work on a channel that is very unfriendly to developers is something that is really quite unique to the rest of the continent. . . . In the United States, Europe, even Cape Town, they wonder, why don't you just do an App when you are doing money transfer?

In a SoundCloud interview,[24] he elaborated on the difficulties of sustaining two-way communication between agents and mobile network operators to enable cross-border money transfers, all while complying with identity and anti-money laundering regulations:

> [USSD] is a very rudimentary channel. You have to get things done in 45 seconds or the channel will close. You still wanna get forex through, the customer confirm, the kyc check, the aml check.[25] You do not know when the electricity will go off, or if the servers will go off. When it rains transactions won't go through because some links to internet are still running on VSAT.[26] If [it] is raining you will get so many complaints.

As an innovator, Okoudjou is committed to working with the agent network. "At the end of the day digital money in Africa was not about the technology but about the agents," he noted at a 2018 conference, where he emphasized that African fintech companies, to scale their products, must perfect their service and experience with accessible and universal SMS/USSD communication protocols if they want to reach a broad range of customers.[27]

Agents and cash-out services are still fundamental. The realities of cost, access, uptake and usage, and Internet and smartphone use question the leapfrogging imagery. Instead, innovators are charting an African path to money. As Okoudjou said, "If we can operate in this environment imagine what there will be [for Africa]—when we have infrastructure." Okoudjou is innovating in the context he has to work with now. He is imagining a better money infrastructure in the future, and building towards it in the present.

Limits of Leapfrogging

Technological change in the South continues to evoke the idea of leapfrogging. With its persistent evolutionary baggage, the concept assumes a constant search for faster or better ways of doing things. But often technological change is much more ironic than it is progressive and linear. During changing circumstances, people may seek continuity rather than a new and better way of doing things. Innovations are often conservative; as anthropologist Conrad Kottack once put it, "An innovation that evolves to maintain a system can play a major role in changing that system."[28] Mobile money uptake itself may be a little-appreciated example. M-Pesa's 2007 roll-out was followed[29] just a few months later by a disputed national election in December and early 2008. Accusations of vote rigging triggered months of unrest and violence that was politically motivated and targeted communities supporting the opposition. It led to 1,500 deaths and thousands of people displaced; roads were blocked, and stores and banks closed. Anthropologist Olga Morawczynski, who was in Western Kenya at the time, found that the use of M-Pesa increased dramatically during the political instability—with hundreds waiting in line to visit agents—and that money flows were also often reversed. Usually Kibera residents sent money and airtime to their rural relatives. But during the political crisis, urban residents relied on relatives in the western Kenyan locality of Bukara to send them money. In turn, they used airtime to keep relatives in Bukara informed about their safety. The money transfer service was a way to sustain the connections and social support of urban-rural family life; a dual system that was itself a means of coping with the legacies of colonial policies that imposed urban wage labor and exile from family. New practices spurred in time of crisis may be more important to the M-Pesa story than is commonly acknowledged.

A leapfrogging mind-set associates progress with the West and perpetuates a view of the Global South as unchanging; yet in business and innovation spaces this trope "endures as a framing device."[30] Tech observers make similar critiques:[31] "There is no shortage of feel-good stories about how mobile phones have changed lives in Africa . . . [which] perpetuate the narrative casting Africa as the orphan opening a Christmas box full of socks and toothpaste, expected to be grateful for finally getting what everyone else takes for granted." Silicon Savanna initiatives reproduce exclusions and divides, for example between the educated employees of start-ups and NGOs on the one hand and the poor targets of do-good tech initiatives, who are paid to participate in market research or in some cases even volunteer their time and labor in producing digital infrastructures.[32] After much investment in Information and Communication Technology for Development (ICT4D), even its leading proponents admit that technological interventions rarely reach their potential.[33]

Calestous Juma eventually moderated his enthusiasm for Africa's digital revolution. In the end, he became skeptical that Africa could leapfrog past secure investments in energy, transportation, telecommunications, water and sanitation, and irrigation. When design and development work around or without infrastructure, their focus on appropriate consumer products for the poor—the bottom of the pyramid approach[34]—can perpetuate a way of life rather than create conduits out of that way of life, especially when the vision embraces empowering individuals but leaves aside the broader settings where people live and fails to engage their civic and political leaders.[35] Instead of providing piped water to slums, the intervention is plastic-packaged water bags sold for a few cents. While this approach meets the poor's budget and needs, their built environment crumbles: "Increasing numbers of Africans are situated in what could be called half-built environments: underdeveloped, overused, fragmented, and often makeshift urban infrastructures where essential services are erratic or costly and whose inefficiencies spread and urbanize disease. The majority of Africans still do not have access to clean water and sanitation."[36]

But even well-off Nairobi residents struggle daily for access to health, electricity, or water, to say nothing of rural communities. Kenyans see these issues as political, not technological. My sister-in-law Bernadette, who taught me to *sambaza*, worked in a government office and paid close attention to her four children's schoolwork and preparations for the national exams. Being the family of a senior civil servant, Bernadette and her children were comfortable and lived in one of the city's older but more affluent neighborhoods, a complex of attractive bungalows near the city center. Nevertheless, their taps and plumbing were dry most days. On Friday nights into Saturday mornings, the water mysteriously gushed out of taps all over the estate. Like her neighbors, Bernadette then brought out long hoses and stayed up late refilling enormous water tanks in her courtyard and on her roof, hoping to store enough water for the week. Watching her troubles, I diplomatically mentioned climate change and East Africa's frequent droughts, but she scoffed. "There is water . . . there is water." She did not elaborate. Infrastructure is also political, a topic I move to in Chapter 4.

Whose Money Is This?

4

The origins of M-Pesa have become legend in business circles. Kenyans have their own vivid origin story that before 2013 was in wide circulation. In 2009, my students at Egerton University told me that a Kenyan student from the Jomo Kenyatta College of Agriculture and Technology had developed the world's first mobile money service. They were not sure of this student's name or whereabouts. An Egerton staff member elaborated a few weeks later, explaining that an engineering student from the University of Nairobi had introduced the idea to Safaricom—which had taken up his insight without including him in the product developments. Among my in-laws, and even online, the story had multiple versions. Some said this student had applied for a patent from the Kenyan government, only to have the application secretly sent on to Safaricom. Then Safaricom, through its international associates at Vodafone, stole the innovation and patented it. Other accounts of the story featured the collusion of a corrupt government figure bribed by Vodafone, or possibly Safaricom, for access to the technological secret. Another Egerton student claimed to know someone who knew the young engineer who had been dispossessed of his invention. Some pointed out that he was from the Luo community, a group associated with the political opposition and with intellectuals. I was promised he would be found, but he never materialized. Expressing my doubts about the existence of this young innovator led to some passionate arguments with Kenyans who were convinced he was real.

My Fulbright fellowship ended in 2010 without the mysterious Kenyan Zuckerberg ever being revealed. I continued to follow the story online, where in 2012 one could still find discussion of the vanished engineer and further appeals to find him. The Kenya-centered origin story gained momentum and became a part of Kenyan political discourse. A Kenyan Member of Parliament, Dr. Shem Ochuodho, praised not only the missing inventor but also the Central Bank of Kenya (CBK) Governor, who was also missing his proper credit: "As usual we credit all the wrong people [and] leave out the true unsung hero: the young university student who 'invented' M-Pesa—the inventor/innovator! Not even his name is mentioned or known! In the history of technological innovation in Kenya, the 'Governor of the Central Bank' (notably Micah Cheserem and the [present governor] will have a special place! [He] was bold enough to let this experiment take root."[1]

At a now defunct website, Human IPO: Home to African Tech,[2] a man claims to have initiated the practice of airtime sending to his parents and says the patent he received from the Kenyan Telecommunications Commission (KTC) was stolen by Safaricom with the collusion of corrupt KTC officials.

In 2012, news reports sought to correct the urban legend of the African student. An official letter from Safaricom circulated online, crediting Vodafone engineers for inventing M-Pesa. The Human IPO website's conclusion: "There is absolutely nothing Kenyan about M-Pesa. It is thoroughly British." A dispiriting rebuke for faithful supporters of the lost Kenyan tech whiz.[3] So is M-Pesa Kenyan or a product of British ingenuity? Who claims this innovation and who gets to shape its goals? Who profits from this channel—local elites, the mobile phone companies, Silicon Valley investors, the financial and payments industries, or the users? Whose money is this?

To maximize suspense, I will reveal the identity of Kenya's lost young computer engineer at the end of this chapter. First, I will demonstrate that for Kenyans M-Pesa is their own money. These counter-narratives to the leapfrogging trope establish M-Pesa as the product of local creativity. They emphasize that M-Pesa is Kenya's cultural wealth,[4] and highlight informal inventions with airtime, and the regulatory experts at the Central Bank of Kenya (CBK) as important examples of Global South innovation.

Unfortunately, the success story is only part of the narrative. Since 2010 the excitement around digital finance in Africa has been tempered. As I explained in Chapter 3, the scaling of many digital innovations has been slower than many had hoped. The growth of new start-ups has not met expectations, and the use of digital finance specifically is not yielding evidence of material benefit, especially for the poor. The high cost of services and the digital divides created by the struggle for access are ever more apparent. Digital microloans caught on quickly but have led to widespread indebtedness and questionable uses of consumer data. Hacking and scams are common.

Furthermore, an increasingly bitter techno-politics over who owns, regulates, and profits from digital finance is fueling public debate. The close relationship between the Kenyan Government and Safaricom has generated conflict. Taxes are continually raised on money transfer services. A major loan provider bank is owned by the family of the president of Kenya, raising questions about the political consequences of money and debt. By the 2017 elections, the M-Pesa brand had become ensnared in these debates over fees, usury, and political patronage: the opposition party accused Safaricom of election rigging and bribery and led a consumer boycott of its services, charging that M-Pesa was a tool of political and ethnic elites. Whose money is this?

The Counter-Narratives: Regulatory Innovators

What is cultural wealth? The symbolic qualities of goods and services, their meanings, cultural and historical contexts, and their rituals of use are an important source of their value. By elaborating and building on the symbolic and cultural value of what they produce, societies have created value both locally and in global trade and exchange. Developing countries have produced significant economic value through the symbolic value of their goods. Building cultural wealth is an important practice of economic development that can challenge relationships of dependency.[5]

Narratives are important ways to contextualize this symbolic value. Another story was recounted by my brother-in-law, a civil servant, although I found a version in an industry report.[6] After testing the money-sending service, Safaricom worked closely with the Central Bank of Kenya on a wider deployment. Michael Joseph, the South African CEO of Safaricom at the time, paid a fateful visit to the finance minister, John Michuki, who was already widely respected for his honesty and competence. As transportation minister, Michuki is known for domesticating Kenya's minibus sector, which had historically been rife with bribery, poorly maintained vehicles, and a shocking record of deadly accidents. His Michuki Rules imposed uniform colors and seat-belt checks. The Michuki

Rules lasted only as long as Michuki was transportation minister, however; after he stepped down, the stuffing of passengers, the joyful artwork, and the substandard vehicles returned. Many Kenyans wish he would have made even more widespread changes as president, but he died suddenly in 2012 and his funeral was a day of mourning across the country.

Joseph's 2007 visit to Michuki was high stakes. The M-Pesa system was in clear violation of Kenya's finance rules, which allow licensed financial institutions to accept only cash deposits. A major exception was going to have to be made for M-Pesa. In the minister's office, Joseph showed him how to send salaries to his farmworkers. When Michuki called his foreman and confirmed the salary had been received, he was so impressed with the speed, ease, and reliability of the service that he gave Joseph and M-Pesa the go-ahead, and Safaricom was granted authorization to launch.

To address M-Pesa's conflict with Kenya's banking act, Michuki's ministry worked with the CBK to reimagine money's definitions and social frameworks. First, the customer transaction with the mobile money agent had to be redefined. In this reimagining, a customer does not buy cash or e-money or deposit any value with an agent—to do so would redefine the agent as a banker, and consequently require him or her to be regulated as a bank and to comply with a variety of rules, ranging from capital and liquidity requirements, to rules about how cash is secured and handled, to checking customer identification consistent with international know your customer/anti-money laundering (KYC/AML) identifications. Rather, Kenyan regulators decided that the agent merely holds the user's cash temporarily in exchange for the token e-money. Safaricom holds liquid assets against this e-money value on a one-to-one ratio in banking trusts at, today, more than twenty banks, ensuring no creation of new value that would disrupt monetary policy.[7] Agents receive e-money Kenya shillings when they deposit cash in the bank trust—paying a 0.5% fee for their float. They then exchange customers' cash for e-money, rather than taking deposits. Cash and e-money transactions are settled daily. In Kenya, Safaricom earns interest on the money held in a trust executed in 2007 "for and on behalf of all M-Pesa account holders"[8] and makes philanthropic grants through the M-Pesa Foundation (in Tanzania, providers like Tigo Money return the interest to their customers). Today the Safaricom trust account holds more than $60 million.

Mobile money launched in Kenya without a real regulatory framework. Instead, CBK figures like Steven Nduati, a payments regulator, decided to adopt a wait-and-see approach. Allowing mobile money to launch without real rules in place, the CBK issued Safaricom a "letter of no objection" allowing the provision of mobile money services without the establishment of a full-scale regulatory framework governing mobile payments. Most important, the letter also allowed Safaricom to contract with agents across the country and build the network.[9] Nduati later articulated that regulation must see how users interact with an evolving monetary framework.[10] The formal legal framework for mobile money came seven years later, in 2014.[11]

Whether Muchuki and his farm manager were really so personally involved or not, Muchuki stands in for all these bank regulators as the hero of the story—a government official reimagining money for the public benefit. The Michuki work-around fits a philosophy of "Better regulation is more beneficial than more regulation," as CBK governor Njuguna Ndung'u put it.[12] The Michuki story, like that of the lost university student, highlights the role of local actors—this time regulators in the Global South—whose reimaginings of money made it possible.

Banks vs. Mobile Networks and the Rise of Safaricom

In business "change happens at the boundaries of endeavors, and innovation often occurs at the intersection of domains."[13] A tangle of domains would certainly describe this evolving experiment in organizing and regulating finance, communications, and banking. The root of this complexity is the protean nature of e-money, mobile money, and airtime, with its potential to transform into currency, digital text message, or cash money.[14] This shifting nature continually produces dilemmas of definition and responsibility. Regulatory difficulties often accompany attempts to build mobile money systems. Can phone companies offer financial services? Who should regulate these activities? As late as May 2015 Uganda's successful mobile money service was challenged by a government claim that a phone company—MTN—had no authority to offer financial services. Similar objections and confusions over who maintains oversight over mobile money services and who assumes liability for customer loss or fraud have embroiled rollouts of mobile money.

As digital finance broadens the array of financial products available via mobile, the bank–phone company collaboration is taking new forms. In 2012 Safaricom and Equity Bank partnered to offer a mobile money savings account; but by 2014 these erstwhile partners battled publicly over Equity's "thin SIM" payment technology, created with Safaricom competitor Airtel. The "thin SIM" sits on top of a SIM card and offers bank connectivity to an Equity account regardless of the user's phone carrier. This clever hack was a way around Safaricom's stubborn refusals of interoperability. It can add to, rather than replace, a Safaricom registration. Safaricom fought the service in court, citing privacy protection for its customers, but lost as Equity and two other banks were given MVNO (mobile virtual network operator) licenses to provide banking services over mobile phones. Equitel money transfer charges a flat fee of 25 shillings, a move designed to undercut Safaricom. However, one must have an Equity Bank account to use the service. After three years, reports of Safaricom's demise at the hands of Equitel appeared greatly exaggerated, and Safaricom had maintained its market dominance. In 2017 one fintech expert in Nairobi told me the Equitel drama was "the slowest Safaricom takedown I've ever seen," citing Equitel's terrible customer service.

Bank-telco collaborations carve out unfamiliar territory for both industries. For example, banks like Equity have emphasized their agent networks. In February 2017 Kenya's banks formed a payment company that launched Pesalink, a real-time interbank peer-to-peer money transfer network allowing phone-based transfers between mobile money accounts and transfers between all bank accounts. It was designed to be "proof that the banking industry has embraced the revolution taking place across the payments industry."[15] At the same time Safaricom has made remarkable countervailing moves into financial services. The Safaricom Investment Cooperative has been in the real estate space since its inception in 2009. Everyday people can buy shares in the booming housing market. Safaricom first offered a unit trust mutual fund account called Mali ("wealth") in 2019. Investors can sign up and contribute via mobile money up to $700 at a time.

Producing the cultural wealth of M-Pesa is a creative storytelling about the vanished engineering genius and about creative regulation. Safaricom also has a prominent public presence through the media, stores, and other spaces. The company's popular media advertisements feature users from different ethnic groups all linking up through digital and mobile media, often situating the use of mobile phones and other devices together with visual symbols of indigeneity such as Maasai pastoralists in traditional garb tending their cattle while on the phone. Although academics find these representations stereotypical, Kenyans love the advertisements. In my experience, they are the only thing on television that will create a temporary lull in the constant conversations that go on over it. One of the most popular ads features soaring vistas of Kenya's national

parks and a gospel choir singing the company song, "Niko na Safaricom"—
(I'm with Safaricom). The didactic "Send Money Home" ad showed how to use
the service and highlighted the bittersweet dilemmas of the urban-rural family dynamic. Its viewers could identify with the social roles of money sending
depicted in the ad, including the rural mother, pious son, and urban worker.[16]

In addition to its media prominence, "Safaricom has the pomp and circumstance of new store openings, the sponsorship of cultural events and philanthropic initiatives, and the routine use of text messages to remind, nudge, and
discipline users."[17] Through these means, the company takes on a prominent
role in public life and aspects of state power.[18] In so doing it produces an "identity myth of a unified nation."[19] President Obama's 2015 visit to Kenya extolled
M-Pesa and the Silicon Savanna's other start-ups; these and other events where
Kenya rises to the international stage are frequent talking points of pride. Several of my interlocutors on the Silicon Savanna referred to M-Pesa as part of
Kenya's "brand." One coworker on a design project told me that Kenya's brand
had four parts: Lupita Nyong'o (Oscar-winning star of the film *Black Panther*),
its long-distance runners, Barack Obama, and M-Pesa. Of all the sub-Saharan
African countries, he said, "you cannot beat Kenya as a brand."

Safaricom also has powerful associations with ethical and humanitarian actions, especially through its charitable foundation.[20] Many Kenyans fundraise
on digital media, including WhatsApp, and in my role as anthropologist for
the online fundraiser M-Changa I began to ask people about their engagement
with these informal fundraisers. Kenyans receive appeals for donations for
medical care or other emergencies daily. In one case I received a fundraising
appeal for a boy who needed urgent surgery on a facial tumor. The detailed
photo featured the Safaricom logo photoshopped in. I suggested to my interlocutors that it appeared fake to me. The reaction was swift! How could Safaricom be involved in a scam? The company would never lend its name to a false
appeal. For many, the Safaricom brand is synonymous with legitimacy. Olga
Morawczynski's account of how a disputed election may have catalyzed the use
of digital money transfer suggests that consumer trust in Safaricom might still
stem in part from the stability, the security against risk, and the connection that
was achieved at that time of crisis.[21]

Such a high bar of trust must be continually maintained. As a near monopoly provider of mobile payments and as the medium for intimate and daily
communication, the company is frequently subject to blame and critique. First
are the company's business practices. People widely resent Safaricom's puzzling

fee structure, frequent network failures, poor customer service, and protection of its near monopoly. Second, the company has entered into the morally dubious loan market, not just as a channel for digital credit but through a popular overdraft service called Fuliza ("continue"), which lent out 29 billion Kenya shillings in airtime in its first three months.[22] Third is the ambiguous indigeneity of Safaricom, which is sometimes viewed favorably as a homegrown free-market success and sometimes as an agent of its foreign parent company, Vodafone. In the story of the lost innovator, Safaricom is Janus-headed, as the partner to the mysterious engineer but possibly a neocolonial collaborator with Vodafone. Could Safaricom be the latest manifestation of global dependency and indirect rule?

Social Dramas over Kenya's Cultural Wealth

Social rifts around cultural wealth have come to the fore as digital money's associations with corruption, exclusion, and political patronage have deepened. While NGOs promote the use of digital technology to promote transparency, in public culture these technologies are much more often associated with what is hidden than with what is revealed. Digital payments enabled by discreet texts are considered more covert than a cash handout. Sectors that have long been linked to graft or theft are increasingly stigmatized by new associations with digital payments, from police extortion of drivers now done as-you-drive instead of at the roadside, to the court system (Figure 4.1), to political gifts and patronage. An elaborate rural funeral might be financed by hundreds of dollars of support from the local MP, quietly sent digitally; the same MP would give a modest public donation at the event. Wealthy and well-positioned families often solicit mobile money donations for study abroad or other self-interests, distorting a practice of community self-help known as harambee. Criminal shakedowns and informal but stigmatized industries like beer brewing are often associated with digital payments.

A widely used digital loan product called M-Shwari is offered through the Commercial Bank of Africa (CBA) on the ubiquitous Safaricom menu. President Uhuru Kenyatta's family owns a large share of CBA, a fact that some of my interlocutors alluded to indirectly. When Nairobi resident Evelyn,[23] thirty-five and unemployed, learned that M-Shwari was owned by CBA, which, as she phrased it, "is said to belong to a prominent family in Kenya," she stopped using the bank, as "this family was using the product to enrich themselves."

Figure 4.1. Political cartoon by Gado highlighting M-Pesa as a channel for bribery.
SOURCE: Godfrey Mwampembwa (Gado), gadocartoons.com. Reprinted with permission.

Other interlocutors knew of links between Safaricom and Kenya Commercial Bank (KCB; another bank associated with prominent players in government and finance that offers loans and other products on the Safaricom menu). Interlocutors of ethnicities associated with the political opposition often associate Safaricom with Kenya's banking and finance elites—a problem that has hampered previous efforts by Equity Bank to scale as well.[24] Interestingly, some of these interlocutors turned to alternative fintech loan providers such as Branch or Tigo. Those already skeptical of the current president's family were quick to point out that M-Shwari makes use of personal data from the SIM card—and seemed unaware that other fintech lenders cast an even wider surveillance net into SMS messaging and social media.

During divisive 2017 elections, the opposition party NASA (National Super Alliance) capitalized on Safaricom's cozy relationship with the government and financial elites. Opposition candidate Raila Odinga challenged the official election results by calling for an M-Pesa boycott, saying Safaricom had transmitted bribes and false election returns. He publicly registered with Safaricom competitor Airtel. Surrounded by cheering supporters, he displayed his new Airtel SIM to TV cameras.[25] On social media, supporters of this opposition-led boycott repainted their bright green Safaricom kiosks the red color of Airtel—leading only to confusion and humorous online memes, as red is also the color of the incumbent Kenyatta presidency. During the months leading up to the reelection, it was hard to judge the success of the Safaricom boycott. My Nairobi interlocutors viewed it as either a populist resistance movement for the ages or little more than a media farce. My sister-in-law Lillian offered that even the opposition leader and his supporters would never *really* give up their Safaricom lines. "He must have another line that he is not using for the moment." If anything, the association between Safaricom and the Kenyan state was strengthened.

The Digital Revolution Becomes the Debt Society

In 2020, more than ten years into the digital finance revolution, observers are taking stock of the impact. Just as the visions of leapfrogging and cultural wealth have had to face the reproduction of divides and inequalities, the so-called pro-poor financial system is not producing greater financial well-being. It actually may be more *pro-poverty*. The risks and dangers that it has created include the high cost of access, taxes and service fees, the rise of a debt society, and hacking and data security breaches.

The high cost of money transfer is ever a flashpoint of resistance and complaint. Fees are assessed at cash in and at cash out, and people do their best to avoid them through social means: one might be politely asked or forced through circumstance to cover fees for elders, children, or one's subordinates. Furthermore, the money transfer fee increases with the amount of money sent—which many users object to.[26] To make matters worse, many cash-strapped African governments are levying considerable taxes on money transfer, now up to 12% in Kenya. One political cartoon suggested that if Members of Parliament were paid their generous salaries through M-Pesa, then they would soon do away with this tax rather than be subject to it themselves. In the summer of 2017 efforts by the Government of Uganda to impose a mobile money and social media tax were countered by street demonstrations, some of them put down with tear gas. In the end the pushback was effective, and a planned 3% tax on cash in and cash out was reduced to 0.5%. The digitization of money is a tempting source of revenue for African governments, which have few other sources.

With the advent of digital credit and the merging of banking and telecommunications interests, along with global investment in digital credit, Kenya's digital money system is now able to reach every Kenyan with quick money as debt—for some interests, this was the goal all along. In June 2017, Visa announced it was moving into the Kenyan market with free money transfer; soon afterward, credit reporting firm Transunion followed. Transunion Kenya chief executive Billy Owino said the mobile money ecosystem had "outgrown necessity-based transactions and peer-to-peer lending and is now transiting [*sic*] into mobile credit and loans."[27] Is it true, as Owino stated, that Kenya's digital finance system has outgrown its roots in the emotional currencies of airtime money?

An emerging debt society is making digital money more expensive rather than less so. Digital microcredit offers small, short-term loans via the mobile money channel. These loans are endorsed by development interests as useful business capital for informal artisans, farmers, and entrepreneurs and as vehicles for female empowerment.[28] The capital flows supporting digital credit companies are framed as social investing.[29] At a 2015 public presentation I attended at the microfinance consultancy group CGAP, digital debt was endorsed as a source of short-term liquidity for low-income households. A financial diary study of 300 poor Kenyan households[30] was cited to demonstrate that digital credit would smooth these incomes.

M-Shwari is not just a debt product but also an interest-bearing account. A similar bank/debt product is offered through KCB. Both of these banks are easily accessed from the Safaricom menu, and they are both regulated. Their credit scoring is based on SIM card activity such as airtime buying and over time will build a customer's loan limit. An advertisement for M-Shwari features a young woman in blue jeans and tattoos saying, "Lock your *chums* [slang for "money"] to meet your dreams." Many other debt providers—as many as 24 digital lender fintech companies in Kenya—are accessible through smartphone app. Only deposit-taking entities are considered financial institutions in the country, so many of these debt providers are unregulated. Many are based outside of Kenya, such as Branch, Tala, and MyBucks. Initial short-term loans may be as small as $10.

A flurry of unregulated loan providers was unleashed after a 2016 regulation capped bank loan interest rates. The banks tightened their lending practices and many people turned to fintechs or the KCB or M-Shwari loans available on mobile phones for credit.[31] Several recent reports based on customer data and user surveys underscore the pervasive use of these loans.[32] About 100,000 digital loans are taken out per day in Kenya and about 70 million digital credit loans were issued in Kenya from 2014 to 2107. At least 35% of Kenyans with a phone have taken out one of these loans. Multiple loans are common, with people taking out more than one loan at a time or taking a new loan to repay a previous one. Young, often underemployed men make significant use of digital credit for betting on sports.[33] Digital credit has become one of the most popular and common forms of loans, displacing shop credit and to some extent friends and family loans, and being used for everyday needs and emergencies much more often than for business needs.[34] Possibly even more pervasive than digital debt is Safaricom's Fuliza overdraft service. This service will automatically garnish your Safaricom wallet. Ironically, people with outstanding Fuliza balances may prefer to borrow, lend, and pay with cash!

Several remarkably critical industry reports discuss a litany of consumer risks that have arisen with digital debt. Data security breaches and identity theft have been pervasive issues. Because security initially took a backseat to openness and inclusion as agent networks rolled out, many agents still routinely copy ID card numbers into hand-penciled ledger books. It is also common to leave one's ID with a building doorman in urban spaces. Since 2017 many M-Pesa users have fallen victim to a SIM swap scam, where a SIM card registration is transferred to another user without their knowledge, and the second user then changes the PIN to access the first user's account balance. Agents and phone company employees as well as hackers have been implicated in these scams. Identity fraud increases the risks of digital debt. Studies of consumer data found that from 2016 to 2018, 26.4% of borrowers had taken "two consecutive loans within 30 days" from the same providers—suggesting a remarkably high prevalence of identity fraud.[35]

A growing debt society is being built on exposed digital identities and vulnerable customer data. A survey of digital loan providers globally showed that they did not have adequate protections and do not take responsibility for breaches in their terms and conditions.[36] Digital loans use customer data in algorithmic credit scoring, and before 2019 changes to the Kenyan government's data privacy policies, some providers routinely delved into text messages and Facebook activity without informed consent. Regulated credit providers on the Safaricom menu use data about airtime and mobile money activity. The same report found that few Kenyans understood that this activity was being scored. In spite of data laws, unregulated providers may still be reaching into SMS, Facebook, or other sources.

Finally, digital loan interest rates are not lower than those of traditional banks, calling into question the rationale for scaling these products. Digital loans provided by banks are regulated and have the lowest fees: KCB's loans cost 6% on a 30-day term and deduct it up front. M-Shwari charges 7.5% of the loan value. M-Shwari might begin a customer at a $20 loan and give 30 days to repay. However, this rate doubles if the loan is not paid within that 30 days and effectively translates to an APR (average percentage rate, the cost of borrowing for a year) of 90%. Customers can increase their loan limits through prompt repayment, but they cannot lower interest rates with any of the digital credit providers except Equity Bank, which initially charges 10% per month.

By 2017 about 10% of Kenyan adults had defaulted on digital loans. Many ended up being listed with the Credit Bureau of Kenya—up to 400,000 people were blacklisted for amounts less than $2—representing a clear case of financial exclusion, not financial inclusion. A payment may be required to again qualify for loans.[37] By 2019 more than 25% of loans were non-performing.[38] Evaluative reports charge that "[p]redatory practices and aggressive marketing have forced consumers into debt traps."[39] Tactics may include frequent SMS nudging, social media shaming, and aggressive language. Credit is widely used by people at all income levels, including informal artisans, traders, and the urban poor, but they are often unable to repay and lack the cash flow to strategize or plan repayment.[40]

In 2015 *The Economist* reported that Kenya was the number two most indebted country in the world after South Africa—80% of Kenyans over the age of fifteen reported taking out a loan in 2015.[41] Kenya's finance landscape, and the rapid rise of unregulated debt, seems poised to recapitulate the story of financial technology in two highly unequal societies, the United States and South Africa. In both of these countries, changing monetary technologies were ostensibly employed to democratize financial services and to provide disadvantaged or marginalized people with opportunities for prosperity. But in both of these countries, financial services have reproduced inequality and insecurity for some while creating enormous profits in the financial industry: a process of *predatory inclusion.*[42]

In the United States, the rise of the credit card in the 1970s accompanied the growth of computer networks that could aggregate, store, and manage ever larger amounts of customer financial data.[43] These networks consolidated in the 1980s and 1990s and as they grew, lobbied away state-level usury laws. Consumer credit has effectively become a world of special monies differentiated by race and class, whether for everyday spending or for home mortgage loans.

Today, riding on digital and Internet payment, the credit card/data society has reached even further into people's everyday money use. Credit money is a privilege, offered at varying prices and with varying perks such points, miles, discounts, or travel lounge access, depending on customer creditworthiness. Financial services have splintered into class- and race-coded products that reinforce inequalities with fees, fines, high-interest loans, and demeaning treatment.[44] Wealth has become concentrated and Americans have very little savings and a great deal of debt; while affluent families can benefit from debt, poor families and black families pay more for debt, and are more likely to be harmed by it.[45]

In South Africa, a 1990s boom in the "right to credit" post-apartheid environment similarly expanded informal and semiformal microcredit and cultural finance like burial insurance.[46] But technology was employed to ensure repayment and help lenders recover their costs. Here debtors are powerless against a plethora of financial companies that can transfer money out of their accounts. A government social grants technology was used in highly coercive ways to burden people with debt and services and to deduct payments without their knowledge.[47] Debtors often support extended families in a society highly conscious of status, family obligation, and shame; defaults and precarity ripple through social networks, along with family conflict, divorce, and even suicide. In the world's most unequal country, finance has become more, not less racialized.[48]

The 2019 report from FSD Kenya was alarming.[49] This extensive survey of consumer finance and digital finance showed that in spite of the greater reach of finance and credit products into people's lives, their overall financial health had greatly declined since 2016. Only 20% of Kenyans—all income levels—were financially healthy, as measured by their ability to save for emergencies, plan, and meet their daily needs (down from 39% in 2016). Many had lost money to digital scams. Although inclusion in terms of accounts and usage of products has increased, people are *not* benefiting. It is hard to reconcile the celebratory narrative of M-Pesa with the consumer risks it soon created. Consumer finance is now rapidly embracing the same practices that have made inclusion adverse or predatory elsewhere, including extractive fines and fees, theft and loss of money, and consumer credit lending that submits online personal data with questionable relevance to financial risk to algorithmic analysis.[50]

Most damning of all, the 2019 Findex showed that people continue to rely on and trust their friend and family networks and informal savings groups far above any formal product. Financial inclusion in Kenya has been a failure. The need to reimagine a better kind of money is even more pressing.

The Real Origins of M-Pesa

In 2012, news reports sought to correct the urban legend of the African student. An official letter from Safaricom explaining the origins of M-Pesa circulated online, explaining how Vodafone engineers had devised the service. The Human IPO website then rebuked supporters of the Kenyan inventor idea: "There is absolutely nothing Kenyan about M-Pesa. It is thoroughly British." But even this correction was unfair. As well explained in Real Money, Quick by Omwansa and Sullivan, in 2003 Nick Hughes, a Safaricom executive, approached Vodafone with an idea for a money transfer service. His original idea was turned down, but it was eventually supported by the UK Department for International Development, which was matched by Safaricom and other stakeholders. By 2005 the product was tested with 500 microloan clients through the microfinance institution (MFI) Faulu Kenya.

Knowing the importance of *sambaza*, you will not be surprised to learn what happened. The clients innovated new uses. Instead of paying back their loans, "they sent e-money to friends and relatives; loaded up their accounts before journeys to keep money safe; and repaid other people's loans."[51] M-Pesa's first rollout emphasized these services: buying airtime, storing value on the handset, and money transfer.

In 2012, Nzioka Waita, director of corporate affairs at Safaricom, put the controversy to rest with the official word on the genesis of M-Pesa as a collaboration: "I would first start by addressing the question of whether the origin of M-Pesa is Kenyan or British. The answer is neither. . . . M-Pesa is the product of years of collaborative research and innovation driven by teams in Kenya, the UK and other parts of the world."[52]

Whose Money Is This?

Official resolutions aside, the question still lingers: whose money is this? On Kenyan Twitter, people share and commiserate over long lists of outstanding Fuliza, Branch, Tala, and M-Shwari balances. They complain about a lack of customer redress, fake appeals, taxes and fees, their disappearing account balance used to offset Fuliza loans, and the SIM card swap scam. And the lost inventor of M-Pesa is still alive and well here, and still celebrated, as in this December 2019 tweet: "I think Safcom should pay the Luo boy who actually actualized M-Pesa some good chums [slang for "money"])." He is a reminder of M-Pesa's origins in informal practices with airtime and of the lucrative market built on local currencies of knowledge and affection.

Could his struggle be a metaphor for reimagining finance as, of all things, a pathway to equality and inclusion? And where will digital payment go from here? Conflicts over fees, taxes, debt, and profit now challenge the unity imagined by "our Kenyan brand." The channel enacts the distributive politics of social class and ethnic tensions, technological divides and barriers, and data capture. But while financial inclusion has been a failure, the cultural practice of money has been a success. Clearly another kind of inclusion is being sought and found. We will turn to the everyday life of digital money in the following chapters.

Money and Wealth-in-People

5

The Three Stages of Money

"I can log on to the fund . . . I can see how the fund is performing. Who is contributing? . . . I can offer my advice to the family on the progress of the fund." As related in Chapter 1, Dr. Andrew Mullei, Central Bank of Kenya (CBK) governor from 2001 to 2004, spoke with me in 2016 about how digital money was changing banking. He stressed the benefits of new digital forms of money and contrasted them to two previous forms: first, the traditional money of his WaKamba community, goats; and second, the subsequent currency money of British colonialism.

Dr. Mullei gave an example of how money as goats circulated in his community's traditions. An uncle can give a goat to his nephew as a gift. After that, an uncle can "be taking a stroll" to his brother-in-law's compound periodically to assess how the goat is faring. "Is my brother-in-law taking care of the goat? Has it reproduced?" An uncle can continue to keep track of the condition of the goat and its offspring, he explained, as long as he stays in good stead with his in-laws.

The visibility of the goat as money contrasted with the lack of visibility with regard to cash as money during European colonialism. Because cash money could be easily hidden, "even in a pocket," Dr. Mullei reasoned, it introduced problems of secrecy and corruption, problems riddling the banking sphere, which he had personally tackled as a reformer. Finally, Dr. Mullei explained that digital technology was transforming money for a second time, now bringing visibility and transparency *back* to money. He used two examples. The first was the real-time gross settlement (RTGS) system, which had given his Central Bank more control over the settlement of interbank transfers and a way to prevent defaults. Through these and other improvements, Dr. Mullei had strengthened the banking sector and uncovered fraud in a well-known consumer bank. His second example was an Internet-based family educational fund, to which all members could contribute. Dr. Mullei logs on to his family fund frequently to see which of his children and grandchildren have contributed their shares. His role is to provide advice for the effort. When his children and grandchildren have not contributed in some time, he can "try to find out why and encourage them to contribute." He was now providing advice to his son Kyai, the CEO of a Silicon Savanna start-up crowdfunding website called M-Changa ("to collect"), which is bringing the family fund shared-ledger model to online fundraising.

In this chapter I will discuss the history of changing money forms. Dr. Mullei told his story as three historical stages of money, with cash replacing the goat, to be in turn replaced by digital money. Like other leapfroggers, Dr. Mullei is an evangelist for digital money. He is attuned to the material agency of money: a goat can be seen, a paper note hidden. Furthermore, he sees the history of money as a set of stages, each version of money replacing what was before. But Dr. Mullei is a money leapfrogger who reverses the narrative's direction: digital money is a leap *backward*. In his telling, technological evolution does away with the corruption of colonialism and the postcolonial state and reverses the pathway, returning Africans to a traditional form of visible money.

All these forms of money were part of a theory of value that can be summed up as "wealth-in-people."[1] This well-known concept is associated with institutions frequently described in sub-Saharan Africa, such as gerontocracy, patron-client relations, and the high-status "big man" who publicly distributes wealth. Here, I use it in a more focused sense to describe a world in which rights in people are the main basis of prestige, power, and access to resources. Consequently, people seek, claim, and call on rights in others—to their labor, support, reproductive capacity, or property. In so doing they use things, especially money, to shape ties of obligation, debt, and alliance with others.[2] In particular, then, wealth-in-people is the ability to do things with, for, and through other people. Money, whether goats, currency, or digital money, is used to influence and mobilize others, and draw on their labor, knowledge and skill, loyalty, affection, and material resources.

Where did "wealth-in-people" come from? Anthropologist Harold Schneider's theory started with East Africa's long history of livestock pastoralism, in which cows and goats were both food and money. For him, wealth-in-people was a political economy based on a form of money that was alive and that reproduced. Working among the Turu of Tanzania, he showed that cattle as living wealth was a naturally expanding money supply. As the size of one's herds increased along with the need for more space for grazing, a larger homestead, and other expenses, they were loaned to others or given as bridewealth to create debts and alliances, leading to "widespread access [to money] and the growth of cross-cutting financial ties.[3] Unlike cattle, which require space and care, webs of alliances could be accumulated.

As webs of credit and debt relationships, the networks of wealth-in-people are not egalitarian. Where people are wealth, there is a social hierarchy around rights in people. Individuals seek to possess or accumulate rights to others but also to *be* wealth-in-people—they seek belonging in a kin group as a fundamental social, legal, political, and ritual protective unit. This "belonging in," then, is paradoxically also "belonging to."[4] Inequality was a continuum from, on one end, full belonging and possession of rights in others, to the other end, where the young or more recently incorporated were wealth to others. Wealth-in-people focuses on "asymmetrical relationships, that is, on the accumulation of power by individuals or groups by making themselves the center of networks of connection—through mixtures of coercion and attraction."[5] Status and political authority emerge around people with the ability to mobilize others and bring together group members with diverse talents and attributes.[6]

In "wealth-in-people," economic exchanges materialize and symbolize rights in people. Wealth-in-people is different from the idea of "social capital."[7] For Bourdieu, social capital described "actual or potential resources linked to the possession of a network or membership in a group."[8] His definition emphasizes material resources, with social ties as a means to gain wealth-in-things. As a cultural theory of value, wealth-in-people is the opposite idea; it was derived from ethnographic descriptions in societies where people "were the pinnacle, and even the unit of measurement, of ultimate value (Guyer and Belinga 1995, 92)." From the analytical view, however, as the sociology of relational work has elucidated, all "economic transactions [are] fundamentally social interactions."[9] As Zelizer explains it, specific material or media exchanges, such as a goat, create distinct relationships with their own meanings, temporalities, and moral qualities—"relational packages" such as "maternal uncle."[10]

Ideas about Value: Bridewealth and Wealth-in-People

Let us return to Dr. Mullei's story of changing forms of money and how they shaped wealth-in-people, beginning with the goat. As Dr. Mullei explained, a maternal uncle can show generosity by giving a money goat to his nephew as a kind of free gift, a gesture of goodwill across a social divide. In his patrilineal society, he explained, a woman is considered to marry out of her own family into her husband's family. Among the WaKamba the groom's relatives initiated a marriage proposal by sending two goats to the bride's family, who would respond with two calabashes of beer to signify acceptance; the bridewealth was stipulated as one bull, two cows, and "some number" of goats.[11] Dr. Mullei also described continual gifts as shows of "respect." Politeness and generosity are highly valued among in-laws. (And yet when relationships go sour, hostility can quickly emerge.)

His account echoed the anthropologists' interpretations. They saw marriage exchanges as building reciprocities between families over time. From this perspective, one's sister's children belong to their father's lineage. In the legalistic interpretation of early anthropologists, the bridewealth transferred rights to the woman, her labor, and/or children to her husband's group. Dr. Mullei's goat, the gift from maternal uncle to nephew, thus moves in the opposite direction, from the bride's family to the groom's, and represents the ultimate generosity— giving to people who actually owe *you*.

But as anthropologists learned more about East African marriage, they realized that the theory of exchange or transfer of rights did not fully explain bridewealth. In fact, in many cases the marriage agreement was less stable. Schneider felt that brothers never feel fully compensated for the loss of their sisters in marriage: "There is an ambivalence about marriage, a feeling that something is not quite right and a tendency always to view the husband as a usurper."[12] Not surprisingly, the often-complex negotiations around livestock transfers arrive at a fragile and unsettled compromise in which husbands give repeated gifts and service over time to their wife's family; at a man's death, "obstruction, litigation and rival claims" over bridewealth often occur.[13]

Dr. Mullei's goat is a not-so-subtle reminder of this unresolved exchange. The condition of the goat can be assessed during a "stroll" to one's brother-in-law's compound. A brother still values his sister and her child and cares about their welfare—"Is my brother-in-law taking good care of the goat?" As a reminder of a debt it is also a way of accounting for the value of relationships and of persons.[14] Bridewealth, then, expresses the value of a woman's labor and her other embodied qualities and abilities along with the commitment and depth of the families' social networks.[15] When these values are disputed, the resulting exchanges can engender asymmetry or ambiguity. The unresolved nature of the exchange often means that rights to women must be constantly reinforced with gifts to keep a marriage intact.

As a generator of wealth-in-people, money first of all expresses altruistic qualities like generosity and caring. Second, it creates social ties and symbolizes the relationship between in-laws and the rights of elders to claim the marriage cattle. And third, money is a contested measure of the value of persons and their embodied qualities and abilities that can be contested and non-equivalent.

Rituals of Wealth-in-People

Most of the research for this book was undertaken in Bungoma County in Western Kenya among Luhya-speaking Bukusu people. Here, cattle are still a form of wealth. According to anthropological accounts from 1930s-era research, Luhya men inherited their father's cattle—"the cattle of the yard."[16] More-recent study suggests that women had their own circuits of cattle, which they could raise, trade, and bequeath.[17] At funerals cattle are sacrificed for blessings and apportioned to children and relatives by birth order and seniority. Twelve cows are considered a generous bridewealth, given from the groom's family to the bride's.

These exchanges initiate continued gifts back and forth. Accounts described complicated circulations of cattle and obligatory gifts among in-laws at various junctures. Among the Nuer of the South Sudan, such gifts were known as "the cow of the cooking ceremony; the cow which one owes to the son of one's father's brother as a counter-gift for having received a share in the marriage cattle given for his sister; the bull to which an uncle has a claim in the case of his nephew's death"; and several others.[18] Cattle were a record of social ties and the embodiment of spiritual forces. Nuer men and women took their names from their favorite cows. Each cow was "an account of kinship affinities" and a mystical link to the spirits of a lineage, who were worshiped by rubbing ashes on a cow's spine.[19]

The numerical qualities of cattle gifts speak to their use as money. The Bukusu ideal number of bridewealth cows was twelve—a number with many factors, one that could be easily divided into sets of two, three, four, or six to be
distributed to relatives and other claimants along varying paths. The avuncular
gift giving that Dr. Mullei described takes place when a Bukusu youth comes of
age. In 2014 a maturity ritual marking this rite of passage was still the norm.[20]
At this time, a boy is first given own livestock and, importantly, a cow from
his uncle. This "thirteenth cow," or cow of *lixoni*,[21] recognizes the son's maturity and fulfillment of his parents' marriage. The thirteenth cow, an odd, prime
number, is that reminder of the continued and open negotiation of the payment, and to Schneider (1968), the greater value of a sister that the bridewealth
cannot fully commensurate. The varying interpretations of the thirteenth cow
demonstrate the conflicting interests of in-laws. Uncles view it (as Dr. Mullei
did his goat) as a free gift that flows in the opposite direction and shows generosity. The initiate's father and uncles may call it a rightful "return" of their
cattle. For mothers the thirteenth cow means that they are still valued in their
natal homes. The ritual provides a field of argument for all these competing
interpretations of value.

Cattle were, and are, a store of wealth-in-people held by extended family
groups. They are also a means of accounting for and building the value of people. As they reproduce and move from one group to another, like humans, they
shape humans' identities and serve as a mirror for society and its relationships
as the value of people and cattle are interdefined.[22] Animal gifts show reciprocity across the life cycle and are a measure of the growing value of a person. For
example, at the Bukusu maturity ritual a boy begins to gradually accumulate
masculine personhood in his body until he amasses the maximum amount of it
as an elder.[23] The end point of the process, which comes two years after a man's
physical death, is called "to cut the rope": the sister's son (who likely received
the thirteenth cow during a previous ritual) climbs to the roof of the dead man's
house and detaches the tip of the wooden center pole there.[24] At this ritual
marking the final departure to the realm of the ancestors, the man's remaining
cattle and other wealth are distributed to his heirs.

Gifts that move across intergenerational time establish the hierarchy of the
generations. They "organize a transfer of output [from older to younger genera-
tions] . . . [by giving] the old some item[—]it need not be material[—]which
they can trade to the younger generation."[25] At a coming-of-age ceremony, for
example, the old trade their masculinity to the young over time in return for

labor, care, and deference. Cattle are a testament to the ultimate gift that is given by the old men to the young: their status as a respected male adult. Cattle are the currency of the growing value of people across the lifespan, a value that is nonetheless debated and contested.

Cash Money and Colonialism

Dr. Mullei's parable moved from precolonial goats to colonial money, which, hidden in a pocket, brings corruption. Indeed, the introduction of currency was a heavy instrument of the European civilizing mission in Africa. The political and military conquest of Kenya, beginning in 1895, established foreign domination and Kenya's role as a producer of raw materials for industrial Britain. Money was intended to impose an imperial identity and control the labor and production of Africans in the colonial economy. As John Lonsdale put it, "Capitalist colonialism both destroyed the old economic dynamic and denied to Africans equitable access to a new one."[26] Through the coercive power of taxation a significant portion of the population was drawn into capitalist and market economies to perform work and produce foodstuffs as commodities. They were dispossessed of their land and rights in the process. Along with other institutions, banking and cooperatives were closed to African participation for most of the colonial period.

In order for colonial money to control people, they needed to use it. Interestingly, Dr. Mullei's pocket issue actually came up for colonial money designers, who noted that East Africans had no pockets, but instead often wore bead and shell currencies on their bodies and clothing, denominating it into strings. As a result, the colonial East African 10-cent coin was designed with a central hole, to be strung and worn in a similar way.[27] Wearing currency may also have discouraged concealment, which Dr. Mullei decried.

East Africans had abundant forms of money. The Baganda king controlled the production and circulation of ivory discs, each worth more than 100 cowries, and he accepted tribute in the form of fine barkcloth, exceptional cattle, or rare beads.[28] Copper coins minted by the Sultanate of Kilwa, on the coast of East Africa, circulated as a means of exchange and were symbols of Islamic purity and kingly authority.[29] Colonial money failed to act as a pure imposition of colonial control and was integrated into these complex circuits. Money remained a sphere of agency for East Africans, who worked out their relationships to colonial currencies in "encounters between different regimes of value."[30] Cash money earned from colonial wages was often set aside and marked, thus separating the colonial market economy from the sphere of wealth-in-people. In the 1970s among the Luo, money earned from breaking taboos or selling cash crops or family land was called "bitter money."[31] In the early twentieth century, among the Nuer of the South Sudan, youths who worked for cash could purchase and have greater personal control over "the cattle of money"—as distinct from the cattle of kinship obligations, which were marked as "the cattle of the girls." Some stigma was associated with currency money, as it lacked the "blood" or life force of cattle; and cattle bought from wages earned by cleaning chamber pots were denigrated as "the cattle of shit."[32] However, newfound cattle of money ended up increasing the use and importance of bridewealth, not reducing it.

By integrating colonial currency into wealth-in-people, East African informal economies and social networks became a means of surviving imperialism and post-imperialism and responding to the challenges of urban-rural migration, precarity, uncertainty, and increasing social inequality.[33] Traders from the region around Machakos supplied the colonial capital of Nairobi with foodstuffs and other goods. Kamba women returned this money to their homelands to sustain their families, build housing and wells, and create roles of social importance.[34] Urban spaces produced new network identities. Women in Nairobi created domestic and caring spaces for male workers, sometimes returning the money they earned to their fathers and brothers, and sometimes building their own lineages and networks.[35] Flexible and novel interpersonal ties have multiplied social hierarchies and created new social identities. These networks of informal economies have sustained relationships of friendship, mutual care, and financial cooperation; ensured food security; forged trade and market pathways; and built sustainable communities under onerous conditions ranging from informal settlements to refugee camps.[36]

New Money Networks

Wale Adebanwi writes that after decades of postcolonial crisis in Africa, "the extremities of wealth and poverty have produced a progressive eradication of the middle ground between human happiness and human misery."[37] With neoliberal reforms and the retreat of state institutions, "the informal economy becomes the whole economy."[38] The Silicon Savanna describes a new era of market-based and technological interventions. Technical experts like Dr. Mullei look to technology, such as bank settlement or ledger software, to reshape money relations around transparency and trust.

In this world of precarity and inequality, people continue to survive through sharing and circulating money in networks.[39] The state's money is blamed for upending the social order; among the rural Luo poor, the bitter money of the 1970s had become by the 2000s a "bad money," associated with social disorder, greed, poverty and isolation, and political corruption. But money is also *uwezo*, the ability to do things and be an agentive person.[40] With money, people can calculate and plan the future and create a sense of hope.[41]

In the twenty-first century, money is still incorporated into the moral economy of wealth-in-people. For example, in increasingly impoverished Samburu communities suffering from climate change, accumulating wealth through exchanging livestock is no longer possible. Young Samburu men who worked as escorts at Kenya's tourist beaches used their earned money to return home and marry, becoming elders early—"young big-men." Some destitute elders went to the beaches too, but found little sexual interest from European women tourists. Returning home, they were berated as "beach-boy elders."[42] Even as young men's affluence subverted the gerontocracy, they still returned home to pay bridewealth and support the interdependencies of their community, where wealth and status are built by extending alliances over time and the life cycle.

Contemporary Rituals of Wealth-in-People

Ritual continues to be a vital part of financial activities, with costly life cycle ceremonies summoning large numbers of people and collecting surprising amounts of money. Rituals serve to display success and prestige, create opportunities for entrepreneurialism and gain, coordinate plans around education, migration, and family investments, dispute social hierarchies, and recognize new identities and solidarities.[43] Above all, they are a financial institution that transfers wealth across the generations.

In 2014, we conducted research at the Bukusu maturity ritual for adolescent boys to understand how mobile and digital money would be incorporated. We followed 46 households celebrating the maturity ritual, and we sketched out how each family handled the financing of it.[44] Digital money became a part of the multiple regimes of value brought together in the event, but it also created conflict in social relations.

Western Kenya

In precolonial times, the Bukusu lived in large, circular-walled communities that would incorporate several clans, with each clan using a separate gate.[45] Photographs from the 1930s show clusters of conical-roofed homes surrounded by patches of cultivation and large areas of forest and woodland.[46] Colonial and postcolonial policies beginning with a 1903 massacre imposed taxes to force these communities into wage labor.[47] Some lands in this area were appropriated for extensive settler farms. Most importantly, colonial land policy broke up the clans to create nuclear-family peasant households. The 1954 Swynnerton Plan imposed individual land titling, initiating several doomed efforts to financialize the land.[48]

Individuating these rural lands destroyed wealth-in-people and created the problem of poverty, which is very much in evidence in the area today. A 2005 survey of 414 rural households in the Kimilili region found that 70% of households earned less than 5,000 shillings ($50) per month from remittances coming in, wage or other labor, or selling farm produce.[49] These rural households farmed plots between one-quarter and four acres in size. About 20% of the surveyed adults had finished high school. Most of them experienced periods of hunger, particularly before harvest time.

The Coming-of-Age

The maturity ritual takes place every two years, and involves a series of events around a large feast, including a visit to relatives; a visit to the mother's brother to be given the thirteenth cow; some kind of circumcision, either at the hospital or in a traditional manner at the river at dawn, which is played up to inspire the maximum show of bravery; and three months later a "passing out" or resolution of the liminal phase, in which the newly created young man is given new clothes. Sometimes a home of his own called "the lion's den" will be built on family lands.

The animal gifts, foodstuffs, and other items required for the ritual must be bought with money. Mzee Nathan is a grandfather in the Bungoma area who is widely respected as an authority on maturity rituals. He has circumcised nine sons, and as he put it, "To show his love for his son, a father has to spend." Although the best thirteenth cow is a large bull, most of the animals given today are young, inexpensive livestock bought at the local market, where the price goes up during the ritual season. The financial imperative of this ritual was experienced with bitter irony by most of the parents in our study. Fathers told stories of the large size of their forefathers' farms, waving their hands toward the horizon and emphasizing how many wives were needed to farm so much land.

The Coming-of-Age Today: Some Households

How do families pay for the event? How do they use digital money to make it happen? Five of the households are described below and in Table 5.1.

Walter is about to start high school. He is the third-born child, and his parents farm two acres of maize, bananas, and sweet potatoes. They sell the last two crops and can earn about 5,000 ($50) per month. They keep two bulls, which they rent out during the plowing season, earning about 7,000 ($70).

In July his parents cut down a tree and sold it for 13,000 ($130) about two weeks before the expected feast for friends and relatives. His father had planned to sell one of the bulls, but then decided not to part with what he called his "moneymaker." Walter's mother also timed her savings club "win" of $60 to this event to buy food and the millet to make ritual beer. She is a member of two other groups and had funds for the ritual set aside in a secret place in her house. Any home that does not provide an abundant feast does not respect the ancestors, and she did not want anything to happen to the money she had set aside. Later in December, another, smaller event required $60.

Franco's family farms about four acres, half for sugarcane and half for small crops and their own consumption. They also earn money from casual labor (around $30 per month) and keep dairy animals (which earn around $20 per month if they calve); these endeavors supplement a monthly income of around $20 from the sugarcane and other crops. About one month before the celebration, Franco's father, Patrick, had $100 on his M-Pesa account, which he said was for the feast. At that time Patrick had expected to sacrifice a cow from the family herd to feast his guests.

When we visited a few days before the event, the paternal uncles were holding an all-day meeting to plan logistics. Patrick had changed his mind about killing one of his own animals and had purchased a young cow for the guests. His animals were good milkers and he preferred to keep them. His mother, Roselyn, would prepare around 80 liters of homemade beer for the upcoming ceremony. She had also purchased flour to make *chapatis* (tortillas). Franco's older brother would soon take him to visit his uncle, where he would be feasted with a sacrificial animal and given the thirteenth cow. Roselyn used her phone to collect some of the e-money gifts he was sent, including $5 from their pastor. Other small gifts in cash were also uploaded to her phone account to make a total of $8 in the mother's M-Pesa account for saving on behalf of the boy. The money was contributed by paternal uncles, parents, sisters, and brothers. The family spent about $170 on the feast, including the cow Patrick had purchased to eat. They would spend about $100 three months later for a final ritual.

Barasa's father bought a cow in April after he received income from sugarcane on another farm he has with another wife. This cow would yield two calves, which could be sold for $100 each. His sugarcane yields about $600 every 18 months from the sugar company. The farmers' cooperative gave him a $200 loan to fund the second December event, which required hiring a tent, plastic seats, and a stereo system and buying about $80 worth of food. His relatives sent the boy money for new clothes on his father's M-Pesa account. His father also gave him $5 to keep and use later.

Kevin's unpartnered mother, Hellen, farms one acre of land and earns about $30 a month from farm income. Kevin will go to a local hospital for an operation, where a pastor will say blessings. A traditional affair is too expensive, Hellen explained. Instead, she had asked her savings group for a $20 payout for the hospital fee and to make a nice meal for her brother, who helped take Kevin to the hospital. She is also keeping $25 in a secret savings place, reserved for buying Kevin new clothes.

Steven is the third child of six. His parents farm one acre of maize, and his father bakes and sells bricks. His family had no feast but served tea, sodas, and bananas to a small group. For the December passing out, his father took out an M-Shwari loan of $35. He signed up for M-Shwari specifically to fund the ritual. He used the loan to buy clothes, shoes, and bedding for Steven, and several of Steven's mother's friends collected $8 for him. Steven's family was the only one in our study to take out a digital loan to fund the ritual.

Table 5.1. Four families' expenditures and gifts (all figures in US dollars) at a coming-of-age ritual, August 2014

	Walter	Franco	Barasa	Kevin	Steven
Total Cost (US $)	250	270	330	45	42 (US $35 from M-Shwari)
Gifts					
Thirteenth cow	Yes	Yes	Pledged	No	No
Cows for feasting	2	2	3	—	—
Other animals "for fees"	—	—	goat	2 hens	—
M-Pesa gifts (US $)	4	5	16	—	—
Cash gifts (US $)	5	12	5	10	8
Other gifts	Prayers Textbooks School bag Soccer ball Shoes "for school"	Songs and blessings Advice "to fit in to society" Blanket Sandals Gumboots Textbooks for school	Prayers and teachings Clothing Exercise books Bedsheets	Songs and prayers 10 exercise books Wooden bed, sweater, socks Books and pens Watch Jacket Bicycle	Prayer service Exercise books Shorts and shoes

The thirteenth cow is a ritual cow given by a maternal uncle. The other gifts come from friends, relatives, and church members.

The Uses of Digital Money and Mobile Communication

During the ritual, mobile phones, the M-Pesa wallet, and digital money transfer capability combined to provide families with the resources for several indispensable parts of the celebration: coordinating and planning the event, ride hailing, setting aside a reserve, fundraising, and gift giving.

Coordinating and planning.   Mobile communication allowed the rapid exchange and circulation of information and money information through text message. During the visiting phase of the ritual, all of the families used mobile phones to invite some of their friends and relatives to the ceremony in lieu of some of the traditional visiting. It was common to invite 50 or more people using phone calls, widening the ritual's catchment area from Western Kenya to embrace international migrants, some of whom sent gift remittances via mobile. Micro-coordination allowed for plans' flexibility and change as needed.[50] Money transfer could save face for hosts and accommodate unexpected happenings—money sent or stored could be spent refilling the beer pot when a set of elders suddenly showed up at the house of a Christian teetotaling family, or when a father and uncles decided at the last minute to purchase more gifts, or when a relative spontaneously offered to rent a sound system, relocate the ritual feast, or pay for gasoline for a truck to carry the boy and his gifts home in style. The feast showed a family's moral and material worthiness. Locations, events, and donations often came together through micro-coordination via mobile phone in the last two or three days.

Marianne (Figure 5.1) and her family provide an example. They were celebrating her third of four sons. Marianne pointedly told me that the thirteenth cow brings blessings specifically to a mother; it means her family has not forgotten her in marriage. Although a generous bridewealth of eight cattle had been given at her own marriage, her family was not reciprocating as her sons went through maturity. Her second son had received the thirteenth cow, but her eldest had not. In recent weeks she had contacted several male relatives by phone and sent her son to visit them wearing his school uniform and bearing his good exam results. In disappointment she eventually redrew plans around holding a joint event with a neighbor.

Ride hailing.   In keeping with the wishes of the elders, all of the families in our study included direct home visits as part of their rituals. Many used ride-hailing services on motorcycles to travel to relatives' houses.

Figure 5.1. Marianne (center) posing with the author (right). At the time this photograph was taken, she was looking for the thirteenth cow from one of her relatives. Bungoma, Kenya, July 2014.

PHOTO CREDIT: Gabriel Kunyu.

Setting aside a reserve.   The mobile wallet was a place to set aside funds. The stored value was used by women for the feast and by fathers and uncles who were planning to purchase an animal. Being prepared for the ritual's social obligations was paramount. One mother noted that she signed up for M-Pesa specifically to prepare for the feast and save money on the mobile wallet. Guests expect to be well fed: "There are under-estimations always. In such a situation, there are rumblings and tumults. . . . I have set aside foods and brew with a neighbor in a secret place." She added that she even saves more on her phone in case these foodstuffs run out: "I can still buy more from what I have saved on the phone to heal the situation." Another important fee for service is the father's responsibility. One said, "I have saved 600 shillings [$6] on my wife's phone for the circumciser . . . so I will not be embarrassed."

Father James tongue-in-cheekly referred to the money on his phone as a "contingency fund." He received 1,050 (or $10.50) in donations from his *bakoki* (age mates) before the beer party; at an agent a few days before the ceremony, he loaded this cash on his phone; he also offered that at the time he had not yet received a $200 loan from his boss, which was to purchase the cow for the feast and to rent a truck to parade the thirteenth cow. The morning after, his younger brother told us that the contingency fund had come in handy—when the age mates finished the traditional millet beer, he purchased some of the local moonshine to keep the party going.

Fundraising.   Households were heavily dependent on social networks to fund the ritual. Mobiles and digital money were widely used to pool and collect money. Men said they were "recalling debts," seeking donations from age mates, and taking out loans from their employers to buy the sacrificial animal and arrange the feast. Women were timing their savings group payouts, ranging from $20 to $100, to fund preparation of food and beer. Women also focused on contacting their brothers, cousins, and others to raise funds for the purchase of the thirteenth cow or to fund the parade of this animal through the marketplace (Figure 5.2), which sometimes involved hiring a flatbed truck or motorcycle, or decorating the animal with cloths and flowers. "Chasing after contributions" refers to the practice of contacting people for help, which often involved repeated requests and stalling. Three days before the feast, Beatrice was very worried that her friends might not help her with money to buy the millet to make beer for her son's ritual. She had made several calls four days before and was getting ready to follow up with the same women, friends from her church and savings groups. Afterward she told us she eventually collected $18 from five of them.

Gift giving.   Some boys received the thirteenth cow (Figure 5.2), and all boys received a diverse set of gifts at both the feast and the passing out three months later. Sometimes mobile money gifts were collected on a parent's phone. Lists of gifts (Table 5.1) focus on preparing a boy for high school with items like schoolbooks, uniforms, new clothes, perhaps a soccer ball "to nurture talent on the pitch," and animals and cash given and pledged "for fees." Goats and cows are given "for fees," with the expectation that fathers will nurture the animals as they reproduce and sell the offspring if necessary. Many initiates were about to begin high school, where fees begin at $300 per year.

Difficulties in Accessing and Maintaining Phones

For many households, access to mobile phones and mobile money technology was intermittent and indirect through phone and account sharing. Although

Figure 5.2. Parade of the Thirteenth Cow, Chwele, Kenya, August 2014. The initiate is in a liminal phase and has been smeared with millet flour. He is returning from his mother's brother's house with the gift of the thirteenth cow, accompanied by singing friends and relatives.
PHOTO CREDIT: Chap Kusimba.

all of the 46 families in the diary study used mobile communication either through their own handsets or by sharing, many reported that handsets were broken or not working, or that they could not use M-Pesa because of a locked account, because someone else had borrowed, lost, or broken their handset, or for other reasons. One mother showed me a SIM card that she kept in a small handkerchief, for use when she borrowed a handset. Phone, handset, and account sharing is a way to distribute access to households that do not have phones or M-Pesa accounts.

Costs of the Ritual

The costs of this ritual for families ranged from $250 to $400. Table 5.2 shows the sources of funds and costs incurred by James, who earns $60 a month as a farm laborer. He took a loan from his boss, and also relied on his wife's savings group payout to meet these costs.

Table 5.2. Expenditures incurred by James for his son's maturity ritual, which totaled US $263 (left-hand columns)

James's Expenditures	Amount in US Dollars	Assistance and Gifts James and His Son Received
Live cow for feast	100	Loan of US $200 from James's boss
Ugali, rice, milk, tea, cabbage	65	Thirteenth cow for initiate from mother's brother
Maize and millet for beer	52	Loan of generator and fuel from a friend
Contingency fund (beer savings) on mobile money account	15	US $15 for truck rental to parade the thirteenth cow from a friend
Mattress	8	US $10.50 for contingency fund from several age mates
Bells and headdress	3	Seats, tents, and cooking utensils from friends
Bangles	1	Foodstuffs for feast from neighbors
Whistle	1	Sheets for initiate from paternal aunt
Transport for two circumcisers	7	Clothing for initiate from a friend
Service charge for two circumcisers	7	Advice and guidance to the boy from a great uncle
Cock to feast two circumcisers	4	Blessings from family, friends, community members
Total Costs (US $)	**$263**	

The right-hand column lists assistance and gifts James received to help create the ritual and the feast. James earns 6,000 shillings (US $60) per month as a farm laborer. Bungoma County, Kenya, 2014.

Families that were able to afford a feast did so by selling off a valuable item, harvesting farm produce, sacrificing a cow from their existing herd, fundraising in their social networks, receiving a remittance from an urban migrant, or taking out a loan from an employer. One family had sold part of their land and had cash available. Fathers might also liquidate a significant asset to prepare the feast, such as a cow or a tree. Other fathers sought assistance from relatives or loans from a boss, savings group, or cooperative at the local sugar company. Some were holding money ($50–$150) in a bank or mobile money account. Others had begun preparations such as cleaning up the household or extending a house to accommodate the drinking party of the *bakoki*. Preparation and planning meant readying animals from the herd as gifts or sacrifice, debating locations, or purchasing livestock before its market price increased ahead of the event. Some uncles promised the thirteenth cow for the near future or pledged school fees. Others brought a goat or hen; one uncle sent $5 via M-Pesa.

Digital money transfer gifts were given by absent relatives or by those concerned with "safekeeping." Sometimes fathers (but more often mothers) were in charge of keeping the initiate's gifts on their mobile money account or in a "secret place." Furthermore, many e-gifts were lumped together with cash and mobile money contributions of others to create a kind of amassed group gift, often on the mother's phone. This group pooling was intended to provide money for the boy's school fees and could also be a way of minimizing the social damage of small individual contributions.

A Summary of Uses

To summarize, the main uses of digital money during the ritual were in intra-household value transfers, transportation, micro-coordination, and fundraising. In addition, the mobile wallet was used to store value, although women's secret money-storage places and bank accounts were also used. This costly ritual is highly valued as a way to create wealth-in-people, in the form of ties created and renewed by gifts of many kinds. Mothers, in general, spoke more openly, proudly, and gratefully about close friends and siblings who assisted them in making the event possible. Many men refused to tell us the source of the funds that they marshaled for their ceremonies or spoke of "recovering debts." In some cases their wives would later reveal that the funds were a loan from their husband's cooperative or his boss.

The Hierarchy of Moneys

The coming-of-age ritual brought together new and old money instruments, such as trees or animals. These forms of money helped people organize multiple time scales. Families thought of using cash, digital, and savings group payments to prepare the celebration; they thought of tuition payments over a period of years; and they considered generational time frames when thinking of inheritances. Fathers focused on shuffling long-term wealth instruments; women circulated cash money in savings clubs and friend networks and raised funds to get the thirteenth cow, a public testament to their ties to their natal homes. The ritual also gave women and youth a chance to claim bridewealth cattle, pay school fees, brew the beer that brought ancestral blessings, and pursue enterprise.

One could arrange these different forms of money in a hierarchy of different time/space qualities, from long-term money, such as land, trees, and animals, to short-term money, such as cash and digital money used as a means of exchange.[51] In many societies the hierarchy of money separated the sphere of long-term collective value from that of short-term individual goals and gain,[52] or "different moral economies of fairness (in the short run) and transcendence (in the long run)."[53] The family land was the ultimate value and belonging, the setting for the collection of people from all over the country and even abroad. Cattle and livestock, digital money, cash money, and all kinds of other gifts were given to initiated boys according to whatever abundance each family could manage—gifts were intended to support a child about to enter high school with money for fees, or perhaps a cow or goat that would reproduce and serve as a store of value. Money and digital money were used at the local market, which sold and rented tents, chairs, sound systems, germinated millet for beer, homemade maize liquor, cooking pots, beer pots, cows, goats, and chickens to be given as gifts or prepared as food, clothing, tailoring, household goods, food, and services, including vans and buses for hire, food catering, beauty and hair preparation, home improvement, and photographs and videos of the events. Women entrepreneurs were especially active, preparing and selling foodstuffs particularly millet beer.

In reality, the long- and short-term spheres of money are interdependent.[54] In the ritual, exchanges of different monies are used to measure the "temporal reach of . . . wealth; over the short run, the life span, intergenerational succession, and in perpetuity."[55] Digital money creates an added pathway in this pyramid of moneys, a means to "manage, negotiate, and move better between different currencies, on a daily basis."[56] For example, access to money is desirable because it can stave off selling an asset. Marianne explained to me that her hen, a reliable layer worth only 500 shillings ($5) in the market, was much more valuable than the 500-shilling note I had just given her as a thank-you after our brief interview.

The elders use their moral leadership to endorse the importance of long-term and often collective investments, assets, and inheritances, such as the family land. During the passing out, initiates don their scratchy new clothes and listen to the elders' didactic lectures about adult responsibility, which includes financial education. As elders and church leaders explain, the boys should now begin a gradual but steady building of value for the long term. Initiates are told to work hard in school, save money, and aspire to start a taxi business, purchase land, or build rental housing. Liquidating assets is discouraged, and is associated with moral dissolution, poor planning, and witchcraft.[57] The spiritual and religious qualities of this ritual mark it as a point along the life span; elder Mzee Nathan reminded me about the event called "to cut the rope," when one's accumulated wealth will be assessed and given out to one's heirs. The assembled gifts, including schooling and animals, are like assets: "investments [and] goods that allow the long term to be envisaged and realized."[58]

Money Forms and Generational Conflict

As mobile money was brought into the ritual and compared in value against other forms of money, such as the thirteenth cow, it generated considerable conflict. Initiates expressed disappointment over money substitutes for the thirteenth cow. The elders were suspicious of digital money in general, in its promises of convenience,[59] and viewed mobile phones as disruptive of the ritual's reciprocal labors. For example, the ritual cycle begins when initiates travel to visit their relatives to announce the event and receive small gifts and promises to attend. Nowadays, mobile phones are used to spread the word, shortening the visiting period to some extent. But many elders insisted on being visited in person, with the initiate dancing right "up to the doorstep." "When we [elders] inherited this [ritual] from our forefathers, they were sending us with bells up to the doorstep. . . . [Then the elders] would give you an animal. A four-legged animal." They explained that mobile phones make easy the work that is supposed to show respect and reciprocity, the important obligation to travel across intergenerational space-time: "You will also be honored when it is your turn. And when you call [an elder] on the phone he will just tell you, I am not a kid to be called on the phone."

Digital money was in these men's eyes a poor substitute for the presence of urban migrants, the commitment among them to the ancestral land and home, and the animal gifts that are supposed to bind the generations and bridge the past and the future. Mzee Nathan also said that M-Pesa will allow a well-wisher to send less than he would bring home on a personal visit. He pointed to the handset: "You will use this phone to deny me a bull"—meaning, you will use digital money to send me less than you would instead give me if you visited in person. The elders said that urban migrants and in-laws are the people most likely to substitute cash via mobile for something more tangible—to send some amount over the phone as a poor substitute for an animal gift, to find ways of using digital money to hide or divert resources from the ritual home. Some felt that such a substitution was acceptable if the cash offered was a larger amount of money than such a gift would cost. Clearly, the elders undervalued digital money and were suspicious of its repertoire. Its incorporation into the ritual, and indeed into everyday life, has introduced contested forms of belonging and presence that I will elaborate on in the following chapters.

Dr. Mullei's parable was misleading in one important way: it was a story of replacement rather than addition. In reality, digital money is not replacing other forms of money or value, but rather adding on to them. In postcolonial Africa, "time is an interlocking of presents, pasts, and futures . . . each age bearing, altering, and maintaining the previous ones."[60] These temporalities intersect in rituals where the hierarchies of money organize time and space in asymmetrical ties of obligation across the arc of the life span. Long-standing concepts of value mingle with the latest technologies for transferring and reckoning that value. In incorporating new money and money relationships, rituals are remade as financial institutions, as "the informal formalization of mutual help arrangements [that] legitimates novel types of solidarities."[61]

In subsequent chapters I will elaborate how digital money is shaping wealth-in-people in new ways. Most importantly, I will discuss how people are using digital media for circulating funds in networked groups of many kinds. The first of these groups is family, which I turn to in Chapter 6.

Hearthholds of Mobile Money

6

Dorcas, a farmer in Western Kenya in her seventies, has been receiving money from her children since 2009. They purchased a phone for her and signed her up for M-Pesa so they could send money for food and household needs and regular inputs for her farm and animals, including seed, fertilizer, veterinary care, and labor. Initially her grandchildren helped her to use the phone, but now she can recognize amounts and understand the meaning of SMS messages. Her youngest daughter, a nurse in Chicago, has used the smartphone app Wave since 2017 to send money directly to Dorcas's M-Pesa account. This daughter eventually contracted local builders to more than double the footprint of Dorcas's one-story bungalow—adding new bedrooms at the back of the house and connecting the property to electricity. Flowers were planted around the front porch. A television and refrigerator soon appeared in the living room. Today Dorcas has nine cows and a thriving six-acre farm that grows cash crops like coffee and sugarcane. Thanks to her daughter, she said, she is the only one of her husband's three co-wives who can offer him a cold drink from a refrigerator.

Dorcas and her family members use M-Pesa money transfer frequently. They circulate money to help members with food and household needs, medical emergencies, school fees and documents, and business projects. Her nine children work as teachers, farmers, civil servants, and a dentist. Two migrated to the United States. In 2012, I sat with five of them and asked them to list the names of people they had sent digital money to in the last year, as well as those who had sent digital money to them. I asked them to omit friends and savings groups and just list relatives. They easily listed their own money-sending connections and even those of others in the group. The conversation fell into laughter, as the people who did more receiving than sending were gently chided. I then followed up with as many of the named contacts as possible, to confirm and, if they were willing to answer, to ask them whom they receive digital money from, and to whom they send money. The resulting sociogram (Figure 6.1) shows the network of digital money transfers that this family created by sending money to one another during the period from June 2011 to June 2012. Each person is depicted as a circle (female) or triangle (male), and transfer directions are represented by arrows.[1] (See a video about these networks at https://sibelkusimba.com/presentations.)

The drawing confirmed what the family already knew—that as a mother and grandmother, Dorcas receives many remittances. She is a central node in the network, which includes many of her children and 44 grandchildren. They also knew that Dorcas is an active bundler and re-sender of funds. The network thus spans towns in Western Kenya, Nairobi, and Chicago. When I spoke with Dorcas, I not only confirmed what her children had told me, but I learned that she is also a unique link connecting her children and grandchildren to her deceased sister's eldest daughter, Elizabeth (Figure 6.1), who in turn sends and receives remittances to and from her own siblings and their children. Dorcas explained that she was very close to this sister, whose children have not been as fortunate as her own. When she becomes aware of any troubles among these nieces and nephews, she helps Elizabeth if she can. Dorcas's husband had worked for Kenya Railways beginning in the 1960s. She told me he had been a good provider until he moved to another town and married another wife. From that point on, she had to rely on her oldest son, a policeman, to pay fees for the remaining children, several of whom received university education. He became a surrogate father of sorts, and a successful government job allowed him to educate his own siblings and many other relatives. Dorcas says she is lucky that her children love her so much and that they did well in school. But she does much more than just *receive* money. She is modest about her own distributive labor,[2] which has shaped this network and through which she supports people less fortunate than herself.

The movement of digital money directly to the handsets of rural women like Dorcas has been one of the big stories of the M-Pesa narrative. This money could be a lifeline for marginalized rural areas. What are the consequences of

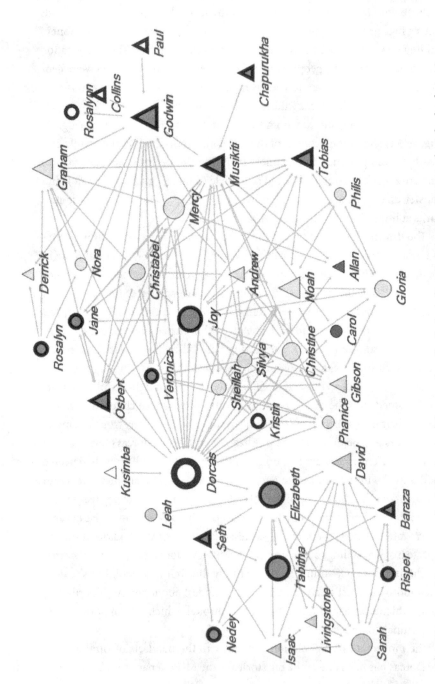

Figure 6.1. Network sociogram of mobile money remittances for a family including Grandmother Dorcas, who is broker between two groups: one is her children and grandchildren, on the right side of the sociogram, and the second, toward the left side of the sociogram, are her deceased sister's children.

these flows of money? What are women doing with this money and the new social role it might give them? Our team began a study in 2012 in the same areas of Western Kenya that I described in Chapter 5, with households that were known to receive remittances from urban centers or even abroad. Often these households were more affluent than the average. What we discovered was that money was forming pathways and networks as it was distributed to friends and families, often not immediately but over weeks and months. Furthermore, these networks distributed money from the more-affluent households to the less-affluent households. These money flows centered around groups of siblings, cousins, and mothers. The research plan followed the money as remittances were broken up and distributed across a network, often moving from more affluent, to less affluent, and finally to struggling families, reflecting ideals of generosity and practices of distribution from those with more to those with less. In this chapter I discuss women's roles as redistributors of money in their communities. Importantly, women are not necessarily benefiting from these remittances in ways we might expect—precisely because of the redistributive roles they play in networks—especially women in overall circumstances of poverty.

A History of Money Transfer and the Rural-Urban Family

In East Africa the stage for the urban-rural remittances of M-Pesa was set in colonial times when money was made a mediator between the urban market sphere and the rural home of kinship and family obligations. The British government, seeking labor for urbanization projects and settler farms, required a hut tax and even a poll tax from households, whose members were thus compelled to seek money wages through mostly male employment. Yet low wages ensured these men's dependency on food from the rural areas, which remained culturally and socially a home for urban migrants.

The urban-rural family struggle is called the *gorogoro* economy.[3] The *gorogoro* is a standard two-kilogram unit for measuring out grain or peas in the marketplace, which people say has grown steadily smaller over time even as the price remains the same. As a metaphor, it describes how dependency on urban wage remittances creates poverty on both ends of the rural/urban divide, as urban migrants set aside money from meager salaries for their rural families.[4] In turn, dependency on urban work at very low wages depletes the manpower available for farming, further risking the food harvest and forcing a humiliating and bitter irony for subsistence farmers—the need to purchase food with money, the *gorogoro* economy.

Forcing clan lands into nuclear family households added to the emerging problem of poverty in Western Kenya. In the gendered dynamic of *gorogoro* households, women were often left in charge of rural farming and care of children, including children of unwed sons and daughters, leaving them dependent on irregular remittances from often absent men, some of whom had other families to support.[5] They relied on older children to care for younger ones, and juggled time and income across their various activities, including farming, trading, and care for family needs. By the late twentieth century, more than three-quarters of families in Western Kenya experienced food insecurity, especially a hungry or lean season in the months before food harvests, which was a "normal state of affairs"; malnutrition affected as many as 40% of children.[6] Families lacked the cash for medical care, schooling, and other essentials. Poverty in rural Western Kenya resulted in large part from women's precarious access to cash, food, and farmland.[7] Today with the ongoing and dramatic increase in population and loss of land and productivity, wage labor is sought to fill the gap in access to income, food, medical care, and school fees, ensuring that the rural-urban dilemma continues.[8]

Over the twentieth century the urban-rural dynamic became an important organizing principle among Western Kenyan families and laid the groundwork of the "Send Money Home" imperative that would emerge with digital money transfer. Urban-rural traveling, often on brightly decorated public buses, became a celebrated part of Kenyan family life in the twentieth century and a mediator of rural and urban lifeways. In the 1960s, migrants to Nairobi told anthropologists that sending money home to Western Kenya—tucked into a letter and sent with a trusted friend or through a package service—was preferable and more useful than visiting. Already, money was a medium of love and commitment for these migrants.[9] They would return home with abundant gifts including such markers of modernity as packaged foods and clothing, along with small amounts of money to be widely distributed (still an expectation today). Competition developed over the abundance of funeral and Christmas feasts; backbiting and gossiping faced returning migrants negotiating the choices and dilemmas of living in two worlds.

Since the 1970s some successful families, especially those with well-employed members or family wealth in the form of land, climbed a ladder out of the *gorogoro* dilemma by "straddling" urban and rural investments. Such families invested equally in formal education and held significant family lands, which they managed by "telephone farming" from their urban offices.[10] In Western Kenya such prosperous families will often refer to a grandparent who was an early Christian convert and an early recipient of formal Western education. The successful coordination of the urban and rural worlds is still a widely held ideal of affluence, now furthered by mobile communication and money transfer technologies—for those who can pull it off. A widely viewed 2009 Safaricom ad featured a businessman who was in the habit of sweet-talking women on the phone. His secretary overheard his conversations with concern, until the females on the phone were revealed as egg-laying hens on his farm. In a similar way Dorcas's farm, described in the opening of this chapter, has been sustained by urban and international remittances, and is a testament to her children's success and their commitment to the rural home. Because of digital money transfer, such upgrades and displays of status have become expected among well-off families, especially those whose members work in the city or even abroad.

But most families do not have the resources to fulfill an ideal as Dorcas's children have. As landlessness grows, the multi-sited and mobile lifestyle is increasing in extent, complexity, and pace. De-agriculturalization is fueled by population increase, structural adjustment policies, and the high expense and low productivity of farming.[11] Urban centers draw migrants for work over short and long time periods. More and more people turn to the informal sector. Older people will tell you that the landless youth are selling sundries in the street, giving motorcycle rides, or washing cars at the river.

Mothers and Sisters as Brokers

Other examples say more about siblings and mothers in networks. Consider the family of Sarah (Figure 6.2), who was thirty-six when we drew her network. Her mother, who is no longer living, was the third wife of a polygynous man. At his death, the other wives chased Sarah, her mother, and her siblings away from the homestead about 100 miles from the town of Kimilili, where she eventually took refuge. Sarah's older sister, Joyce, married a Dutch man when working as a secretary at an agricultural science institute. Joyce now lives in Holland and sends Sarah $200–$300 several times a year. Sarah uses the funds to support her friend and fellow seamstress Cecilia ("like a sister to me," she explained), her brother, her mother's brother, and her mother's sisters' children.

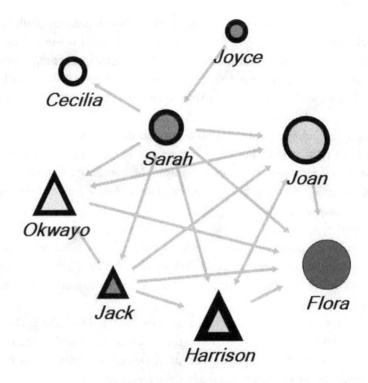

Figure 6.2. Network sociogram of mobile money remittances for siblings Sarah, Jack, and Joyce; their cousin Okwayo; their maternal uncle, Harrison; their friend Cecilia; and Joan's daughter, Flora. The sociogram depicts siblings in the same shade of gray and shows generational distinctions by varying the thickness of the black outline of each node. Harrison is in the senior generation in the network and has the thickest outline, and Flora is in the youngest generation, with the thinnest outline.

Her twenty-year-old niece, Flora, attends an accounting college and has the most receiving ties in this network—she reported receiving money from five different people in it.

Sarah's network map illustrates important features of money transfer networks. First of all, it is multi-sited, with members who live in different cities in Western Kenya and connect to a node in Holland.[12] Although very few Kenyan families receive international remittances, it is common for in-country remittances to connect people across different regions and to connect people who are highly mobile as they seek employment and other activities. Second, the network shows density—many connections through which an individual might access help and support. In our original study of twelve families, each individual had an average of 5.4 money contacts. The interconnectedness that people can achieve with mobile money remittances is remarkable. Third, many of the money transfer ties are bidirectional, indicating reciprocal sending (visible in Figure 6.2 as bidirectional arrows). Figure 6.3 shows the family relationships of the sociogram.

Sibling and cousin relationships are the connectors of family networks in Western Kenya. Often, these siblings and cousins connect to parents—especially mothers and people connected to mothers, like mothers' brothers. Mothers' brothers are key sources of money transfer—and more common than fathers in family network graphs. Women with many connections may be old or young—like Flora, who has the most connections in Figure 6.2. On the map of Sarah and her siblings, resources flow to her niece, the youngest and most central node in the network. Flora cultivates generosity in her aunts and uncles by keeping in frequent contact with them and sending them free SMS such as "Please call" or "Greetings." They return with small amounts to help with her daily needs at school.

Generosity and reciprocity are often demonstrated by older people, who have cultivated a lifetime of relationships and achieved elder status, often ending up as central nodes like Dorcas, who is also a unique tie between two

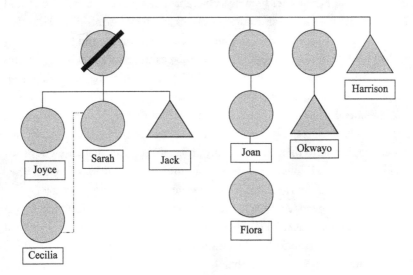

Figure 6.3. Family relationships for the sociogram depicted in Figure 6.2. Horizontal lines indicate sibling relationships and vertical lines indicate parent-child relationships. Dashed line is friendship. The mother of Joyce, Sarah, and Jack is deceased.

groups—a broker. Brokerage in social theory is often associated with positions of control or individual advantage,[13] but Dorcas is the type of broker who distributes her advantage across the group rather than seeking to maintain her unique position as a bridge. At her urging, her children and those of her deceased sister have created a family association to collect school fees for the children and grandchildren of this pair of sisters. At the deceased sister's funeral these two clusters of siblings, who live in towns in Western Kenya as well as Chicago and Nairobi, discussed the high cost of education. They then formed a credit and savings group in which each of them agreed to contribute 1,000 shillings a month to a common savings account from which school fees would be paid on a rotating basis. The members meet once a month, where they all put in 1,000 shillings toward a banked fund for school fees. The treasurer can receive money transfers from absent members.

In another example of an international broker grandmother, Sister Lucida is a 47-year-old nun and student in Chicago who sends about $300 a month to her mother in Homa Bay County, Western Kenya. Sister Lucida is too busy to hear and assess numerous requests for school fees and pitches for business investments from her relatives. She allows her mother, a widow, to use the money she sends as she sees fit to help the family. After her father died, Sister Lucida explained that her mother became vulnerable among her in-laws, who chased her away from her home and stole her dishes and home furnishings. Sister Lucida and her siblings purchased a new plot of land for her and built and furnished a new home for her that they describe as the envy of the village. Sister Lucida sends her money for "upkeep," and is aware that the money ends up helping others in the family as her mother sees fit.

The social network study's interviews elaborated on money as a way of making relationships, especially about the sense of belonging and commitment people had to their mothers and siblings. People explained money's social meanings and how its use centers around support, help, and gifts. They send money to express generosity, to show happiness at having seen a long-lost friend, to buy someone a treat. Others said (paraphrasing), "I send money [to my grandmother] because I love her," or made similar expressions of emotional closeness as the reason for sending money, especially to mothers.

The obligation to one's mother is also called "being useful." Childhood upbringing stresses being useful in helping with domestic work and younger siblings.[14] In adulthood these responsibilities continue. E-money gifts can express usefulness. A sixty-two-year-old woman, whose oldest son has lived in the United States for 12 years, described his ongoing presence in her life, saying, "He is very useful around here, very useful. He bought me a gas cooker . . . and pays my workers." A remittance as transformed into a gas cooker can represent one's work and usefulness and show belonging and presence in the place one was born.

E-money remittances connect specific relatives, especially siblings, mothers, grandmothers, and mothers' relatives, such as maternal uncles. While men and women are equally represented in the networks, men appear as brothers and mothers' brothers more than as fathers. The mother-children unit is known as the "hearthhold," referencing the social power that African women derived from food and cooking.[15] Historically, women in many African societies that traced descent through males left their natal homes at marriage. They built up new social networks, their hearthholds, by circulating important resources such as food. For example, Fulbe pastoralist women tended cattle, and fathers, husbands, and sons depended on them for milk: "If she refuses to give a certain person some milk, the husband can do nothing about it. Although a man has the power to give milk from his own cows to a stranger or relative, it does not equal the social significance of a gift of milk from a woman."[16]

Fulbe women gave milk as gifts to create ties with in-laws and sustain their own ties to their natal homes, building the relationships of a hearthhold as a material and social support network, and giving their children connections to both their mothers' and fathers' kin. Milk also had symbolic associations with hospitality and female beauty. For the Fulbe women, who married into their husband's lineages, milk was "the social glue" of their hearthholds.[17]

Milk has an ancient history in pastoralist societies. Nonetheless, the idea of building a hearthhold by redistributing the currency of everyday sustenance sheds light on the gendered patterns of e-money circulations in Western Kenya. Women like Dorcas not only circulate mobile money in their networks; they also reciprocate e-money sent to them with other resources, such as food. And these mother-centered social and economic relationships go beyond just transferring money; they help to create social roles and social power. These central nodes are often mothers and grandmothers who are both receivers and senders.

Social network analysis can map flows of money that men and women send and receive. E-money remittances create dense networks of reciprocal transfers shaped by the distributive labors of grandmothers and others in the hearthhold.[18] These patterns trace the social obligations to hearthholds of siblings, mothers, and mothers' kin. Money moves across generational time; money flows to mothers and grandmothers and back to young people as a form of support. E-money has emotional value and expresses usefulness, generosity, and reciprocity.

Network Self-Portraiture

In a network perspective, senders and receivers hold unique positions that are shaped by social norms. I wanted to know more about how these networks form. How do a mother and grandmother build a central position in a network over time? I also wanted to know more about how people use different kinds of money. How are the networks of digital money transfers different from networks of digital loans, cash money, foodstuffs, or other valuables circulated? What kind of valued transactions do people recognize?

In 2016 I tried a new approach to these questions. I asked women to draw their social/financial networks—their ties to others formed by different kinds of money. The drawing exercise included many iterations with participants of varying levels of education. I asked women to draw themselves at the center of networks of others whom they help and support and from whom they receive help and support. Women depicted themselves connected to friends and relatives, informal groups such as church and savings groups, employers if they were employed, financial service providers including M-Pesa money transfer, M-Shwari, or KCB digital bank if they used it, and so on. I asked them to use different colored markers to denote types of support they give and receive, both material and non-material, as media of exchange.

In Figures 6.4a and 6.5a, Consolata, the headmistress of a school in rural Western Kenya, portrays herself as connected to other members in her social network, which she has drawn around the perimeter of the page. To depict different media of exchange that produce these social ties, Consolata used assorted colors of pen to denote food, information, money, mobile money, other digital financial services, and emergency loans (my categories). Consolata drew emergency loans in red; she can access her siblings, her sister-in-law, her nephews, her savings groups, or the digital credit service M-Shwari. Her network also includes her church, two welfare societies that help with funerals, and a SACCO (a savings and credit cooperative). She also offered her own media of exchange: security and advice.

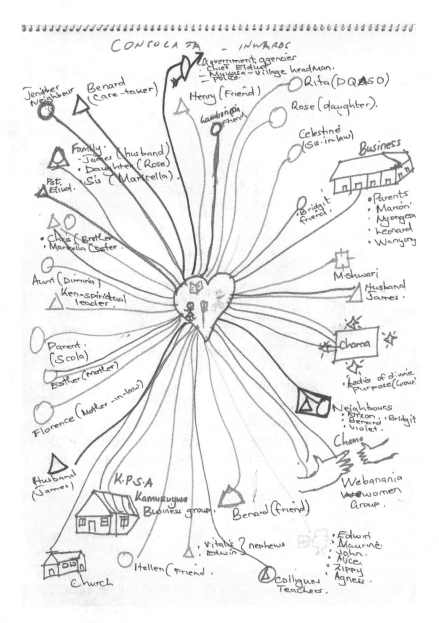

Figure 6.4a. Network self-portrait of Consolata depicting ties she creates by receiving.

Figure 6.4b. Consolata drew M-Shwari as a lockbox with three perpendicular lines through the sides, which she said were three locks.

The drawings use symbols to depict different kinds of money. The savings group is drawn as a pair of hands extended to help. She drew M-Shwari, the digital money bank and loan product where she keeps money saved, as a box with three locks on each side (Figure 6.4b). A popular savings group method uses a box with three locks to keep the collective fund and gives three members each a key.[19] The locked-box analogy came to her as we discussed M-Shwari as a secure place to keep money.

Consolata drew herself as a heart in the center of her drawings. She said her love of her students (inside her heart as two stick figures along with a book and pen) was her motivation as a teacher. Her work strives to bring achievement, love, and hope to this impoverished rural community. She is often called on for material support in this poor rural neighborhood. During the week of our first interview (Figure 6.5), Consolata contributed 200 ($2) to a passing neighbor toward raising an orphanage; sent 2,000 ($20) in mobile money to "comfort" her friend Fiona, who had lost a husband; sent 1,000 ($10) to the mother of a pupil and friend of the family to prepare a wedding; and took another 1,000 in cash to her brother, hospitalized for a spinal injury. The previous week another neighbor had lost a child. They came home to bury the child but could not return to Nairobi, so Consolata gave them 200 ($2) to assist with transport; similarly, she gave a neighbor with a sick parent 150 ($1.50) for food, as they had nothing to eat. She frequently gives out small amounts of money that supply a portion of the immediate and urgent need of a friend or neighbor. On her graph, I asked her to list the names of friends and neighbors she frequently

Figure 6.5. Consolata (right) discussing her use of digital finance tools with Chap Kusimba (middle) and Gabriel Kunyu (left). Wabukhonyi Village, Kamukuywa, January 2016.

PHOTO CREDIT: Cristabel Waluse.

supports. She began to list many names (lower right-hand corner, Figure 6.6a) but soon grew tired, put down the pen, and sighed. She stopped listing names and over them with another colored marker, drew herself as a boat, which as she put it "carries many people over rough waters" of poverty and need (Figure 6.6b).

It is useful to reflect on the differences between a network self-portrait, like Consolata's, and the network sociogram for Dorcas drawn using social network analysis. Both of these diagrams show women with important roles in mobile money circulations. But there are three important differences between Figure 6.1, the sociogram, and Figure 6.5a, the network self-portrait. Whereas the sociogram would draw her as a large circle with many arrows going out and in, her own self-portrait reflects the meaning and self-identity she finds by sustaining many others with money—as a vessel that protects and brings mobility to other people.

Consolata's maps in Figures 6.4a and 6.5a show visual symbols depicting the meanings and moral qualities people give to different kinds of money, and

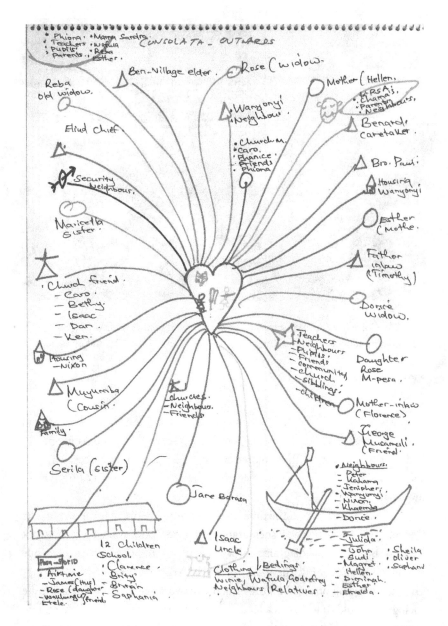

Figure 6.6a. Network self-portrait of Consolata depicting ties she creates by giving and sending.

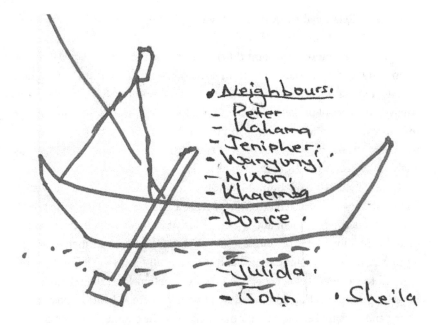

Figure 6.6b. Consolata grew tired listing the many names of friends and neighbors she routinely assists, and instead drew herself over them as a boat "who carries people over the rough waters of poverty."

the kind of behaviors and actions expected around those monies. For example, a savings group is associated with collective concern, help, and support, drawn as helping hands coming together; the M-Shwari digital loan product is associated with a secure lockbox.[20] Working on these maps with my participants created a conversation about women's financial relationships in which they spoke about their motivations for helping others, for asking for help, and the sense of self they wanted to create.

The sociogram shows a network, a set of nodes and ties among them, as a finished product, and can reveal the actions of someone—say, a grandmother who gives out money—in the light of her network position as a central node. The self-portrait drawings, on the other hand, can reveal something of a process behind the product, the work of making economic relationships around exchanging particular kinds of moneys and asserting their meanings.[21] Zelizer has called this process relational work: "In all areas of economic life, people are creating, maintaining, symbolizing and transforming meaningful social relations."[22] Relational work uses distinct *media*, defined as "accounting systems and their tokens," or *currencies of exchange.*[23]

There is one more important difference between Dorcas's network sociogram and Consolata's self-portrait. In social network analysis, the sociogram depicts nodes as distinct from the flows and relationships that connect them. Analysis of types of brokerage, for example, looks at how different amounts of information flow and cohesion can bind an individual to their group either weakly or strongly.[24] However, most network theories still view individuals as analytically detachable from the networks they participate in.

Consolata's own depiction of her role is not as a separate node, however. She drew herself in the center of the page, as I had instructed, but then drew two students inside herself, and spontaneously produced herself again on top of and containing other people as a boat. Vehicles are frequent metaphors for agency across social boundaries,[25] and in Kiswahili both vehicles and people are said to carry (*kubeba*) others. A vessel or container for the relations of a network gives protection and movement to others. Being a boat is a position of caring and of shared economic risk that spills over the boundaries of nodes and ties. Such multiple depictions of the self have been called "distributed personhood . . . as agents, they were not just where their bodies were, but in many different places and times simultaneously."[26] The boat that contains others depicts "personhood as the aggregate of external relations."[27]

The Limits of Women's Roles

Women like Dorcas and Consolata are hubs within networks with significant resources. They prioritize redistributing and passing on the benefit to poorer relatives, as Dorcas did in starting the savings group connecting her children with her sister's children. For women with fewer resources, such a role may be a burden and its social benefits fleeting. Grandmother, farmer, and trader Violet of Bungoma lived on a quarter acre when I met her in 2016. She was raising two grandchildren, including Christabel, who had sickle cell disease and was frequently very unwell. Violet's home was closer to the clinic in town than Christabel's parents' house; Violet was also at that time trading quite a bit in vegetables from her farm and had a more stable income than the girl's parents. She used remittances from Christabel's parents and her earnings from trading to take her to a clinic in Bungoma town for care, including blood transfusions.

Yet Violet often found herself unable to help her children, who would come to her with many challenges. She said her heart often hurt when her phone alerted her to her daughters calling. She once had to find money for medical care when another granddaughter was burned by boiling water. She had no money but found help by leveraging her network of obligations: "I did not have money at the time—but I sent [my daughter] to a place to be given two bags of maize that she could sell." Her reasoning was that her daughter could sell the maize in small amounts to repay the clinic. Two years later, in 2018, Violet had moved away from her unhappy marriage—"my brother came and returned me to my people." Back on her father's land and away from town, she was no longer fostering Christabel, who had returned to her parents. She was not trading, as there was not much market in this more rural area. She explained that her children called only rarely now, as they knew she had very little money.

The remittances that flow to mothers, which give them central roles on the maps, do not always benefit them. They bring myriad expectations and responsibilities. Many remittances are sent to help raise granddaughters born to teenage mothers, who because of stigma and lineage descent rules are often raised by grandmothers. Rural mothers and grandmothers also manage medical emergencies and chronic illnesses, foster relatives' children, and supervise the family farm. Sending money to enable caring can be a way of avoiding responsibility for the work of care, which is often left to women household heads.[28] Women like Violet have long been vulnerable to role overload as caregivers, farmers, and workers in the rural home even before digital money made such arrangements even more common.[29] Remittances can also leave prosperous grandmothers like Dorcas open to the distributive claims of other relatives and neighbors experiencing want or medical and other crises. In 2016 at the behest of the Chicago daughter, the family stopped sending Dorcas money. Dorcas was frequently diverting funds in response to requests from less-fortunate friends and neighbors, who often got wind of an imminent remittance before it even arrived. Furthermore, Dorcas had shared her PIN number with so many friends and neighbors who needed access to the service that her account could no longer be used safely. Instead, her children now send money to a local shopkeeper, who brings Dorcas meat, tea, and sugar. As women respond to the obligation to recirculate money in their communities, the benefit may also become diffused, and the goals of direct, personal transfers may not always be realized.

The Rise of Money Networks

Mobile money networks are characterized by reciprocity and density. Money remittances trace the sibling and mother ties of the hearthhold, and like the parade of the thirteenth cow make visible these often-backgrounded connections to and through women.[30] Using money, women become important in their communities as they become like a boat that carries others. Acts of caring and responsibility involve distributing resources across the network. These central nodes are positions of wealth-in-people: those who hold rights to others also take responsibility for others. Bringing home money but also receiving it, being generous, solving problems, mobilizing groups of people—all are opportunities to show leadership. Urban migrants and rural grandmothers alike demonstrate that social prestige in this part of the world is about "the act of mobilizing people and resources, the capacity to take initiatives and the knowledge to decide when they are necessary."[31]

The hearthhold concept originally brought attention to the value of food, cooking, and motherhood to women's social power. In Western Kenya, an honored guest will be fed generously. Regardless of who cooked the food, it is important to thank the lady of the home personally. If she is out, one waits and makes small talk until she returns. Like food, e-money is a medium of women's everyday exchanges that are crucial to social reproduction.[32]

Forced labor migration created the rural-urban family, and the circumstances of poverty that it endured. As the network study showed, the *gorogoro* economy is now a multi-sited family sharing resources across a dispersed web of money flows. Affluent grandmothers can help sustain their communities, and ties to and through women are important in networks—but these ties are tenuous for poor mothers like Violet. Just as the *gorogoro* economy spread families thin—leading to failure on both ends for all but the affluent[33]—there are many risks for the multi-sited family in managing a complex network of often fragile ties. I describe these distributive labors further in Chapter 7.

Distributive Labors

7

"If I was an employee of Safaricom, they would be giving me a bonus." Toby is a rural man in his twenties who works as a farm laborer. "Oh, I do so many things with it. I don't just buy airtime. I put money on M-Pesa, and I keep it there. I use the 'let's reward ourselves' promotion." Toby did not use M-Pesa much before 2016. There was not much use for it: "Where we live is very far," he explained. "The nearest shops are very small and do not accept M-Pesa."

But one year later it was a different story. Toby's friends drew him into the soccer betting craze; they often bet together on SportPesa. He also realized that M-Pesa could take him into town: "I can go to town to the supermarket. I will send the *boda boda* [bicycle or motorcycle ride hailing] fare by M-Pesa. Then he will come and take me to the market. I can take the *boda boda* back to my house." Toby taught himself how to send money, buy airtime, and earn promotion points by "playing" with the interface. "By playing with so many things, I have learned. Like now I am playing here, with Lock Savings [another menu feature]."

As a result, Toby said, he was now an expert in using mobile money. He not only places bets for other people but also transfers money for people who lack accounts and for people who cannot afford or risk travel to distant agents: "Many people give me their money and say, please send this money using M-Pesa for me. They ask me to send 500 to a friend who needs help urgently."

Toby was unpleasantly surprised to be left with the fees for these sending services—thus he says Safaricom owes him a bonus. "Safaricom will deduct the transaction fee and this person has not left you that money. When I get the transaction, 11 shillings [$0.11] have been deducted. When helping someone, I am actually losing money because of these hidden charges." Because he is helping people and because they are grandmothers or they are less well off than himself, he cannot ask them to add on the fee amount.

Building Wealth-in-People

The network perspective revealed the distributive networks of women and grandmothers. In this chapter, I will describe these distributive labors[1] more fully. In this chapter and in Chapter 8, I draw on our team's fieldwork in rural Kimilili and Bungoma, but I also include the words and experiences of individuals who were a part of the M-Changa project, where we conducted 31 semi-structured interviews in Nairobi (see Chapter 10).

The networks of money transfers and exchange are continually remade by everyday acts of money sending. Toby extends the network into his rural area, teaches himself and others how to use digital financial services through the trial and error of "playing," provides access to others and pays their fees, and connects the digital payment channel to the network of *boda boda* drivers. These activities extend access and produce network ties and connections.

People shape their networks around three overlapping objectives: to belong, to survive, and to get ahead. They circulate money to show caring, presence, commitment, and to do the obligations of kinship. Networks provide material support and can generate value over time in savings groups, financial clubs and cooperatives, welfare associations, and other financial groups.

Ways to Belong

Emmanuel uses money to belong. He is in his twenties, unmarried and a care-taker at a private primary school and church, where he earns 6,000 ($60) per month. Emmanuel was educated up to seventh grade but dropped out for want of fees. "I am looking for something that my parents have. Once I acquire what I want, other things will follow." His struggle to find bridewealth, claim his adulthood, and start his own family is common for young African men now experiencing a delayed adulthood.[2] But Emmanuel's story is complicated. He was born to an unwed teenager and raised by his maternal grandmother after his mother eventually "married elsewhere." Since he is someone born "outside" (illegitimate to his biological father) in a patrilineal society, his relational work with money sending is a complex negotiation of claims to belong to his mother and her family on the one hand, and to his stepfather's relatives on the other. He uses money to achieve his adulthood in the eyes of these two families, but he belongs to neither of them.

Out of a strong sense of obligation to his maternal grandmother, Emmanuel sends her money every month before she needs to ask. His feelings toward his mother, on the other hand, are more complicated. When we first met him, in 2016, his e-money remittances to his mother were reluctant. He would wait for her to call first to ask him. She calls him "with a false excuse of checking on me . . . but then . . . inquire[s] if I have anything for her." Furthermore, "if what I send is not enough—say 200 [$2]—she will not call back to give thanks. If she does not call to say thank you, I will know she is not satisfied with the amount."

Emmanuel's mother had recently called and requested assistance, barely two weeks after Emmanuel had sent her 300 ($3). As a way of encouraging him, she also called her brother—Emmanuel's maternal uncle—and he in turn called Emmanuel to persuade him to send her money, explaining that she needed to buy fertilizer. Because of his uncle's call, Emmanuel said, he broke into his savings and sent her 1,000. Women gain important roles in money sending hearthholds through a combination of such practices around obligation, emotional closeness, and influence through their own networks and kin.

Emmanuel's story also reveals the importance of fatherly ties. Emmanuel has always struggled for full acceptance in his biological father's family. Acceptance comes when you are asked to build a house on your father's land; "then you know that is your place." Emmanuel's father finally offered to build a house for Emmanuel as testament to his belonging. But something was amiss from the beginning: his father offered to build the house himself instead of hiring someone. Emmanuel initially refused. "You cannot climb on the roof of your son's house," he explained. This taboo of avoidance between fathers and sons is designed to create the respectful distance for a son's autonomy. Fathers cannot go inside sons' homes. Instead they wait in the garden to be received as visitors.

Emmanuel gave his father the money for a house of 16 iron sheets—but it was built with only seven. His father misappropriated the money, tricked Emmanuel by building a smaller house, and took the rest of the sheets for his own new family. Emmanuel bitterly recounted how his stepmother had told him, "Thank you for building a house for my children."

One year later, in 2017, we reconnected with Emmanuel. He was still working as a caretaker and still felt betrayed. He recounted the story of how he eventually left his father's house. "I said to myself, there is no future here. There is no
honesty." Furthermore, a stroke of bad luck had befallen Emmanuel's father—
gender imbalance. His father and stepmother had eight male children and no
girls. "There are eight boys and there is no daughter in the home, so how will
we manage?" No daughters meant there would be no bridewealth to help these
brothers marry; furthermore, the land would have to be split equally among
the eight boys in inheritance.

After a week, he decided to leave his father's house for the house of his stepfather and (biological) mother. His relationship with his father is still estranged.
The two barely talk. "Nowadays when I run into my father, he just waves at me
because we have no relationship . . . because I decided to follow my mother."

In 2018 Emmanuel was in his new home at his mother's house, with a new
set of half-siblings, trying again for acceptance and using money to show his
usefulness to the family. He was now spending two-thirds of his monthly salary
on his siblings' schooling and food and sending his mother regular small transfers. His stepfather had recently showed him about half an acre of land where
Emmanuel could build a house. He seemed optimistic that his work for the
family as a firstborn son would bring him his stepfather's acceptance: "It is not
easy when a father is not your own. But he has come to appreciate me. . . . I am
helping so much. . . . In fact today he treats me as if I am the *simakulu* [firstborn
son]. . . . As the firstborn I have the ability to do something. As the firstborn—I
have the ability to change the look of this family."

I asked him if he is wary of another fatherly promise of a house—will he
again be betrayed by a trick? He only said, "I need to be careful. You never
know how members of his [stepfather's] clan might react." Ultimately, his position in his stepfather's patriline will always be precarious.

Emmanuel's connections to land, inheritance, and legitimate belonging
are all at stake. Much of his money sending involves showing his usefulness to
his stepfather's family as the firstborn son. He is fostering and educating two
stepbrothers, and he frequently sends money to his stepfather, in spite of his
outsider status. Furthermore, this year he made some major upgrades for his
mother—he bought her a solar light, rented a plot of land for her, bought her
seeds, and paid to weed the crop. This cost him more than 12,000 ($120), but
his mother was pleased. "When they eat this maize they will realize I am part
of them," he said.

Belonging is at the heart of the "Send Money Home" imperative, which includes both the hearthhold of sibling and mother ties and the belonging to land and ancestors often traced through fathers. One's adult personhood still depends vitally on the judgment of others. As such, both men and women take the care of parents to be of utmost importance. Emmanuel said, "I do not want my parents to have a hard life. They should look like people who have assistance. I want them to know they have a son who is working and who is helping them in small ways."

Siblings often connect with one another to share the responsibility for providing for parents materially and to show "appreciation" through general giving. These distributive labors also help perform social class identities. Cathy is an administrative assistant in a government office in Nairobi. She sends money to her parents in Western Kenya once every two months. Last month, she said, there was a family function and her mother needed a new outfit, while her father needed new shoes. Cathy organized the money pooling on behalf of the siblings—although she is the second-born, she is considered the most responsible and is often a source of advice.

Similarly, Nairobi resident Wanja contributes monthly via M-Pesa to a family fund run by her siblings, who are scattered in several Kenyan cities. The money is sent to her parents in Nanyuki for groceries, utility bills, energy, and a medical insurance policy, with some of it saved for house repairs, improvement, farm work, or other needs they might encounter. Wanja eschews decision-making, preferring to contribute generously and let her siblings see the plans through. Such lifelong sibling networks extend to siblings in their seventies who look after nieces and nephews and their children. Gabriel, of rural Bungoma, is seventy-six but still cares for his younger siblings' families, as he is one of the few among his siblings who earns regular monies, as a plumber. He often juggles urgent family needs for school fees, medical care, and food. Our interview was briefly interrupted when he sent 1,000 ($10) to a brother in a medical emergency. He had been planning to use the money to pay his farm laborers.

Family fundraising pays close attention to rank. Older brothers and fathers coordinate responses to family crises, assigning target donations to various family members based on their presumed ability to pay. Employment or school success, a marriage to a wealthier family, international or urban migration, and personal qualities can also bring expectations to lead. Going back to Emmanuel can illustrate this common new family dynamic—fundraising via mobile remittance. As one who is deeply tied to his hearthhold, Emmanuel is frequently pressed by his maternal uncles to help his mother. Her 2016 hospital stay led to a bill of 36,000 ($360), a debt that his two maternal uncles decided to apportion across the extended family based on seniority and members' presumed ability to pay. Emmanuel was assigned an onerous target of 6,000 ($60)—equal to his monthly salary as a caretaker.

Social networks became entangled as Emmanuel sought assistance from his friends and peers to pay the debt placed on him by his maternal uncles and siblings. He called on six different friends to help him make the 6,000 target; two had promised to help, but at the time of our interview one month later none of them had sent any money. Emmanuel had returned to discuss the situation with his uncles. His biggest concern was making his uncles understand his genuine lack of the means to help; he was worried that he would be viewed as selfish. He reminded them that he was helping to support his mother's farm and paying school fees for his mother's children. One of the maternal uncles then offered to pay the 6,000 on Emmanuel's behalf, but on condition that Emmanuel would repay the money. As he recounted the story, he admitted that there were few acceptable ways to push back against his uncles.

Emmanuel's sense of filial piety does not extend to his biological father, however. Rarely will Emmanuel give or send money to his father except on some accidental meetings. After all, his father had abandoned him and failed to pay his school fees. But he budgets carefully to send his grandmother money every month, because "she raised me, I cannot forget her even a single month." As for his mother, well . . . it's complicated. Money is Emmanuel's opportunity to show his stepfather's lineage, and his own mother and her relatives, that he can be a useful son. On the other hand, he never feels he has enough to meet their demands and senses their suspicions that he may be keeping more aside. In a society where relationships to fathers define one's public identity but fathers are increasingly absent, money-sending networks in hearthholds reveal the continuing and even increasing role for mothers' brothers. As protectors of their sisters, they exert their elder power over sisters' sons.

Rituals of the life cycle are financial vehicles and "the ultimate test of belonging."[3] Across sub-Saharan Africa they are becoming more important and diversifying in form.[4] Kenyans contribute to life cycle rituals regularly, especially funerals, where they are often involved in bundling and fundraising. Travel to the native home shows presence and continued commitment to the home and family. Crowds of thousands are easily found in Western Kenya on any Sunday afternoon.

E-money gifts are now expected at funerals. They are sent to the family of the deceased or to assist with the cost of treating or releasing the body. Money is bundled and raised across social networks. E-money is sent through friends, intended to help other guests afford the cost of travel, or given privately to rent tents and chairs, prepare food, arrange for photography and loudspeakers, purchase ritual animals, and meet other needs. In many communities live animals are purchased as gifts or sacrificed to honor the ancestors. A religious specialist may perform prayers and may require compensation. Cash money is publicly donated and recorded in a book, as are e-money remittances. Ongoing e-money gifts to the dead ensure the upkeep of their graves, homes, and gardens or complete their remaining bridewealth commitments. Mark, a Nairobi resident in his twenties, earns money sporadically as an office temp. His young nephew in Siaya died prematurely and suddenly without having built a house in the family compound. Mark assembled seven e-money contributions from his male friends to fund the building of a house for his prematurely deceased young nephew. This would ensure his nephew's memory and presence into the future, but also enable the nephew's younger siblings to marry and build homes while still respecting the rules of seniority. Mark felt it was his responsibility, and an honor, to personally further the passage of generational time with the help of his friendship network.

From the social networks point of view, money transfers are a part of the give-and-take, what has been famously called the economy of affection.[5] These e-money gifts express and represent people's work and care in the economy of affection. This personalized nature of the gift remittance is a part of oneself or one's presence, especially when sent at funerals, when the money transfers are sent to "condole" people or "offer them comfort," "because I could not be there," or "to show my concern." Rural farm laborer Evans is in his twenties. He contributed to the burials of his maternal aunt and maternal great-grandmother with M-Pesa transfers. His mother had asked him for 600 ($6), but he sent her 800 ($8) to "comfort" her and his maternal grandmother with 400 each. His mother would use 200 of it for her transportation to the funeral. He added on 200 ($2), he said, "because I could not be there."

Work and other responsibilities frequently prevent people from being present at events. These absences are often painful. Often the fee or fare for bus and minibus fare back to the rural areas for a funeral will be compared to the amount of donation or "appreciation" that could be shown to the family of the deceased. Ellen, a fruit seller in Kitale town, explained that the cost of returning home for a funeral about 80 kilometers away would reduce the money she could bring home, but at the same time it would prevent neighbors from backbiting and gossiping about her absence. The math problem hardly solved the dilemma, though; rather, it forced her to weigh her reputation in the community against her mother's material need for the money. She also reasoned that her mother would find a way to communicate the size of her donation in the neighborhood and therefore relay Ellen's generous intentions. For these ultimately very social reasons, sending money can still be preferable to visiting.[6] If there is a coming-of-age ritual, septuagenarian Mzee Nathan of Bungoma said, "they [an urban migrant] may send like 1,000 or 1,500 [$10–$15] to buy something like sugar instead of traveling [to attend the coming-of-age]. This cuts the costs. Sometimes they may be funerals during hard times of life. My child may send me money to cater for the costs. He is supposed to come and witness an event within a couple of minutes and get back. It is better he sends the 3,000 [$30] and continues with his activities."

Whether e-money gifts replace a person's presence at a ritual, or paradoxically underscore the person's absence, is an unpredictable judgment and a constant source of uncertainty and anxiety.[7] The money amount can influence how it is received and accepted, but like all money meanings it is open to interpretation.

Welfare societies are more formalized groups that can organize these donations. For example, a welfare society collects emergency funds. Typically relatively small monthly donations are collected from upwards of several hundred members, such as urban migrants, kin group members, church groups, or neighborhood. A welfare society in the Kawangware neighborhood of Nairobi has more than 500 members and is almost totally digitally mediated by a group of several treasurers. It offers its low-income and itinerant population of Western Kenya migrants burial insurance. A text message signs people up and accepts monthly M-Pesa dues of 50 shillings ($0.50). When a member's family experiences a death, the society will provide a funeral donation. Some welfare societies also communicate via WhatsApp.

Many people send regular remittances to close contacts. They maintain their parents' farm with coordinated payments for groceries, labor, and other needs; they pay regular school fees and take care of people with chronic illnesses. They manage and coordinate investments in family property, mediating the investment across rural and urban settings. Support may range from sustenance to small gifts, pocket money for nieces and nephews, assistance with medical needs, and so on. Often these regular remittances are linked to a sense of obligation as a son or daughter, spouse, friend, or sibling. Mobile phones and mobile money mediate a relationship to home and make showing a commitment to that home possible and, in an age of mobility, paradoxically ever more important. The ability of digital finance to straddle multiple worlds, like the telephone and the automobile before it, creates the imperative and the obligation to contribute and show presence.

Ways to Survive

Robai is seventy-two years old and a farmer and potter in Bituyu, Kenya. She is the matriarch of her extended family, the leader of her potters' guild, and an elder at her church. "I had twelve children and God took three and left me with nine," she explained. Off and on over the years she has been caretaker for some 30 grandchildren, many of whom play about the garden when sent home for lack of school fees. Robai became a potter to gain cash income and has taught her daughter the craft. Their workshop earns her household a net income of about $60 per month. She is widely known in the region as a master, and her signature styles mark her handiwork, which is sold at the local market for cooking, storing water, and brewing beer. I once made the mistake of asking her whom she turns to for advice. She corrected me sternly. "I never ask for advice. I only give advice."

Robai is widowed and the third of five wives. Each of her four sons inherited one acre of land. She lives with one of these sons and two daughters. When I inquired as to her household size, she said about 200 people; after further discussion around who frequently sleeps there, she decided that her household size was 37. Touring her farm, she showed me maize, avocado, watermelon, and 16 other edible food plants. She keeps chickens, goats, and cows. But in spite of her farming, Robai needs money. She also pays school fees for her grandchildren whenever she can. At the weekly market her family buys maize and sugar, shoe polish, body lotion, and toothpaste. To support her pottery manufacture, she needs to purchase clay, grass, and firewood and transport it to her home.

In June 2016 I asked Robai to tell me how she had sent and received M-Pesa and cash money over the past month. Placing her elbow on one knee, she immediately enumerated five examples, folding over her fingers to make a fist.

Recently she had sent 3,000 ($30) to her friend Mary, who was hosting her in-laws. Robai and Mary visit each other regularly, share ideas, and help each other often. She explained that in-law visits are about showing generosity, prosperity, respect, and moral character.

Without pausing after all this, Robai went on. A close friend's husband had died, requiring Robai to visit and "console her with a blanket and clothing" costing 3,000 ($30); she also gave her 2,000 ($20) in cash. She had considered sending her 5,000 ($50) through her phone, but instead opted to visit her after selling several pots to afford the fare. Next, she had sent her daughter Phylis in Kakamega 4,000 ($40) for her to repay a loan to her savings group—Phylis planned to ask them to let her "win" the cycle early to pay a bill for her husband's medical care. Furthermore, last month she gave her daughter 2,000 ($20) in cash to prepare dinner for a friend. She also recently gave 3,100 ($31) to her grandchildren's' school. Then she made a fist with her hand—fifth, she contributed 1,000 ($10) for a friend's child's school fees. She added that she had sent two pots as wedding gifts; her reputation for craftsmanship makes her work valuable.

Receiving had also been frequent for her over the same month. She received 1,500 ($15) and on another occasion 3,000 ($30) from a close friend and 1,000 ($10) from a daughter. Like many mothers, Robai made it a point to say that she does not need to ask her children for money, but that they send it without her asking. She further volunteered that she is a member of seven savings groups who collect monthly contributions as well as emergency funds for homecoming events, long journeys, school fees, church events, potters' needs, funerals, and weddings. Recently she gave the group 2,500 ($25) to help a member's son buy a bridewealth cow. Last Thursday another of her groups contributed 1,000 ($10) to her, about half the hospital bill facing her son when two of his children were hospitalized. Robai said she could speak of many more groups she is a part of and shares money with routinely—the members of her church, other sellers at the marketplace, and neighbors, with whom she gives and receives plants, foodstuffs, clothing, and dishes.

Robai supports more than two dozen on her farming and potter's salary, yet also is part of multiple overlapping money networks that can quickly crowdfund large sums of money—more than $250 in the case of the bridewealth cow. None of her children completed eighth grade, yet she is widely known as a successful businesswoman and local matriarch who routinely helps generate large sums for friends, neighbors, relatives, and group members.

This remarkable capacity to engage a network is common. In certain emergencies, people can mobilize seemingly moribund ties almost immediately. For example, consider Shadrack, a Bungoma carpenter. In 2016 his three-year-old son, Mike, swallowed a nail and was successfully treated. The hospital costs accumulated to 30,000 ($300). Via SMS, Shadrack asked eight of his close friends to help him clear the bill, and they responded quickly. His son's teacher sent him 5,000 ($50). Three friends he had not seen for months sent their contributions immediately. Two friends sent help after two days. He had also coincidentally met a longtime friend at the hospital the same day, and that friend immediately sent him 3,000 ($30). Together, these friends amassed a total of 34,000 ($340). Shadrack used the extra 4,000 ($40) to buy timber for his carpentry workshop. As in this example, surviving with everyday finance often involves bringing together three, four, or more people around needs and crises large and small, including medical needs, school fees, documents and bribes, making bail, late contributions to a savings group, contributions to funerals, transportation emergencies, and lack of food or fuel. Indeed, this informal fundraising is so common in rural areas that much of M-Pesa traffic involves pitching in along with a few other people to supply some portion of a need.

The *gorogoro* economy of the rural-urban family was a product of forced work migration in colonial and postcolonial times.[8] Today a new model is emerging, that of a multi-sited family sharing resources across a network. People are by necessity investing more and more in income generation, education, mobility, work, and the money economy. M-Pesa remittances support these investments. The *gorogoro* economy may also be frequently inverted—a rural family often finds that city relatives ask them for assistance. A cow can be sold for school fees if the rural side of the family is willing. The rural home, when it exists, is now less the rural farm of the *gorogoro* setup than the site of various "projects" aimed at making money—everything from ride hailing to cash cropping and animal keeping. Rental houses[9] are the new status symbol and are put up by private individuals. A long, narrow cement structure is segmented into several one-family units, each with its own door. Such houses, designed as shelter for the landless, are now visible near marketplaces big and small. One of Dorcas's daughters told of an entrepreneurial neighbor who was continually frustrated by renters' inability to pay. Behind the local shop he had built several rows of the houses, but his boarders could not pay. He could not evict them, because the houses deteriorated when no one lived in them. "So he has no choice but to let [renters] stay without paying anything." Dorcas and her daughter then reflected on the morality of it all. Perhaps it is not Christian to make one's landless neighbors pay to simply live.

Fueled by population growth and landlessness, and enabled by digital money, family and friend networks often shift around short-term work stints. More and more people turn to the informal sector, as there is no longer any land. Grandmother Dorcas described the problem as *congestion*. With too many people on the land, many had no means of supporting themselves. In the past one's cows could graze on a hillside and come home at night of their own accord; but today that hillside is full of the homes of strangers, and your cows must be inside the house to prevent them from being stolen. Dorcas then spoke of petty jealousy, which in her mind arose from the social inequalities and divergent fortunes now fracturing communities. Her own situation provokes envy: "When neighbors realize that three of my children are gainfully employed . . . they become very jealous. They are practicing witchcraft . . . because my children have gone to school." In all this change, the home remains an essential site of security and belonging; it is where people are nurtured, physically and economically. Rural families sustain claims to attenuating rural assets in whatever way they can. Being there matters greatly, but sending money can also be an accepted form of presence. Only someone truly rooted in the community can move around—and still have permission to return and fully belong.

I once asked Robai about the importance of finding cash money and mentioned her pottery production and her son's salaried labor on local farms. She tossed the words aside with her chin and clucked in annoyance. What really mattered was her land, she corrected me sternly. As a widow, she has had to fight to keep her home and property, her stability and livelihood. Then she related that her co-wives had connived to take her land after her husband's death. Furthermore, people sometimes visit Robai to buy her land—they are victims of fake land sale scams. Her response is, "Look at my farm so lovingly cared for. . . . Is this the kind of land that anybody can sell freely just like that? . . . Look, this is my husband's grave . . . and his mother's. I cannot sell!" Robai's farm is the grave of her children's ancestors and the site of her ongoing projects, including trees, maize, and coffee. It is a fundamental asset that is constantly under threat, a lifeline to defend, and a refuge for the members of her large social network of friends, children, and grandchildren. Her son lives on a neighboring plot given to him by his father, and her daughter Helen returned to assist Robai in potting after her marriage failed. Helen's married home near Lake Victoria had been full of mosquitoes and flooded all the time. Helen's children were constantly ill, and when her husband died and her children grew up, she returned to Robai. Although daughters are expected to marry out, they frequently return to the natal home, where they will always belong.[10]

Robai warned me about the chimera of money. "There is nothing peculiar about having money," she counseled me. "Money can just disappear." In a vivid story, she related money to gluttony and witchcraft: A neighbor had sold all his land for money, except for a rectangular patch just big enough to one day serve as his grave. He gave a big stack of this money to the butcher, so that he could go there every day for the rest of his life and eat meat without paying. He is still regarded as a witch in the community, and when he enters a bar or shop no one else will enter for fear of witchcraft: "If he comes to your bar, your business will fail that day." His children, left landless, resorted to giving *boda boda* rides along with the many young men waiting at every junction. For Robai, her land is what really matters. As Peter Geschiere writes, "The soil . . . seems to raise deep feelings that easily surpass economic calculations."[11]

Ways to Get Ahead

In the wake of widespread landlessness and the increasing imperative of money, financial groups and solidarities are proliferating across sub-Saharan Africa. Savings groups have a long history; other, often novel, economic arrangements include voluntary associations, welfare associations, burial societies, new forms of savings and credit groups, new national and international remittance channels, financial cooperatives, crowdfunding platforms, and solidarity entrepreneurs.[12]

Groups use varied media, combining face-to-face meetings, WhatsApp groups, cash, and money transfer. Some groups contribute to investment projects such as land plots, stock market investments, animal projects, and selling household items. Some savings clubs circulate donations for a few weeks or months, while longer-term welfare groups of several hundred members offer aid in irregular or emergency situations. Some WhatsApp groups are based around mother's side or father's side family groups.

Of the 61 people we interviewed in the Nairobi portion of our research project, all of them had been members of groups, and half were currently members of one or more groups. Savings groups, or *chamas*, may range in size from as few as 5 people up to 25; their common name belies a wide variety of purposes. They may help members buy consumer goods, start a business, purchase land plots, or buy shares on the Nairobi stock exchange. Welfare associations have several hundred members and collect small regular donations for funerals or health emergencies for co-residents of an urban neighborhood or for members from the same extended family or home area. Although some groups discourage mobile phone donations and prize face-to-face meetings,[13] many other kinds of groups are emerging that rely in some form on the digital channel. They are based on diverse forms of homophily including ethnicity, profession, co-residence, and mutual hobbies; one savings group in Kitale called "Muscles" involves recreational weightlifters who are saving to buy their own gym. Many savings groups rely almost exclusively on digital and mobile communication. From our 2012 field notes here are examples:

- Twenty-two men who own a *matatu* [minivan] contribute 1,000 ($10) daily at 4 p.m. to one of their members. The 23rd day's contributions are sent from mobile phones to a treasurer's phone, and on to the group's bank account, and the cycle resumes. After four years, the members have been able to pay off their loans on their *matatu*, and the group plans to purchase another one with their banked savings.

- A group of 23 bus drivers e-transfers 1,000 ($10) each week to a fund. Half of the pool goes to one member and the other half goes to a bank account. As bus drivers they are rarely in the same place on payday when contributions are due, and the "win" is apportioned via mobile.

- Seven female and five male college students e-transfer 500 ($5) each Friday and circulate the win. They only contribute during the 12-week semester, creating a new group of 12 members the next semester. One member uses her money to run a school supplies shop in her dormitory room.

- Ten male friends from the same home village in Western Kenya call their savings club "the brothers." As adolescents, most of them had been through the maturity rituals together. Today they live in Bungoma, Kitale, Nairobi, and other areas. They circulate a monthly win, keep an emergency fund, and communicate via mobile phone to allow each other flexibility in keeping current with contributions.

E-money is employed in "solidarity entrepreneurialism . . . whereby individuals make investments and share transactions in collaboration with others."[14] Groups like university students can form and reform easily around time frames of weeks or semesters, thanks to mobile connections. Among mobile transportation workers, mobile communication supports "always on" connection. The bus and *matatu* drivers' groups have frequent short conversations throughout the day, updating one another on locations, mechanical problems, weather and road conditions, passenger numbers and fares gained, and planning the circulation of contributions and wins.

In urban and other areas, WhatsApp groups are proliferating. They coordinate fundraising campaigns and often use Safaricom Paybill (payment till number) to collect donations sent via money transfer. Paybill was designed to help merchants receive payments, but Safaricom now advertises the service as "short-term," along with a photo of a bride and groom. Kenyans with smartphones are highly engaged with WhatsApp groups of family, friends, savings groups, school alumni, and so on.

Eva, a mother of three in her late forties, communicates with nine to fifteen WhatsApp groups on any given day. She checks her group chats every morning and takes a daily call from her middle daughter in college. When the groups have specific targets or contribution pools, they set up a Paybill and she does her contributions, if any, in the morning, after checking up on the group activities. Her membership includes a group of coworkers of her own ethnicity that is pooling resources to buy a plot of land; two women's savings groups; her neighbors; her siblings and their children; and her five sisters-in-law, all married to a set of brothers. She is estranged from her husband, but through the sisters-in-law group she keeps up with goings-on in her husband's family, which holds important resources that she wants her children to lay claim to. She stresses her need to "be someone who knows what is happening."

WhatsApp groups engaging in e-commerce use Paybill to take payments. They also use Paybill to collect for celebrations, school fees, and medical emergencies. These WhatsApp groups range from the most spontaneous and informal—for example, two or three people may come together around someone who is stranded without transport—to groups that agree to regularly pool money via mobile phone, mimicking a savings group model.

The Internet and Facebook are hosting investment groups riding the Nairobi housing boom. Evelyn works in Nairobi and is close with her five sisters. She is part of a women's investment group that she joined after seeing a Facebook page. After a year, the Facebook group met in person, and then every month for a year to establish "who we are and our characters." About 50 members contribute monthly, topping up the following month if they fall short. Evelyn's sisters help her to avoid falling behind on payments. Evelyn's group has four different land purchase projects that they made through a group investment product run by Safaricom, which offers several options of varying cost. So far, Evelyn has completed her payments for two projects. For one, she is waiting for other members to complete payments before the group is given land title. Where the banking sector is notorious for ethnic bias and prohibitive mortgage interest rates, the mobile network operator Safaricom has stepped in.

Savings groups, table banking groups, welfare and wedding societies, SACCOs (government-registered Savings and Credit Cooperatives) at their most formal instantiation—group finance is on the rise. There are groups who invest in the Nairobi Stock Exchange, groups of women who met on Facebook who are buying a plot of land, groups of poor urban migrants who send regular small donations to a welfare society even if they have never met in person—even if they are temporary or recent residents in the city. People see the opportunity to "own" a minivan along with 21 other people. Even the wealthy make investments with siblings, group members, and friends, preferring a part of a larger investment—such as a hotel or apartment complex—to a smaller, individual project. In Nairobi, these group investments are democratizing home ownership but fueling dramatic housing price increases. Savings groups employ the mobile phone in novel ways to create new bonds of friendship around work, hobbies, and other forms of connection. Mobile phones have diversified solidarity entrepreneurialism beyond women's groups and are attracting young people, informal workers, and men.

Nairobi resident and baker Annette belongs to about 10 *chamas*. She is often asked to join these groups, as she has a reputation for punctual contributions. For one of the groups, composed of Annette and 11 other women that she grew up with, each person sends 5,000 ($50) monthly using a Paybill number. These women have purchased land in Kitengela through Safaricom's Investment Cooperative, which they plan to sell off later when the value appreciates. Annette heard about the cooperative in another women's group: "Safaricom can purchase land on our behalf to be repaid by the group." She also participates in two investment groups she heard about through Facebook, which are building accounts and looking for a plot. In one case the group contributed to a fund and discussed plans for it online for a full year before their first face-to-face meeting. Another group of 40 "old girls from secondary"—her high school classmates—takes contributions of 30,000 ($300) from each member for an annual group trip. This year they plan to go to Zanzibar: "Once you pay the money to the Safaricom till, you forward the confirmation message to our secretary for record keeping." With 20 primary school classmates Annette contributes on a monthly basis to a welfare association so that they can help one another in time of need.

Distributive Labors

Digital finance providers tend to view their customers as individuals. Their practices are set up to flag sharing of accounts or SIM cards as potential fraud. As a representative of the South African digital credit provider MyBucks explained: "If the same IMEI number [a unique 15-digit code associated with each phone] . . . popped up more than once then the second one must be fraud . . . well, we declined those lines but then it turned out that people are sharing handsets. . . so we had to switch that part of the technology off because of sharing of phones."[15]

The distributive labors and distributed identities of users like Toby, who sends money for others, or Grandmother Dorcas, who shares her account and PIN with her neighbors, are keys to access and to use of digital money for many people who would otherwise not be using these services. Through these distributive labors, digital money networks are built and extended into space to reach people far away from agents. They interdigitate money transfer, mobile banking, digital credit, payment tills, pay-as-you-go solar or water services, and WhatsApp groups.

Struggles and strategies to belong, survive, and get ahead create digitally mediated networks. Networks are built through distributive labors. The distributive labor of Robai, Emmanuel, and Shadrack is a response to material want, but is also productive—of people, livelihoods, and communities. It is a "crucial social activity that is constitutive of the social and not only the economic order."[16] For the poor and the landless, having many homes redistributes risk: a child born out of wedlock or a bride in a difficult marriage can return home or create another home. The interdigitate can distribute their investments in many groups or ventures or sustain many places to call home.

Through social and financial connections, people create strategies of relationship and belonging. Money sending is a new imperative and a means of day-to-day survival. Urban folk are financializing rapidly, not through banks but through WhatsApp and Facebook groups where they not only help friends and family but build assets. In contrast to rural people, they have markedly greater agency with diverse financial technologies such as WhatsApp and can access and generate much greater amounts of wealth-in-people. It is easy to see how the use of digital finance will, over time, amplify social inequalities.

Distributive labor is an expression of presence and commitment to home. Boundaries to giving and boundaries to belonging help define who is included and who is excluded. To show caring and generosity and thus to achieve belonging, now requires money, more than ever before. At stake is nothing less than social death because a real person contributes materially to his community. As Grandmother Violet of Bungoma, who had nurtured her grandchild who had sickle cell, put it, "When you have done something worthwhile the community will recognize you as a child of a person." She spoke bluntly of freeloaders in her community. "Those who don't help others, well—you don't have anything to tell us because you are not a person. Who are you? You are speaking as who?"

In other words, there are weighty risks to these distributive labors. A powerful moral economy motivates giving, and as a result, money circulations produce conflict and feelings of betrayal. Furthermore, people encounter more requests than they can meet. How do people negotiate the imperative to participate in their networks when to do so will exceed their means? Chapter 8 will explore strategic ignorance.

Strategic Ignorance

8

"My last-born brother came to me for money for dowry." Fred is a Nairobi teacher whose family contributed via digital money to help his younger brother raise bridewealth. "It was hard for me because we had set a limit as family members, and I made sure to contribute that stipulated amount." Fred explained that life was getting too expensive. In maturity he found himself "caught in the middle," taking care of family members both younger and older than himself. Setting targets for contributions was a way to ensure fairness. "But even after paying the dowry, he still called telling us that we had to chip in a second time. This second time I was unwilling!"

The siblings then turned to friends and other relatives. "Other people also contributed, but he kept disturbing me, and I was able to help him even though it took some time." In the end Fred had to find a way: "Since he is my brother and whenever I have a problem, I share with him, I decided to help but it took time."

As Fred explained, the wealth-in-people of digital money takes time to create and to sustain. People create a powerful moral economy when they speak of money as caring for others and being present for others. But because resources are limited, people are also wary of burdening others and of becoming a burden themselves. They must find acceptable ways to break these norms of generosity—ways to *not give*. They choose presence or absence—to take a call or to turn off the phone. Strategic ignorance describes a way to retreat from the information, resources, and relationships of one's social ties in order to lessen the obligation to give.[1] In retreating, people blame technology—the unreliability of networks and the distortion and deception wrought by mobile communication. By delegating responsibility and agency to their devices, people negotiate strategies of non-use.[2] In this chapter I will describe how changeable strategies with mothers, fathers, friends, and co-members reveal the moral weight and social dilemmas of these negotiations, and ultimately, the fragility of wealth-in-people.

A Moral Economy

"Yesterday . . . I ran into someone in town, and he told me, oh today is your day, I'll buy you lunch. He asked me, should I send you by M-Pesa? I told him my phone is dead. And he said, I will send it anyway so that when you charge it, your lunch will be there. So I praised the Lord because he has given me this gifted life." Emmanuel, a firstborn son whose struggle for belonging in his stepfather's lineage was described in Chapter 7, explained that his reputation for generosity and kindness brought him many money transfers from friends: "If I was a bad person—if I was mean to my brothers—I'm pretty sure that blessings such as this would not occur."

Friendship, support and caring, and the interventions of God are all expressed in money transfer practices. Digital money transfer accompanies phone talk through which people create common lives over time, sharing their troubles and plans. Perhaps this is why it is spoken of not as money but as words of feeling and emotion. Money sent will be referred to as "friendly appreciation"; the action of sending money is not referred to as such but with words like "support," "condole," "comfort," "a friendly handshake," "just a bit of airtime," "just a top-up," "sugar," *majani* (tea leaves), "I would feel inhuman if I did not help," "I know he needs my kindness right now," "I was relieved." Money sending has important meanings and creates bonds of trust around support, help, and gifts.

Money sent stands in for a person and represents that person socially. Like the classic gift of anthropological theory, it carries a great deal of the sender in it.[3] Sending is "another way for me to be there." Julia is a farmer who recently sent money to Janet, her closest friend and relative, when she was going for surgery in Eldoret. Janet did not ask for the money. Julia felt that since she was not accompanying Janet, the "other way of doing so" was through the 700 ($7) she gave her to cover any expenses on the way.

People send money to show that they are generous, appreciative, dependable, dutiful, and caring. These expressions are important in friendships. A single mother from Nairobi in her thirties reflected on a close friendship she has maintained with a female friend from school. "We've been friends for a long time, and we've been helping one another through thick and thin." Money transfers are at the heart of these demonstrations of caring and helping: "We are very close and if I have any problem, I tell her, and she sends me money to help me out whenever she can. We trust each other well, so if she comes to me with a problem, I help her without any hesitation. I will also send if we are not together."

Distributive labor produces friendship networks of different kinds. Some ties involve long-term relationships with intimates. Other, shallower networks fundraise sporadically or around smaller amounts across a larger group. One strategy can balance the other: Nairobi IT student Jackson asked several friends for money when he recently had trouble paying his rent. He reflected that asking for smaller amounts from many people is easier than asking a few people for large sums.

Networks of friends are often same-gender groups who grew up together, went to school together, or went through a coming-of-age together. Bungoma farm laborer George, twenty-two years old, earns about 5,000 ($50) a month. His age mate Wekesa works in Nairobi as a dealer in motor spare parts and sends him airtime and money through M-Pesa. In January, Wekesa sent George 2,000 ($20) through M-Pesa. Wekesa had called George to check on him and in the conversation, George asked Wekesa to send some money. Wekesa agreed easily, assuring him that he was just "sharing some of his beer." However, George did not have a Safaricom SIM card: he therefore asked Wekesa to send the money to George's mother's Safaricom line. The mother retained 500 ($5), thereby fulfilling George's monthly obligation to her. George has never sent Wekesa money, simply because Wekesa appears to earn more than George does. George also sometimes activates more-distant ties, receiving on occasion from Wechabe, a friend he met when visiting an aunt. Wechabe has sent George money three times in the past five years even though they have never met during that time. Wechabe sent more than he was asked for to express friendship.

Evans, who is in his twenties and a part-time farm laborer from Bungoma, reflected on why he sends money to people, noting that someone may have helped him in the past: "Sometime back a friend had assisted me [with] some money to contribute towards my savings group. Later on, when my friend's family lacked food, I remembered his kindness and rendered just as I was rendered to." Money transfer gifts are the sign of a socially connected person who is cared for. Evans added: "These days, nowadays, if someone sends me 500 or 200, when someone sees a message saying, confirmed, you have received 200, people look at me and they say, yes, this person has people who care for him. And life goes on."

God is the ultimate source of reciprocity in these networks and inspires people to check on one another and send money when needed. Rural farmer Ben gave a stranded man 50 ($0.50) for bus fare, saying that "helping a stranger pleases Providence," who divinely intervenes in his life. Baraka, a Nairobi sound engineer, sends and receives money from family members on a nearly daily basis. His Christian beliefs have taught him that "giving is receiving . . . and that blessings await those who give." People often think of the bad consequences of *not* sending money—being sent home from school, medical suffering and emergency, disappointment, anger—and these bad consequences, and the possibility of being held responsible, are part of the emotional work of deliberating around money sending.

The Gender of Money

Money transfers also express gender roles, in particular that men be good providers. Ideas about gender inform credit and debt relationships from the day-to-day to the long term. Most of Kenya's cultural groups are called patrilineal; through cultural symbols like the central pole on the thatched-roof house, "creditors are symbolically likened to males and debtors to females."[4] But as Parker Shipton writes, those who are entrusted with wealth—the land—are obligated to distribute and circulate it. Gender norms are informed by this sense of an underlying obligation, which more recent practices of gender and work have reinforced. These gendered norms position women as receivers in mobile money circulations. A study of low-income Kenyans found that women received 33% of their income from digital remittances—as compared to only 4% for men—and were "more likely to receive help when they need it."[5] Digital money exchanges tend to reproduce these status distinctions of sender and receiver, but at the same time, within gendered social norms of generosity and reciprocity, bestow the obligation to pass on and circulate. Possession of resources may simply engender debts to others. In the common etiquette of money sending, senders include the cash-out fee that recipients pay the agent along with the amount sent, and if they forget, they might be politely reminded to forward it along—"Ongeza ya kutoa" (Add on the cash-out fee).

We have seen how women like Consolata create roles of importance in their communities using financial relationships. These gendered norms enhance and deepen relationships for both men and women. By invoking these obligations women can ensure that they receive funds. For example, Daniel, a land surveyor in Bungoma, frequently sends some money to his estranged wife and two children some 80 kilometers away. In the first year of their separation, his wife reported him to his parents and village elders for neglect. They demanded that he attend to his family's fees and other needs. For the past three years, he has sent school fee payments directly to the school so that his wife does not need to call first. He transfers money to her weekly or biweekly.

Men may carefully consider their position in vertical networks of unequal prestige around age, money, and other economic resources. Nairobi construction worker Barry will ask for money from people who are in a lesser financial position than he is, especially if the amount is small. For example, if he needs "just 500 shillings" ($5), he will not call a relatively affluent friend; he will rather "save that call for a bigger favor." He will look instead to a friend for whom this sum is significant. Barry said that these friends of lower income and means than himself "understand that people have challenges regardless of their status," and they will respond immediately. As someone of greater means, he is a valuable friend, and they are likely to need his assistance at some time in the future for a bigger favor and so are eager to help him out. Similarly, Nairobi DJ John asks for money from those who "understand me and know my life struggles." He cannot ask those who are less well off; he compared such a request to "asking for money from your house help": "The water guy comes, and you don't have money on you, but you cannot ask her [your house help] because it's 'wrong' and things are working in reverse."

Tobias, a rural man in his twenties who was looking for employment, recently received assistance from his brother, who sent him bus fare; another male friend, who helped him with a college loan; and his boss and cousin, who chipped in for his bus fare to his sister's mother-in-law's funeral. But he has been able to send money to several women during the same period, starting with his mother. He also mentioned sending 700 ($7) to a lady friend and helping another female friend and former classmate who was stranded late one evening with 500 ($5). Finally, he sent 1,000 ($10) to a friend and college student. She had asked him to support her when they met in town the previous month, and she had reminded him again recently with a phone call.

Expressions of providing and caring inform many relationships, including the brother-sister bond and romantic or spousal relationships. Barry works in construction in Nairobi and through money transfers and other media supports two sisters who are three and ten years younger than he is. His support protects his sisters' reputations from "sponsors" (sugar daddies). Barry also regularly sends his fiancée e-money, saying with pride that it "is my responsibility [to take care of her]. . . . She is also very open about what she needs the money for whenever she calls to ask for money. When I do not have the money, I call and explain to her so that the relationship is not strained. . . . When I can, I just send her the money for her to go and take care of whatever she needs to."

Avoidance practices that give women privacy make it quite inappropriate to judge amounts or ask about intended uses. Barry says that women often have needs that cannot be explained. Similarly, Tobias doesn't wonder what women need money for. "She did not tell me what it was for and I did not ask. Ladies have needs they do not like to discuss."

M-Pesa gives men of relatively little means the ability to send money to others—helping someone who is stranded or who needs something unmentionable. But for some men—urbanites like Barry and John, for example—relational work also produces social ranking that can make it harder to seek assistance. "Subtle linguistic expressions . . . give away the asymmetry between the participants in relational work."[6] Euphemisms might be used to minimize the value of the money sent, depict its value as a social gift, and perhaps blunt any shame a receiver might feel. Wechabe told George that the money he sent was just a gift of friendship, saying, "I am sharing some of this beer." In a similar example, Pithon, a university student, was broke and called a lady friend and asked her for airtime (which tends to circulate in much lesser amounts, mostly as greetings and gifts). In fact, he needed money. She sent him 300 ($3), which he used to buy soap and toiletries. He also called a male friend, who sent him 500 ($5), reassuring Pithon via text that the money was merely "a friendly handshake" after a long period of not meeting. Barry said if he was "broke" he could admit it only to his sister. He could not think of any women he would feel comfortable asking for money.

Exclusions and Betrayals

Because the emotions of e-money are so closely associated with belonging and the moral economy, they can also quickly turn sour. Money sending can also cause stress or make one feel neglected, forgotten, or left out; it can cause jealousy or bitterness; being asked for remittances may mean "they don't understand my pressures"; or "they overestimate my means." Jealousy is the by-product for those who are denied, left out, or given less. M-Pesa has made helping a choice; with it, people "can assist neighbors, even in-laws . . . and ignore their own parents," Grandmother Violet complained. One young woman is known to be particularly close to the grandmother who raised her; her cousins assume she receives large remittances, but she confided that she does not. To avoid conflicts, a man sending money to his mother, intended to support the family farm, must balance that with e-gifts to his wife so she can purchase something for herself. It can cause jealousy or become a means of comparison that makes others feel inadequate. Similarly, Evans will send money to the parent whose phone is functional at the moment. Right now that is his father: "When I send money, I will call my dad, I will send you 200, 100 is yours and 100 is mom's. You know what the old man needs is just his medicine, you know what I'm talking about [locally brewed alcohol], and mom has her own needs. So what I do is to balance."

The pain of exclusions and betrayals is much greater with relatives than with friends. Grandmother Violet explained that people from the same hearthhold are "from the same stomach" and therefore they should always be there to help one another. Yet Violet says that siblings naturally envy one another because of their inherent differences in ability, talent, and luck: jealousy is what undermines sibling relationships. The dangers inherent in sibling intimacy were also addressed by potter Robai's son Bernard. Bernard's homestead is a short walk from Robai's and on the same land that she came to live on at her marriage. At her husband's death Robai's four sons were each apportioned one acre in inheritance. Bernard has a wife and five children, and often stays at a commercial farm about 40 kilometers away, where he earns 6,000 shillings a month ($60) as a manager. He had recently come back to his home when his two youngest children got typhoid. Without any money for their treatment, he visited his half brothers for help, but they refused, saying they had no money even for their own food at the time. Bernard then asked his neighbor, who paid for the antibiotics; he still owed the doctor money for the visit. He joined my conversation with Robai one day when his children were convalescing. Still troubled about their illness, he said his father's co-wives were riddled with jealousy, even hatred, and that his half brothers have been plotting to disinherit him from their father's land for some time. Bernard said it was getting to the point where he could see himself killing one of his half brothers. Such tales of conflict are common. Grandmother Violet thinks jealousy is endemic to plural marriages. She explained that because so much is expected from people who are "from the same stomach," they are the very people who will disappoint you, betray you, or even hurt you. "If a child of a particular wife is successful, the children of the other wife will begin to say, they have bewitched us, or they have done something cunning to us." Others said, "The jealousy between wives is passed to the children" or "The children of this wife eat while we are starving."

Children of a hearthhold who are "from the same stomach" should care for one another, but caring takes money. People living under the assault of landlessness and joblessness strain to live up to the constant imperative to participate in money circulations. The disappointments, jealousies, and exclusions they generate build up walls around patrilines or hearthholds, leaving many disappointed or excluded.

Another common breach of the moral economy is lying. Lies are a constant risk in mobile money circuits, ranging from false calls about an accidental money transfer ("Please return the 500 I mistakenly sent you"), to charity scams, to agents who miscount money cash-outs. You may send money to a rural relative for a house help's bus fare, but she never shows up. A hapless relative diverts money sent for school fees toward a poorly conceived business plan. Many people navigate these rough waters of trust by confirming that claims for help are honest or deserving. Emmanuel's close friend Rose once asked him for 2,000 ($20) to help her go for a medical checkup. Emmanuel promised to give her the money the next day. However, he suspected that she might want the money for reasons other than medication. He found out through mutual friends that Rose was really looking for bus fare to Nairobi, so he turned down the request and severed his friendship with her (they eventually reconciled). Emmanuel uses three excuses when he needs more time to investigate the veracity of a request. He tells the asker he has not received his wages; he says the person may check in later; or he claims that he is expecting money from someone else soon. Emmanuel's generosity has limits—he must know the purpose of a transfer, and it must be a purpose that he believes in. His common response to "Why did you send him money?" is "I know he could never do a lie against me."

Strategic Ignorance

Most people receive more requests for money than they can grant. The expansion of connections and networks has brought an expansion of responsibility and with it the dilemmas of responsibility. The awareness of a need, and the awareness that others are aware that you are aware that there is a need, creates a powerful obligation. But someone who is unaware of a crisis cannot be held accountable for not helping. Some senders want to know as little as possible about the reasons why people are asking for money, so as not to be become entangled or implicated in their plans, should those plans involve gambling, drinking, affairs, or a shaky business scheme. Others feel a donation for school fees will commit them to educating a child into the future. Strategic ignorance is the deliberate retreat from requests and information and is widely used to lessen the obligation to support others.

Strategic ignorance is enacted with the help of technology.[7] Turning off one's phone is the most common way to produce strategic ignorance and find some distance from excessive pressure for remittances. Aaron, a rural schoolteacher, was sending his daughter off to high school and was "looking through my phone" and calling his contacts. He needed at least 9,000 ($90) for the girl's uniform and books. Everybody's phone was off. Aaron explained that it was school-opening time across the country; after schools opened, he said, he might be able to get one of his contacts to answer; unfortunately his daughter could not report to school without a uniform. Nairobi dweller Kinyua lost some money and sent four friends he had recently helped a text message asking for 500 ($5). Two of the friends sent him portions of this amount. The other two did not pick up his call, and Kinyua said he might not ask them again.

To minimize interactions, people will hide phones or feign losing them, refuse calls, turn phones off, and discontinue or change their mobile money registrations. An unanswered call rings repeatedly and eventually gives the caller the *mteja* ("customer" in Kiswahili) message (as in "the customer is not available"). The caller can interpret this generously: this person would probably like to help but might not have the money. Meeting that caller in the market later, the embarrassment of the *mteja* message can be easily shaken off with joking or gentle chiding, "You were *mteja*—what happened?" One can say the phone was charging or misplaced. One day schoolteacher Aaron was himself trying to avoid someone in town. (The shoe was on the other foot.) This person came to us eagerly, inquired about Aaron's family, and then mentioned he had been trying to reach him by phone. Aaron claimed his phone had fallen down the pit latrine. After the man left, I pointed out that he had just used his phone a few minutes before. He told me he was referring to another phone! Not responding to a call can implicate you—"Why didn't you answer?" Therefore, turning off one's phone is the safer path, leaving both parties in the bliss of strategic ignorance.

Sometimes someone can disconnect the phone line, which is interpreted as wanting to end the relationship. Samuel farms one acre of land in Naitiri Village and can earn 12,000 ($120) a month as a cutter for a sugar company when there is work, but his pay is often late and he is sometimes paid in sugar. To buy a cow to sacrifice for his son, he reached out to his younger siblings. He explained that his initial calls were met with the *mteja* message. Eventually two of his brothers changed their SIM cards to avoid him. He was visibly saddened as he told the story. He instead borrowed 20,000 ($200) from a local informal lender and relied on many other friends to cover the costs of his son's ritual.

Oscar is a university lecturer who disconnected from M-Pesa and threw his handset away in frustration (temporarily) after a barrage of requests. He says that the culture of M-Pesa has enabled a "culture of dependency and a total inability to plan" among the rural folk. "We live a culture of crisis. We just move from crisis to crisis." His complaints are common among the more affluent. Strategic ignorance finds ultimate expression in the habit of keeping multiple handsets, more than one line, or handsets with two SIM cards.

Just as remittances communicate meanings, their absence is equally weighty with uncertainty. Perhaps *mteja* really *was* charging the phone. Or perhaps some dynamic of the previous relationship may be behind a conscious decision to refuse a call. Maybe this relative disapproves of the argument you had with your father last month and wants you to heal the rift, or heard about that misguided advice you gave a friend, which didn't really work out, and perhaps you're being blamed for the fallout when a mutual contact doesn't answer your phone call. The uncertain meanings of *mteja* proliferate, and responsibility is directed away from moral choices and behavior in the direction of notoriously unreliable networks, unpredictable batteries, and the pit latrine.

Askers tend to make general statements of want or trouble and then explain what they have already done to address the situation themselves. A common tactic is to avoid asking for specific amounts: "Send whatever you can." After all, they know little of their relative's means or other demands on his resources. One might also avoid mentioning whether or not others may be contributing, again hoping to inspire a large donation. The giver will wonder about the veracity of the stated purpose of the money gift and its real cost, and the number of others who might also be sending or intending to send. Risper, a rural woman in her twenties, asked a male friend to help her "facilitate our Boxing Day celebration." Since she did not ask for a specific amount, the friend decided to figure out how much one person could use on groceries for the day and gave her 800 ($8). Risper was satisfied with the amount, confiding that she had expected to receive less. Strategic ignorance worked in Risper's favor. When asking someone who can be presumed to have more resources, she explained, one might be better off avoiding any discussion of costs—after all, such events can vary in cost and scale.

It is widely believed that askers describe particular needs—such as school fees—but in reality, divert that money or even originally intend it for something else. Strategic ignorance shapes both sending and receiving with international migrants. Kenyan immigrant families in Chicago field numerous requests for "school fees." But remittances are often folded into household consumption and diverted to community needs, such as church donations, funeral and wedding donations, medical help, and local public works projects. Senders complain but are nonetheless resigned to the diversion of "school fees" toward what they deride as "status displays." Stay-behinds counter that these contributions ensure that "his people appreciate him"—reinforcing the migrant's belonging in the home community. Furthermore, both sides consider their relationships to be a particularly fragile tie. Stay-behind relatives often fear that their relative in the city or abroad will "become lost," and no longer respond to call, text, or e-mail. They greatly fear being considered too dependent and too needy. For emigrants and stay-behinds alike, "school fees" seems to offer a morally acceptable use of funds that quietens both sides of the exchange and protects the relationship.

The mobile money account allows an individuation of agency that is considered socially dangerous. Like the mobile communication of which it is a part, a mobile wallet can be "a direct and indeed a very individualized medium . . . [to] maintain social networks."[8] People-with-phones can choose what to do with the money reserve and for whom. For example, the money storage account was used during the coming-of-age ritual as a semiprivate "contingency fund."[9] But even the money reserve is often claimed or claimable by others. Responding to an emergency request or need in the social network, people will send "what I had on my phone at the time." Nairobi resident Daniel sent his friend Job an urgently needed police bribe of 2,000 ($20), saying it was "ready" on his phone for such emergencies. Evans "balances" remittances to his mother and father with a minimum of 100 ($1) each, and therefore needs at least 200 ($2) in his account before he sends money to them: "When it [the money balance on his M-Pesa account] has not reached 200 yet I do not send because it must be balanced." Emmanuel leaves 50 ($0.50) on his phone each month for his girlfriend's airtime.[10]

Because the money in the mobile wallet is already claimed or claimable by others, many avoid keeping money on their phones if they receive many requests. Grandmother Dorcas's son, a well-off dentist in Kimilili, banks 2,000 ($20) daily from his dental business if he can, so that he will not be tempted to send it to someone or buy something. In 2012 each phone-to-bank transaction cost him 70 ($0.70). The individuation of money and decision-making is given varying moral judgment depending on its usage and who is benefiting. Emmanuel, his reputation for generosity and his many labors for his parents and step siblings aside, also admitted: "Yes, M-Pesa helps me very much. If someone asks me for money, I say I don't have it. But I know that I have something on M-Pesa."

Circulated e-money remittances not only forge connections but also disrupt relationships. The mobile channel is widely associated with bribes and illicit payments, affairs, and hiding money from spouses, usually to the benefit of siblings or secret families. Women and men often maintain their hearthhold ties with remittances kept private from their spouses, a pattern we found to be pervasive among 33 women farmers in the Kitale area whom we interviewed during the social network mapping study.[11] Women hide money from husbands and privately send money to mothers and sisters to educate nieces and nephews, and those in precarious circumstances of polygyny and widowhood reach out to siblings and cousins. A retired policewoman described "a lot of wrangles over money" with her two co-wives. Before e-money, her husband would forcibly take her cash to support his favorite wife. She relies on secret transfers from her brother and son. A fifty-two-year-old widow was forced off her husband's land at his death; she returned to her father's land, where she assists her brother and his wife. Her brother remits her children's school fees, unbeknownst to his wife, "who despises my presence here. With this M-Pesa account I have been able to educate my children with my brother's help without his wife discovering." The exclusion and privacy typical of digital gifts shape social networks through negative reciprocity.

Again, people tend to blame not human failings but the agency of mobile phones for the betrayals and exclusions produced by money networks. Rural elder Mzee Nathan disapproved of the agency, mobility, and information that the phone was giving to women and youth. His two wives use the phone to compare his provisioning of their households. "Because of the phone,"[12] he said, he must now bring them equal amounts of meat—one whole kilo each—in order to "balance." "Because of the phone," his wives have a newfound mobility: "Women have become very unfaithful using phones. Because you can come to her house and ring her. She says, 'I'm at home.' But you are in her house and she is not there! So from there you start thinking twice about these phones."

Women and youth are not really bad, Mzee Nathan reasons, but with phones they are now moving around without telling him their whereabouts, and soliciting funds for false projects and needs. Men and women complain equally about money gifts that fund affairs. A rural woman in her fifties mused that "this M-Pesa service should only be for women" because "it is destroying many marriages . . . you find the SMS has gotten in, and this person is not sister or cousin. Why are you sending money to her?" These gifts create powerful relationships: "A bond begins when a husband sends money to the other lady . . . it goes on until the marriage breaks."

Notwithstanding the role of the phone in "lying and cheating," Mzee Nathan sees an opportunity in the technology to know where his wives are: he has heard that there is a phone with a screen on it that can show you the surroundings of the caller (in explaining this new kind of phone he used his fingers to outline the rectangular shape of a smartphone screen, which he had seen pictures of in the newspaper). He suggested that all phones should show you these surroundings, so that the phone can keep women and youth from using phones for lying, and instead be a means to "confirm the presence of where this caller is." Mzee then corrected his stance on phones, reasoning that perhaps the solution is not to get rid of them but to get a better kind of phone.

Even though secret transfers are often just as easily conducted with cash money, the belief that phone money is especially socially disruptive is widespread. One rural couple shares a phone to cut down on costs and allow both husband and wife to see the record of their children's' remittances and thereby "keep the devil out of our home." Widespread sharing of handsets and SIM cards also poses dilemmas and opportunities for strategic ignorance.

Emmanuel's friend and workmate Wycliffe has no phone, and Emmanuel frequently lets Wycliffe borrow his. Wycliffe's family members often call Emmanuel when they need help with money, and Emmanuel feels their requests are meant equally for him. Once Emmanuel sent money to Wycliffe's family himself to treat a child sick with malaria, because he knew Wycliffe had no money. After this incident he set his phone to divert calls from Wycliffe's family, to avoid the responsibility imparted by these calls.

Why Strategic Ignorance?

In supporting strategic ignorance, the mediating and delegating roles of technology come to the fore, raising dilemmas of responsibility.[13] If strategic ignorance creates so much indeterminacy, why do people continue to enact it? Uncertainty allows both senders and receivers to strategize, to hide the amount they might really have or be willing to send, to keep their relatives' expectations low, and to prevent accurate assessment of their generosity. Both askers and receivers seek "room to maneuver . . . [to] make others think or assume that this person must have boundless resources."[14] Ambiguity fuels shifting judgments of a gift's adequacy and its social intentions, which can then leave the meanings of these remittances continually open to interpretation. Senders and receivers complain about helping too much, not helping enough, asking for too much, or not being clear on what is needed. As a result, the social relationships produced by money transfers are always open to reshaping through the many animated discussions that precede and follow these remittances.

Strategic ignorance is a part of the flexible and open-ended arrangements around money. Money sent may be cast in whole or part as a loan. But a loan goes frequently unpaid and will then by agreement be reframed (in whole or part) as a gift in order to preserve a relationship. In this setup of flexibility in framing and reframing there is often no clear boundary between generalized and balanced reciprocity—or negative reciprocity, for that matter.[15] Nairobi DJ John gave a loan to a friend, who avoided his calls: "If you lend people money, they block their phone or blacklist you." John said debtors should keep you up to date on their efforts to repay. These various forms of stalling, which are called "giving a lot of excuses," "playing games," or "coming with stories again," are the norm, but John said they are preferable to silence. Eventually the amount to John was adjusted downward, and the friendship was patched up.

In this landscape of uncertainty, being trustworthy becomes an important part of maintaining one's networks. Kate, a farmer in rural Bituyu, Kenya, was surprised when her friend Amos asked for 500 ($5) for bus fare—because she knew that Amos earned good pay. She felt "it was a test of my generosity"—as he has frequently helped her out when she requested. She reasoned that Amos really did need the money and promptly sent him the exact amount.

The ambiguity of time can also help frame and reframe agreements. Promises and claims can be realized weeks, months, or even years later; a longer duration makes a claim more valuable. DJ John says, "The longer you wait to get something in return, the better the payoff." A debt repaid can increase over time; promises can be reneged upon or closed off by resolving the debt. Promises to repay can also stall or stave off a claim but may eventually be dropped.

Because of the indeterminacy of informal relationships, money can shore up or instead smooth over the social boundaries they traverse, such as creditor/debtor, rural/urban, or barriers of generational obligation, thus making who owes what to whom open to reinterpretation. For example, rural and urban kin tend to speak of their worlds in stark dichotomies. Grandmother Dorcas expressed sympathy for her working sons in Nairobi and other towns. "You must buy everything there, water, food, even the air you breathe . . . while all of that is free here for me. I have no money here and yet imagine I have so much food here at home." Such comments perform empathy but also represent urban and rural lives as incompatible opposites, obscuring their interdependency. Her son the dentist received this remark as strategic ignorance. Was he to pretend that the comment was intended to be taken at face value, or that it was meant to remind him of his obligations—and inspire a money transfer?

The strategy of distributing your money investments among many networks—thus preventing others from knowing your real means and assets—has long been a privilege of wealthy telephone farmers to obscure their real means from demanding kin.[16] Through strategic ignorance, the well-off can choose how and when to participate across the phases of an elaborate ritual. Wafula, a fifty-year-old Nairobi resident whose businesses include rental houses, explained that at this point in life, he is juggling numerous requests for money, as nieces and nephews seek school fees and job placement, and as elderly folk continue to need support. He has a "system," as he calls it, for dealing with "celebrations back home." He explained how it worked during the 2012 coming-of-age of his nephew (who would refer to him as "father"):

"As the day approached I refused my brother's calls and those of my sister in law. I just kept quiet. I missed the whole thing. But then during the passing out [another event in this ritual that occurs three months later] . . . I called my sister-in-law. . . . I asked her to prepare a shopping list of everything that would be needed. . . . She sent me an SMS with the list that came to 6,000 shillings ($60). I sent her that [via M-Pesa]. So there was a big feast and that 6,000 paid for everything. My brother called me to say thank you."

Wafula estimates he saved around 20,000 ($200) by staying home, avoiding the cost of transport and numerous requests for assistance before and during an event attended by several hundred people. He would have been expected to give money to older women for their "sugar"; help people with transport; and assist the church and the family with last-minute expenses, food, and medical costs for the boy. Initiating the call at the passing out event and allowing his sister-in-law to set the price of the remittance makes him appear infinitely generous, even as his own estimates, he explained, would end up too high for the actual cost of groceries in the rural areas.

Mobile finance has democratized the distributional tactics of strategic ignorance. Michael, twenty-four years old, is an apartment caretaker at a Nairobi complex. For about seven years he has been sending Robert, an M-Pesa agent and age mate from rural Western Kenya, 2,000 ($20) monthly (about 10% of his monthly salary). Robert will do a variety of things for Michael at home, including maintaining his rural farm. Michael also prefers to send Robert to look after his parents when they tell him they need something. He has a bank account with KCB that he accesses through the Safaricom menu on his phone. He avoids sending money to his parents from this account. With Robert as his proxy, Michael can meet social obligations more cheaply and insulate himself from the dramas of rural politics and the vagaries of his parents' needs, which he claims "interfere with my savings targets." His motivation in keeping his rural network earmarked is not self-interest, but rather to extend himself across networks of family obligation, on the one hand, and those of choice created through friendship, on the other. He has prioritized having money for his immediate local networks. He impressed upon me that because of his careful planning, he was recently able to help his wife's brother with 1,000 ($10), as this brother-in-law needed to bring a gift to his in-laws. I asked Michael what Robert thinks of the whole arrangement. Michael replied that he is saving money to buy a piece of land for Robert one day.

Friends, Relatives, and the Search for Accountability

The burdens of kinship are heavy for both rural and urban folk, who alike frequently say they prefer their friends to their relatives. You cannot choose a relative, but you can choose a friend. Friendship is an expression of willing association.[17] You cannot ask a relative to return money, but a friend will repay to preserve the relationship. Bernard sees greater value in the possibilities of friendship. In the conversation we had when his children were sick, and referencing his half siblings' refusals to help buy their medicine, he told us: "A friend can enable you to travel in places you have never been . . . but those you have been born with would much rather see you dead and buried."

Savings groups promise a detachment from the hierarchical obligations and disappointments of family life. Informal finance has found fertile ground in the friend zone. Nairobi baker Annette avoids asking her relatives for money: "Relatives are very hard to deal with . . . they will not pay back—they feel they are entitled to the money." She once lent a relative 40,000 ($400) that was never refunded. Whenever Annette calls, this relative disconnects—"This lady has blocked me." She tries to rely on her 10 friend savings groups, including a group of like-minded women she met on Facebook. Their arrangements slide flexibly between gifts and loans and can also lend money to help the friends and relatives of non-members. In addition, she regularly receives money from a childhood friend. Sometimes she repays this friend, or she may bake breads and cakes for the friend's office and church groups instead. Annette's group lends significant sums informally outside the group, even for ongoing medical care such as dialysis treatment.

One cannot overplay one's hand with strategic ignorance. Its uncertainties risk being interpreted as breaches of honesty and trust. In particular, the obligations of family life based on generation and gender are now an everyday imperative to negotiate roles in digital money networks. Many people seek ways to disentangle some of their money relationships from these networks even as they also engender and participate in them. They seek greater regularity and predictability in their access to money: they seek to accelerate reciprocity, and they seek the formalized and rule-based relationships of savings clubs.

Financial groups are often self-organizing. They use rules and rituals to set apart from everyday life the relationships and monies of the group so that they can be applied toward savings, investment, or other goals.[18] Families now frequently try to self-organize as well. In a family *chama* (family savings group), family members contribute equally and share the payout on a regular basis, following the common rotating savings and credit association (ROSCA) model. Baker Annette tried to start two "family *chamas*": maternal and paternal. The members of the paternal *chama* contribute 400 ($4) monthly. The money is sent to a Safaricom Paybill number and is supposed to be for funerals and emergencies only, but recently the grandchildren used the fund for a member's wedding gift after some discussion. Annette's maternal *chama* fell flat and, as she put it, "failed to monetize" because not all members "on that side" had M-Pesa accounts; she offered that many of her relatives often failed in "looking for a way to send the money." As Nairobi teacher Fred related at the beginning of this chapter, digital contributions for family obligations like bridewealth can help meet the costs of these rituals, but they mean new imperatives to grant assistance.

Many of the people turning to informal groups and clubs are urban entrepreneurs, like Annette. But the rural poor are also seeking regularity and predictability. Farmer Praxides lives near Bungoma with her mother and relies on her farming, trading in firewood, a part-time job as a teacher's aide, and assistance from her brother of about $20 per month. She noted: "In today's world people are so busy. People are goal oriented. People want to achieve things. They don't have a lot of time to look for money or follow up on unpaid debts." A rural family in Naitiri, Western Kenya, began to rotate donations equivalent to $2.50 monthly after their brother was beaten to death by thieves, leaving his siblings, parents, and maternal aunt without savings for his burial. A rural farmer and elder in the same town, along with his sons and their wives in Mombasa and Kitale, use M-Pesa to circulate 500 ($5) a month, mostly for medical bills and school fees. One member consolidates the payments and keeps track of the account.

Family groups often form at funerals, when "lost" family branches resurface and hierarchies are sorted out. Sacrificial animals are offered in order, and those given the honor to offer the first animals receive the most blessings. By working out such arrangements at funerals, family members bring up or assuage discord. Nowadays, family members will use the newfound closeness to start savings groups with mobile phones, often with a hearthhold focus. "These [family *chamas*] happen at funerals and emotional times—but they just don't succeed," said Praxides. In her own family, a relative absconded after receiving his payout. Relatives do not take their obligations seriously; your own brother cannot be held accountable. As family life becomes more and more monetized, people ironically conclude, as Praxides did, that "relatives and money don't mix . . . [because of the hierarchies of seniority and generation, and] the jealousy and backbiting and too many differences of opinion."

People in networks are drawn into money circulations, but the obligations they receive are always greater than they can match. They use strategic ignorance to lessen both the obligation and the social damage of refusals. Strategic ignorance creates indeterminacy and flexibility, but also a cloud of doubt and ambiguity. Although the goal of strategic ignorance is ultimately to protect and care for wealth-in-people,[19] the result is a kind of liminality and uncertainty with regard to people's social ties.

Besides groups and collectives of many kinds, another increasingly popular option for people needing money is digital microcredit. Digital debt offers immediate, private remittances over the phone, and like the formal arrangements of savings groups, it promises some detachment from the negotiations and shifting readjustments of the informal sphere. Digital loans are widely insinuating themselves into social networks—in Kenya about 3 million digital loans are processed every month through M-Shwari alone.[20] But the freedom they promise can be illusory. In Chapter 9, I will consider the use of digital debt—and its effects on social networks.

Reimagining Debt

9

The Rat and the Purse

"M-Shwari is like a rat," Brendah finally decided. "M-Shwari is a rat that hunts for money at night." We laughed. Brendah is twenty-seven years old and a schoolteacher. She is married to another schoolteacher, and they have a daughter. Brendah drew her financial and social relationships on a network self-portrait that also included her friends, relatives, and other financial tools (Figure 9.1a). Her most important financial sources were her savings group, or chama, which she drew as a purse, and the M-Shwari account digital money account, a source of small loans and a place to store value, which she drew as a rat. These sources of liquidity helped her care for her daughter, find transportation, run her household, and contribute to her savings clubs on time. Brendah had bought into her most successful savings group three years ago with the minimum bid of 50 shillings ($0.50). Over time she had increased her performance in these groups and was now successfully repaying loans of up to $100. She drew the savings group on her network map in Figure 9.1a as an open purse. In Kiswahili the chama is often called mfuko wa chama—the purse of the savings group—to denote the collective fund.

Brendah's savings group meets regularly. Members are supposed to draw scheduled payouts or draw lots, but they often claim funds out of turn by explaining their troubles and needs. Brendah explained to me that her *chama* has helped her to fund celebrations and funerals in her family and among her friends, to take care of her parents, and help out with medical needs of friends and relatives. She waits her turn for many needs, but in an emergency or when

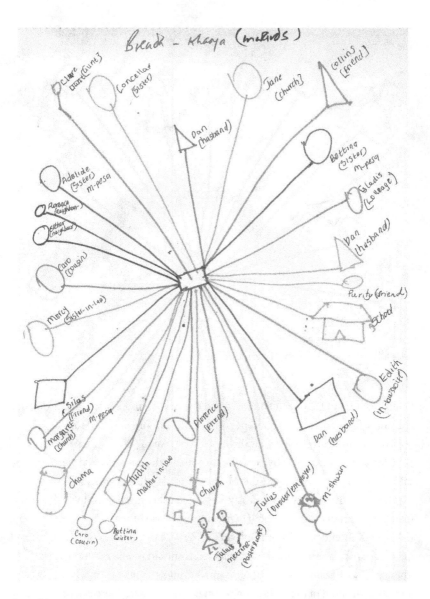

Figure 9.1a. Brendah's network self-portrait showing the *chama* or savings group as a purse.

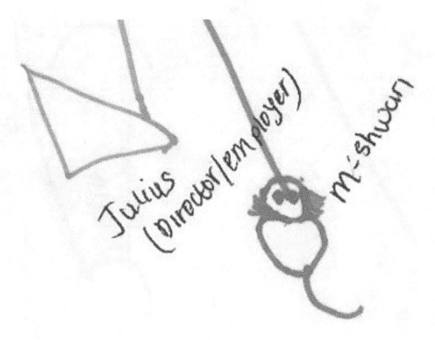

Figure 9.1b. Brendah drew the M-Shwari digital microloan as a rat.

facing an unexpected need she can go to the *chama* and explain her problems, and she will often access a good portion of the amount she asks for.

The M-Shwari microloan, on the other hand, was a private money source. On Brendah's map it was a furtive cat like this one in the corner or, better, a rat. She said she could save money in the M-Shwari bank without others knowing—its PIN access is an extra level of security. She could also draw on M-Shwari loans immediately without having to explain her needs to the women in her savings group. But overall, Brendah did not think that using M-Shwari loans often was a good idea. In particular, she said, these digital loans should not be for younger women. They would be easily tempted to buy small things to make themselves beautiful, attracting the kind of men who ruin reputations, or worse. There is an epidemic of young women accepting sponsors (sugar daddies) these days, she said.

Wealth-in-People and Digital Debt

The popularity of digital microcredit has raised concerns about debt and ndebtedness. How can we know when debt is being used positively and when it is harming those who use it? One common approach is to examine the data on repayment. Are loans being repaid? Are people building creditworthiness and growing their loan amounts? But evaluating the impact of these loans just by looking at customer data is complicated by several factors. First is the common practice of taking out multiple loans, often accessing new debt to repay existing debt. While data sharing among debt providers could reveal how people play multiple sources of debt off against each other, these data-driven approaches still leave a great deal hidden. The hidden labor is distributional labor, whereby people access their social networks both to give out borrowed money and to amass money to repay.[1]

In this chapter I look at the use of digital microcredit accessed through mobile phones, using a social networks approach. To understand how digital debt works its way into money networks, I asked several women such as Brendah to draw their network self-portraits to capture the networked array of monetary technologies and people through which they access and send out money. The co-produced drawings depicted cash money, digital money or credit, food or gifts, even advice and security, as they connected women to relatives, friends and neighbors, clubs and churches, and financial service brands such as M-Pesa and M-Shwari. Our discussions around how monies are used and the kinds of relationships they form led us to choose visual metaphors on our drawings, where monies are represented as airplanes, buses, and eyes. These metaphors represent the technological affordances and moral qualities of money and reveal how different material forms or *media of exchange*[2] shape women's networks. The drawings allowed me to discuss the moral and social dilemmas of debt in relation to those of other kinds of money—the rat and the purse. The privacy of M-Shwari—the rat that hunts at night—can be contrasted with the collective purse of the savings group.

As digital money and digital loans become popular, they are joining other, already existing financial and social instruments. Thus, the consequences of digital microloans go beyond economic indebtedness in the narrow sense. Debt is often accessed to give aid to a friend or relative; then the debt is distributed across a social network of friends, family, and even mobile money agents to extend time for repayment and avoid fees. Distributing formal debts across family networks can enable access to funds for repayment and create greater flexibility in repayment terms. On the other hand, social obligations may also draw people toward the use of private credit, because it is an easy way to access money to help someone in need. Debt, as it weaves itself into existing social and financial instruments, becomes a part of the way people build, sustain, and protect their social networks.

Digital Credit and Financial Inclusion

Debt has become a way of life for many people in the world. In the Global South, many low- and middle-income families use small loans for survival needs. They often have "an ongoing need . . . to find ways to translate small, irregular cash flows into usefully large sums."[3] Small loans have been actively promoted as a solution to poverty. Today, hundreds of millions of people in the Global South use microfinance. Its benefits are debated.[4] Recipients of loans often use them to support their basic survival or as only a temporary solution to a lack of money—creating a debt spiral.[5] Furthermore, credit ends up creating speculation, risk, and migration,[6] repayment struggles that entangle friends and family,[7] and even exploitation, gender violence, shame, depression, and suicide.[8] The current consensus emphasizes that these loans have tended to support consumption, providing needed liquidity for day-to-day life and emergencies, and that their success in spurring entrepreneurial investment has been exaggerated.[9]

Women have been an important focus of microfinance, as they continue to be in digital finance. At a March 24, 2017, webinar on women and financial inclusion by Innovations for Poverty Action (IPA), the hosts expressed disillusionment with microfinance through organizations, microfinance lenders, or traditional banks as a poverty alleviation tool. Globally, microloans were not leading to "higher incomes or more product investment." The webinar hosts suggested a new approach: digital finance delivered via mobile phones. They proposed that digital finance could bring women empowerment, control, and agency and lead to positive social change: "We want to create financial tools that will create agency and control for women and shift gender norms."[10]

Through reports, studies, and research evidence, development professionals are articulating a new project to bring digital finance to women in the Global South—especially poor and rural unbanked women. They are using data sets of bank account ownership to identify gaps in women's financial inclusion, and they claim that social and gender norms are barriers to women's agency with money.[11] Development thinkers hope that digital finance on mobile phones will bring women a private and secure account so they can control their money and "rapidly connect to digital financial services that enable them to more easily store, transfer, secure and build value digitally, beyond money payment transfers," bringing "empowerment and equitable decision-making in households."[12] The emphasis here is on using digital finance as a device for storage, personal control, and money accounting. Similarly, digital credit instruments are promoted as money management tools. The objective of these digital microloans is to smooth incomes to meet sudden or periodic needs for liquidity.

Such affordances are depicted in Figure 6.4a, Consolata's network self-portrait. Even though M-Shwari is a digital savings and loan product, Consolata drew M-Shwari not as a phone, but as a box with three locks on it. This three-keyed box is part of a widely used savings group method in which three members each keep a key to a rectangular metal box that stores the group's money.[13] Consolata's drawing shows how understandings and behaviors like saving money emerge from engagement with development interventions and their devices.

Digital microcredit's short record has not been favorable.[14] Unregulated providers in the Kenyan space such as Tala, Branch, and MyBucks are mostly accessible through smartphone apps. Their practices have raised security and privacy concerns around access to data and the inscrutability of credit algorithms. (In 2018, Google Kenya announced it would no longer allow loan providers like Branch access to text messages and government regulations passed a consumer data privacy law in 2019.) But the sharpest discussion has emerged around indebtedness and blacklisting, which has led to some rethinking of the goals and limits of financial inclusion.[15] For example, microcredit among Zambian farmers is mostly used to survive and to fund rituals, not to build businesses.[16] The rise of digital credit in Africa seems to be following the same path to debt as microfinance has done. As a CGAP professional put it, "This is not the kind of credit that helps people invest and grow. This is the kind of credit that helps them manage day to day and get by."[17]

Should such loans really be easily accessible on a phone menu or should there be redlining or limits to who is given a loan?[18] To address the debt problem, the more than 20 Kenyan microcredit providers have pledged to share customer data so as to understand a customer's (or SIM card's) total debt burden. But such sharing would still only partly assess the effects of microcredit. To understand why, I now turn to a network perspective.

Juggling

Digital debt becomes part of people's social and financial relationships in varying ways. Taking on debt—or deciding not to—is a decision made with reference to the net of other financial instruments, especially friend and family borrowing. "Juggling"[19] refers to complex strategies of debt management: "People . . . balance expenses and resources, often through moral and physical earmarking. . . . Juggling debt also helps to manage budgets. People combine various financial tools to support ongoing borrowing, repayment, and reborrowing (one borrows from one place to repay elsewhere). Juggling practices often reflect conscious strategies to multiply or diversify social relationships and strengthen or weaken the burden of dependency ties."[20]

Guerin's concept of juggling adds a calculative dimension to how people shape their networks. How does digital debt become a part of this juggling of informal loans? Consider first Kinyua and Annette, who rarely use digital credit. Nairobi student Kinyua has a flexible and shifting social network for informal loans. He will occasionally ask his parents for help when he is short on cash but prefers to ask friends. Friends who are working or from better-off families are more understanding—they know he will have trouble repaying. He mentioned that he had recently sent four friends text messages asking for help in coming up with 500 ($5). Two friends contributed to reach the goal—the other two did not respond even though he had helped one of them out recently. He explained he would not pay these friends back but would wait for them to call him when they needed help. Kinyua has used an M-Shwari loan only as a last resort. Similarly, Nairobi baker Annette regularly receives money from a childhood friend and is a member of ten savings groups, from which she draws both regular and emergency cash. Some of the groups also lend money, and she is earning a small profit from the group's informal banking activities. Like Kinyua, she avoids digital credit and prefers the flexible terms of her friendship network. Both Kinyua and Annette mentioned the costs and fees and rigid timing of digital microcredit and the fact that friendship loans are frequently renegotiated. All or part of the loan may move from "gift," to "loan," or back again.

Using the opposite strategy is Nairobi inhabitant Kate, an unpartnered mother, who prefers to rely on M-Shwari loans rather than her social network. She took an M-Shwari loan for her daughter's school fees after her friends and family were unable to help. She has used both the savings and loans products and finds the loan product very reliable—the money is readily available. (Interestingly, many people also describe the money in a savings group as "available" or easy to access.) Kate knew the terms of different lenders. She explained that M-Shwari gives her more time to repay—one month—as compared to fintech lender Tala, which required her to pay back a recent loan in a week. Kate preferred digital loans because they were private and immediate. But most importantly, Kate, unlike Kinyua and Annette, is not confident in her wealth-in-people. She has asked friends and family for money for her children's fees, who stalled her for several weeks or even refused. Importantly, Kate experienced "shame" in these experiences of "looking for money from people"—especially those who, she admitted, "have not heard from me in some time." For people like Kate, digital debt can be a way of protecting fragile ties and reputations and avoiding the risks of failure involved in what is also called "chasing after money" or "chasing after contributions." But repayment struggles often follow the decision to secure an immediate, and private, loan—and may mean returning to the social network to solve the problem.

Digital credit decisions, then, involve calculating and earmarking various social/financial media in one's networks, such as friends, relatives, savings groups, and financial services. To illustrate, I will explore the diverse media of exchange in the networks of Praxides, a rural woman who uses digital credit, as well as other financial tools. We drew her networks and followed her in a brief diary study of 22 weeks, as she struggled to repay M-Shwari loans.

Praxides

Praxides was twenty-nine years old in 2016 and lives in a semirural area near Bungoma, Western Kenya, that has many small farms of one half to three acres, crisscrossed by murram roads and small marketplaces. Land fragmentation and increasing population have squeezed this community. Those with land can grow cane for a local mill, receiving payments only every 18 months. For the others, the search for money might involve petty sales of goods, ride hailing with a motorcycle, or selling cannabis. Praxides is unmarried, the youngest of seven. She lives with and assists her mother, Janet, who is the third wife of Malaba, a farmer and plumber. Like many women, Janet struggles to maintain a working phone due to the costs of airtime, repairs, and batteries, and her phone serves the household. She receives 2,000 ($20) monthly from her eldest brother, Mukite, a police officer. She also contributes substantially to daily household needs. After all, she explains, her father manages two other households.

Praxides has a certificate in library science but could not find employment in her field of study and eventually returned to school to study early childhood education. Over time she has traded goods at a home kiosk, selling basic household commodities, but bad debts to informal lenders and meager profits pushed her to start hawking vegetables and cereals. She used these proceeds to raise capital for a firewood business. She currently sells firewood at home and bakes and sells bricks, which has enabled her to buy sheep and a cow. She farms kale, tomatoes, and cowpeas and teaches part-time in a private primary school, earning 2,000 ($20) per month. She also raises animals for sale and plants cash crops like beetroot. I asked her about marriage plans, but she responded that her father's farmland is her security.

Praxides's M-Pesa connections include friends and siblings with whom she circulates frequent small transfers. Just this week, she offered, she diverted a planned savings group payout to her sister for a medical emergency, and her close friend Esther asked her for anything she could manage to celebrate her new home. Earlier in the month, her cousin at college needed 1,000 ($10) urgently, so she asked a friend, Andrew, to help. She will figure out how to repay Andrew later. Her father had also sent her 1,500 ($15) for her mother's medical care.

In Figure 9.2, I have drawn the social network that Praxides has formed using ties of mobile money, cash, and in-kind gifts (foodstuffs and clothing) with family members, friends, and *chama* members.

Evelyn and Esther are Praxides's most important friends, customers, *chama* members, and fellow businesswomen. All three women sell produce and trade in maize, firewood, bricks, and other ventures, circulating liquidity through their *chamas*. Praxides's sister Wilkister is her bridge to her firewood suppliers. Nephew Dommy, her sister Ann's oldest son, works in local government and also supports Praxides and her mother. Praxides used to give him pocket money when he was a schoolboy. In her network Praxides is a daughter, aunt, and sister, a savings group member, a businesswoman, and a friend.

I suggested to Praxides that her sociogram drawing in Figure 9.2 depicted a thick web of social support. She just scoffed. She felt quite alone, she said;

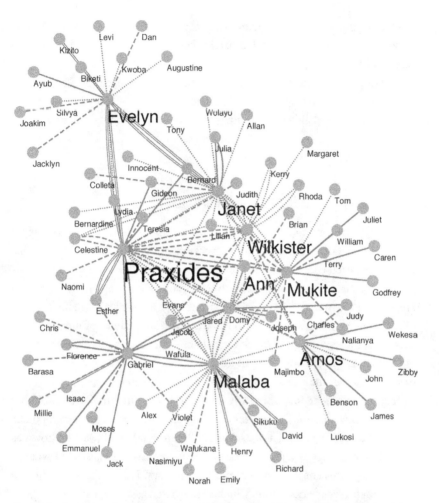

Figure 9.2. Sociogram for Praxides, depicting her mother, Janet, and her father, Malaba, and siblings Ann, Mukite, Wilkister, and Amos, along with friends and *chama* or savings club members. Her ties to friends are drawn with solid lines, ties to *chama* members as parallel lines, ties to siblings as dashes, and ties to cross-generational relatives as small dots.

finding people to rely on was very difficult. "Those days of people helping each other are gone," she said. "Life is very expensive these days . . . people live on their own and they are very independent." Furthermore, people, even relatives, are undependable. "If your brother assists, that's fine. If they do not assist, that is fine. You cannot predict." She added that youth are failing to find livelihoods, creating permanent dependencies on their parents: "Life nowadays is almost impossible. . . . You might find that parents continue to assist their children into adulthood."

Praxides began the firewood business to give her a livelihood but also to set aside some money of her own. She said she would one day like to grow a business that would also support a regular income in teaching. As we will see, it did not work out, especially after she found employment in a school and gave managing the business over to her mother.

The Shape of Money: Network Self-Portraits

The self-portrait method can be one way to understand the use of digital money, as part of a constellation of diverse currencies of exchange or media. For Zelizer, each currency creates a different relationship: "Every currency attaches to a circuit of exchange and every circuit of exchange includes a concrete set of meaningful social relations."[21] Zelizer's concept of distinct media of exchange can also draw attention to the material qualities of money.[22] Furthermore, the circuits of digital money are one part of larger circuits involving other media. The drawings sought to depict these circuits and also to enable a discussion about the qualities of different kinds of money.

Figures 9.3a and 9.4 show the outbound and inbound networks that Praxides drew to describe her monies and media. On her inward map she drew eleven different media of exchange (Figure 9.3a). M-Shwari is shown as a watchful eye (Figure 9.3b)—Praxides's repayment struggles, which I will explain later in this chapter, will elaborate on the eye. I also asked her who she could get emergency cash from, which she depicted as an airplane for its speed (Figure 9.3c). She listed M-Shwari loans first, followed by the name of an M-Pesa agent, followed by her mother and another friend. She drew cash money as a basket—and listed her savings groups as sources of this cash, a place she always goes where she knows she can get money when she needs it. Her drawing of savings groups as a basket, a kind of collected, common reserve, is similar to Brendah's drawing of the savings group as a purse (Figure 9.1). Her other media of exchange include food, gifts, security, support and advice, which she represented as a heart, and information, which she represented as a phone, explaining that she uses her phone to keep in contact with people from whom she buys maize and firewood.

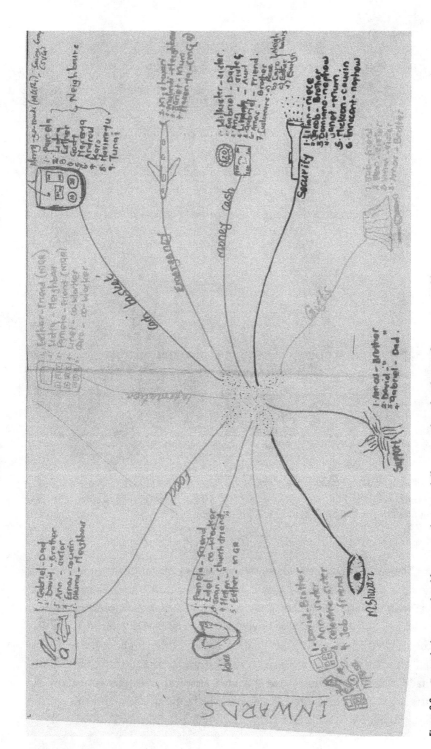

Figure 9.3a. Praxides's network self-portrait showing different media of exchange flowing toward her.

Figure 9.3b. The M-Shwari loans Praxides struggles to repay are drawn as a watchful eye.

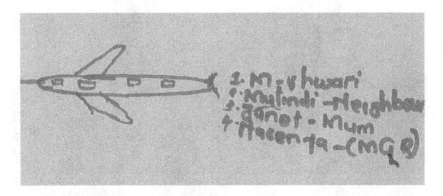

Figure 9.3c. I asked Praxides where she would turn for emergency help. She listed M-Shwari loans first, followed by a neighbor and relative who is also an M-Pesa agent, followed by her mother and another friend.

The social/financial maps show that varying social ties (be they people, groups, or formal services) create an assemblage of complementary media. These drawings add another important level of relational work involved in weighing the use of digital credit versus friend and family loans. Praxides was confused by my directive that she draw herself in the center of her maps. Finally, in the open space at the center of the drawings she added a diffuse flower made of small dots, whose petals extended out toward the other symbols on the drawing (Figures 9.3a and 9.4). She described this flower as representing "the beautiful life I would like to have."

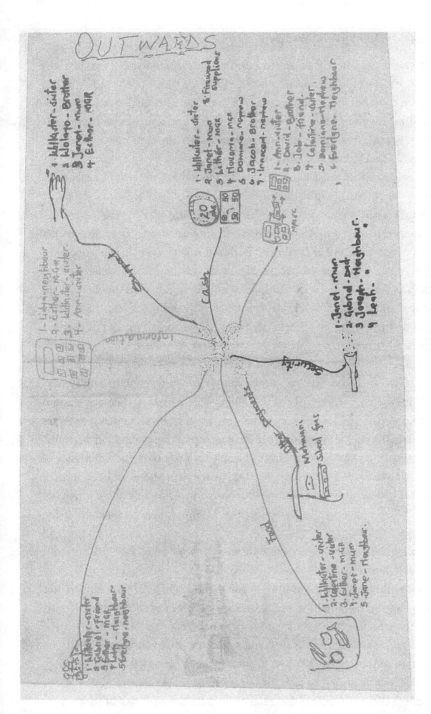

Figure 9.4. Praxides's network self-portrait showing different media of exchange flowing outward from her. She separated out flows of information (the phone), support (a helping hand), people who give her cash money, those who send her M-Pesa, along with food and security. She drew her savings club as passengers on a bus.

Struggles with Entrepreneurship

M-Shwari is marketed as an aid to informal entrepreneurs. In Praxides's village income-generating and entrepreneurialism are widely promoted by NGOs and even churches. But many people, like Praxides, who are drawn to income-generating are also farmers with a variety of income sources and social obligations. Praxides's struggles with entrepreneurship can show how microcredit loans often lead to indebtedness.

In 2015 Praxides finished her studies and found full-time employment at a primary school, receiving a salary of 2,000 ($20) per month. But, she found, "I can hardly assist my parents—I am left with nothing after buying the basics." She decided to start a firewood business, buying firewood at a nearby market and transporting it to her local neighborhood, where she split the wood with an axe and sold it. She took out the M-Shwari loans, which she referred to in English as "capital," to use as transport. Praxides highlighted the digital loan product's affordances around safe, private storage and quick loans. She mentioned that M-Shwari could help her build her business, "instead of meeting every family need."

Praxides was aware that M-Shwari loans must be repaid on time to avoid being blacklisted, and that loan limits can be grown through prompt repayment. She used the service for one year and by 2016 had grown her loan amount from 2,000 ($20) to 7,500 ($75). She observed that M-Shwari interest rates are lower than the rates for loans through local table banking groups. Furthermore, Praxides showed an understanding of bank rules and noted the importance of self-discipline around repayment. She told us she pays M-Shwari back in small bits; she becomes conscious of time to repayment; a closer deadline forces her to pay in larger amounts. Small wonder that M-Shwari appears on her drawing as an eye.

During the 22-week diary period in 2016 when we asked Praxides to record her use of digital credit, she borrowed from M-Shwari seven times and repaid M-Shwari three times. It was hard to say if she really used it to support her firewood project; sometimes the reason she gave us for taking an M-Shwari loan was expressly to help a friend—she borrowed from M-Shwari to assist friends and relatives with medical and school fee emergencies and needs for medicine, and then strategized repayment through friends, her savings group, or an M-Pesa agent. In one case she borrowed 8,000 ($80) from M-Shwari for her sister's daughter's school fees. Her sister paid her back half of that, which she repaid to M-Shwari. Speaking of the remaining repayment of 4,000 ($40), which was due within a week, she said she would ask the M-Pesa agent to repay for her and then wait for her sister to receive a savings group payment in the following month to repay her. She borrowed from M-Shwari to repay her firewood supplier and her savings club, and also borrowed money from friends and relatives to repay M-Shwari loans. Praxides was juggling.

During the diary exercise Praxides maintained between five and nine social connections per week through cash, in-kind such as food, and digital money exchanges. Her overall money balance was mostly negative throughout the period—in fact, her firewood receipts were consistently less than her costs. The diary exercise was not long enough to understand the economic impact of digital credit. However, it did show that, along with the money transfer service and her exchange of gifts, food, and security with her neighbors, the digital credit product was a way for Praxides to create and maintain her network.

Praxides's relational work extended to her relationships with mobile money agents. Through them, she also sought to reduce M-Shwari fees, extend her time to repay, and even convert a balance owed into an informal loan. During the diary period in 2016 an agent had helped her repay an M-Shwari loan of 4,000 ($40). She then immediately borrowed 4,500 ($45) from M-Shwari again to repay the agent. She now owed M-Shwari 4,500, but, she explained, she had another 30 days to repay the full sum and one week before her reminder SMS message.

In 2017, 2018, and 2019 Gabriel Kunyu followed up with Praxides about her business and her M-Shwari loans. By 2018 she had increased her M-Shwari loan limit to $95. Business was highly irregular. She had bought a large quantity of firewood for sale, anticipating the rains when demand would be high, but unfortunately no one had bought it. She was trying her hand at reselling maize using M-Shwari loans for capital.

> Gabriel: So how is your business going?
>
> Praxides: I am not doing very well.
>
> G: Did you eat the capital?
>
> P: No, I have not done that, but the stock I have is low. I haven't eaten the principal capital, but sometimes the stock is not so good.
>
> G: I thought that during the rains, that is when you should be doing very well. People buy firewood when it rains.
>
> P: I just got the stock recently. I have it at home.

G: Are people buying a lot of firewood?

P: No. I got to a place where I stopped buying firewood and I began buying maize, but even the maize is now finished.

Praxides's attempts at entrepreneurship are running into a frequent problem—the material limits of her clientele. She also struggles with repayment:

G: How did it go with M-Shwari? What is your loan limit?

P: It's still at 9,500. I repay slowly. I have stayed at 9,500 because sometimes they say they want to increase my loan limit, but I refuse because I will struggle to repay. But I try. I pay regularly. Even yesterday I paid.

G: Did you pay on time?

P: I just, just made it. I paid yesterday.

G: Last time how much did you borrow?

P: I borrowed 9,000, with interest, it reached 10,000. I paid 400 every day. I still owe 4,000 because the balance was 4,200 and then I borrowed and then there was also the interest and so with interest they wanted 4,400.

G: So did you take 4,000?

P: 4,100 and then they added 300 [300 shillings is the fee].

G: *Umejikaza* [you have been very determined].

The Ambiguous Role of Mobile Money Agents

In this follow-up, Praxides also elaborated that she has over several years been borrowing money from two M-Pesa agents to meet M-Shwari loan deadlines. One of them is related to her as a nephew—Edson. Edson had often fronted Praxides money to help her pay her M-Shwari loans, but she discovered through another friend known to them both that Edson was gossiping about her and boasting to others that he often helped her pay—and that he was not tipping her in return. To Praxides the gossip was unfair—she did not feel she owed her nephew a tip—but also humiliating. Because of his gossip, she has sought new relationships with other M-Pesa agents.

Praxides also recounted a subsequent incident with an M-Shwari debt of 4,000 ($40). Because of late fees, she had incurred a penalty that brought her total debt to 4,400 ($44). She was able to bring together the 4,000 from her savings group and firewood sales. Owing 4,400 to M-Shwari, and to avoid Edson, she went to a new agent, Mama Lisa, near the school where she worked. She had never used this agent before but explained that she needed 4,000 to pay for school and that she did not have the 400 in what she called interest (which was actually the remaining half of an M-Shwari fee plus a penalty). Mama Lisa listened to her story and then told her to return the next day at 2:00 p.m. When Praxides returned the following day with 4,000 in cash to repay, Mama Lisa added 400 to cover the fee/penalty. When Praxides left, she thanked Mama Lisa, who said, "No, thank you, because you are giving me business."

Agents such as Edson and Mama Lisa encourage clients to use their services, and often offer new customers gifts and favors to build a client base, as Mama Lisa did. As a result, they add flexibility to M-Shwari's terms to help people repay successfully. Agents may be friends or relatives; they may front money for fees and payments or absorb these outright; they may facilitate direct transfers, so clients can avoid loading fees—even though these practices are forbidden by MNOs.[23] Agents are important intermediaries and bridges between formal and informal loans. On the other hand, the liminality of the agent, as both informal and formal financial instrument, can present numerous social risks, as in Praxides's case when her nephew exposed her to gossip and maligned her creditworthiness, leading her to then seek out another agent in a neighboring town.

The social risks of digital microcredit were visualized on the network self-portraits. Recall that Consolata drew M-Shwari as a lockbox savings tool (Figure 6.4b). But other drawings depicted the dubious moral qualities of M-Shwari as digital debt. Consider Brendah's "rat that hunts in the dark for money" (Figure 9.1b), where M-Shwari is a private and secret loan. Brendah's association of the private M-Shwari loan with young women, urban or urban want-to-be, who use M-Shwari loans to plait their hair or wear extensions and buy clothing and shoes from the secondhand shops, is widespread and partly fueled by Safaricom advertisements depicting young people with tattoos and wearing blue jeans. The illicit potential of the "rat" lies in the gossip around women's reputations, as Praxides experienced—and their association with sponsors or *fataki*—older men who maintain these women in intimate relationships. Far from empowering women, then, these digital microloans are contributing to stigma for women who dress or present themselves in a certain way.

The final dimension of digital microcredit, depicted by Praxides, is the eye (Figure 9.3b). When I asked her why M-Shwari was an eye, she simply shrugged and said an eye was useful. But her drawing may be communicating more than she felt comfortable articulating. Did the eye represent the watchful eye of Safaricom with its reminder messages and of CBA, the bank that issues these loans and keeps the calendar of repayment? Was she communicating something of the exposure or risks of exposure and shame that she experienced as she sought assistance from agents to help her manage repayment and fees? The eye in her drawing could depict what she could not explain—the pervasive power of digital debt.

Praxides sought help from her family to run her firewood business while she was at school, but found her profits were disappearing. She soon discovered that relatives were buying personal items like airtime with her firewood profits, claiming to have purchased household goods. She could never discuss these issues with those who used her money in such a way—it would be inconceivable to confront her mother over such. In 2018, she finally closed her firewood effort and began to rethink the value of entrepreneurship. She said she had stopped taking loans from M-Shwari and was looking for better-paying employment instead.

Ruefully, she said she had nothing to show from her M-Shwari loans. She mused that maybe instead of running the business, she should have used M-Shwari loans to make herself beautiful like other women her age—recalling the dubious behavior Brendah mentioned in describing the rat. Praxides said, "So I used to borrow money [from M-Shwari], yes, but what did I do with it? Did I buy a piece of cloth or shoes?" She laughed sardonically. "I have reached a point where I am now saying to myself . . . I will use my money to buy beautiful clothes, to plait my hair . . . if I had used that money that I borrowed to buy clothes, for plaiting my hair . . . that money would have still gotten finished."

Juggling Debt and Agents

Digital debt is drawn by individuals, but it often becomes distributed through the social network as they try to repay. These debts widen the individual's financial choices, but they may also reinforce the dependencies of the informal sphere. Successfully issuing loans to women like Praxides will rely on their work of juggling. Furthermore, the work of the agent in this juggling also comes to the fore. His role is a paradox. Does Praxides find a means of debt resistance, or claim a right to liquidity by finding an agent who can repay or defer her fees? Or instead, do agents present a danger to face and reputation, another way that financialization can be destructive to social bonds?[24]

The network self-portrait drawings describe characteristics of money media—a purse of the collective fund, the watchful eye of a digital loan, or private loans that women fear are being used to plait hair, buy new clothes, and threaten respectability. They communicate the moral qualities imparted to digital media. The entrepreneur thinks for herself, the savings group member extends her hands to others and shares her troubles, the rat plaits her hair as an urban and modern woman with her own money. In the end, Praxides's entrepreneurialism was a failure. When she became employed, her mother and others used her profits for their airtime and other needs, eating up the thin margins she was earning, so she resorted to the juggling strategy with her M-Pesa agents. Praxides realized she could have indulged herself and made herself beautiful by plaiting her hair, with no greater loss. For all her trouble, she says, she should have chosen the rat.

Reimagining Giving

A Design Project

10

Mary: An Expert Fundraiser

In August of 2016, I met Mary for cappuccinos at one of the new malls in the affluent Nairobi suburb of Karen. She is a loyal customer of a crowdfunding platform called M-Changa—a Nairobi start-up that helps people raise money online. Recently Mary led a fundraiser on M-Changa to raise funds for her father's funeral. To honor a father with a fitting burial is one of the most important duties of any child, she explained.

Mary had previously led five M-Changa fundraisers. She is known for rallying others around her own and their causes. Mary said she has never let people down. In fact, they look to her for leadership when problems come up, especially her women friends, who share and solve problems together. Mary had started out using the M-Changa platform on her personal computer after a visit to her alma mater, one of Kenya's best high schools. After seeing the poor state of the buildings and grounds, she connected with her alumnae friends via WhatsApp, and they decided to gather contributions toward refurbishing the school—eventually raising more than 50,000 Kenya shillings ($500). Other fundraisers followed to help relatives with medical needs. For a close friend living abroad, she led a fundraiser to help her buy an airline ticket to return home for a father's funeral. She also raised money for her daughter's coming-of-age retreat at her church. Most of these events also involve her putting out the call to WhatsApp, where she is a member of several groups, including her church.

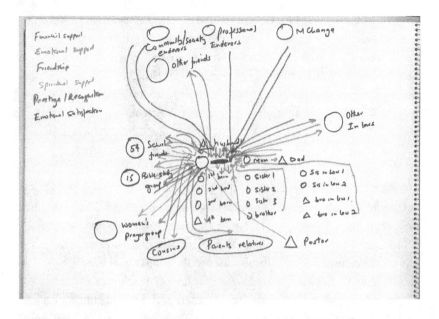

Figure 10.1. Mary's network self-portrait includes two WhatsApp groups with 54 and 15 members each and the fundraising platform M-Changa, which she drew as a source of prestige and recognition.

She drew these groups on her network map as circles (Figure 10.1), along with the M-Changa platform, where she collects donations.

Mary's fundraising activity has raised her social profile. Through holding numerous fundraising calls on the website, "now people know me from school, from church, my neighbors, even back home." People come to her, Mary explained, because she can mobilize others on behalf of other people's causes. She realized she had become someone important in the eyes of others during her own time of trouble—her father's passing. Her father needed a funeral befitting his dignity, and so she turned to the fundraising network. "When my dad died, they really rallied. People I had not seen for years contributed, because of who I am to people." The M-Changa fundraising call for her father's funeral brought in more donations than she had ever expected. Next to the M-Changa symbol on her network map, Mary wrote the words "prestige and recognition" as we talked (Figure 10.1).

Could the wealth-in-people theory of digital money design a financial inclusion product? In this chapter, I will describe how the network approach was applied to a fintech design. I came to consult for the M-Changa company in

2016 and 2017 as part of a Gates Foundation effort to scale a crowdfunding (Internet/digital fundraising) platform for a larger customer base, including low-income or rural clients. This Nairobi start-up had recently broken even and had provided hundreds of successful fundraisers. However, the Gates Foundation reasoned that M-Changa's small size hampered its potential development impact. Could a fundraising app offer financial inclusion, if it could scale up and build on the social networks of mobile money? Could informal financial ties build a market product—crowdfunding with an African twist?

In assisting the project, I worked with human-centered design (HCD) and behavioral economics consultants, along with many M-Changa users and non-users who agreed to participate in focus groups and surveys. I will first introduce crowdfunding and the M-Changa company. I will then review the design project's objectives and activities, and the findings and understandings that emerged. Finally, I will discuss obstacles to the project goal of scaling and assess the potential of a crowdfunding site for financial inclusion.

On a Kenyan crowdfunding website, users seek to fund rituals of the life cycle like funerals and weddings, educational fundraisers, and medical crowdfunding for surgeries, medications for chronic illness, and catastrophic care. The M-Changa design showed that there is real potential in anthropological knowledge to reimagine the definition of success in design projects, and to reveal the social and relational dimensions of money. The social meaning of money can point to new ways of financially including women and others through a broader definition of value. Beyond just money value, fundraisers amass contributions of nonmonetary gifts such as labor in cooking and preparation at events and a variety of material gifts, including, yes, goats; along with an instantiation of the value of financial/social ties that participants can generate and leverage from hearthholds and other groups and collectives.

The website also offered proof of the legitimacy of fundraisers with documents from hospitals, funeral homes, and other institutions, which users believed were important builders of trust. A crowdfunding website also creates a space where altruism and giving are valued as a form of "social finance," a vehicle for new commitments and solidarities.[1] The website and platform also rethought the relationship between financial services and clients. Could the M-Changa platform reimagine itself as a member of client networks— rather than as just a provider to individual clients? To pursue this question, the design team developed several ideas about a currency or digital loan value that could circulate amongst client networks and increase in value through the circuit.

The M-Changa design project also showed that a crowdfunding website presented challenges to financial inclusion. In engaging with low-income people, our design team learned that technological barriers like network and platform access often hindered scaling. Furthermore, fundraising is an activity associated with people of prestige and abundant social ties. Those with less wealth-in-people—the very communities the project sought to financially include—expressed a reluctance to risk their social ties with a fundraising appeal that might fail to generate value and cause embarrassment or shame. Strategic ignorance emerged as a means of withholding and retreating from ties and calls. It preserves fragile relationships, but it is also a real barrier to giving. It is most common among the very people that financial inclusion projects seek to embrace.

Crowdfunding, Fundraising, M-Changa

Globally, crowdfunding is a surprisingly popular new financial technology. The term "crowdfunding" refers to fundraising platforms accessed through mobile or desktop Internet connection. Fundraising websites in the United States such as Kickstarter and GoFundMe have raised more than $17 billion for a variety of projects, including artistic works, entrepreneurialism, philanthropic giving, religious charity, medical needs, and funerals.[2] In the United States and China, fundraising websites host communities of artists, entrepreneurs, religious followers, or people facing medical challenges. In China, crowdfunding has scaled dramatically. The health care fundraising company Drop of Water raised $8 billion from 100 million Chinese givers in just two years.[3]

Kenya's emerging entrepreneurial and fintech scene is called the Silicon Savanna, or Digital Kenya.[4] Here, leapfrogger ideals of innovative disruption are recast toward local visions of cultural wealth, development, and problem solving. M-Changa is one of many new fintech start-ups, and the largest digital crowdfunding platform in sub-Saharan Africa. Started in 2012 by Dave Mark as chief technology officer, Kyai Mullei as chief executive officer, and Kyai's father Dr. Andrew Mullei as advisor, it has six employees. Some of M-Changa's clients are humanitarian organizations and charities; most are individuals seeking to raise money from across their networks of family and friends. A customer survey of 558 existing users showed an educated, well-off clientele. Most have tertiary education, 75% have a laptop computer, and two-thirds own a car.[5] Seventy-four percent are members of two or more savings groups, most have bank accounts, and two-thirds have used M-Shwari loans. Nevertheless, a majority had an urgent need for money in the previous year, particularly because of a medical crisis in the family, and 87% went to friends and family for help, either via M-Pesa or in person. Only 13% went to a bank, and 50% said that commercial banks were not trustworthy. (In 2016 two major consumer banks were put into receivership for fraud.) Although more-affluent Kenyans have access to formal finance, they remain enmeshed in friend and family networks.

M-Changa offers several major forms of value for customers. First, its fundraising ledger makes accounting of contributions from multiple channels much easier. M-Changa accepts mobile money, bank drafts, Visa/Mastercard, and PayPal. It keeps these funds in merchant accounts with these channels until customers request to withdraw them, at which time it transfers funds to customers through the company's bank account. Second, fundraiser managers choose up to three treasurers, who help to view the ledger and are permitted to withdraw funds. Customers can send out free SMS appeals and their fundraiser page is linked to Facebook and WhatsApp. M-Changa also flags potential fraud on its platform such as SMS messages that promise gifts. Finally, M-Changa validates each fundraiser, verifying and posting documents such as medical bills and death certificates. In the company's first six years, its customers fundraised about $3 million. Most of its clients access the company's Internet website on a desktop computer. However, M-Changa can also communicate with clients via mobile by using SMS. The company does not have a smartphone app.

Medical needs are the most common purpose of M-Changa fundraising, making up close to half of all fundraisers. Kenyan citizens are encouraged to contribute to a National Hospital Insurance Fund (NHIF) with a contribution of 500 shillings ($5) a month, but the coverage is inadequate, and most health needs are handled through out-of-pocket payment. Catastrophic illness is often financially devastating. Weddings, graduations, and coming-of-age rituals together make up another third of M-Changa fundraisers. These events entail renting hotel space; feasting siblings, friends, teachers, and relatives; and funding travel from rural areas or overseas. Finally, the platform has attracted efforts to support business start-ups, charitable concerns such as school drives or school fee support, community infrastructure such as road projects, and church fundraisers, in that order (Figure 10.2).

Crowdfunding on M-Changa

Digitizing fundraising and using a crowdfunding website is an involved process of coordinating human and technological networks. M-Changa offers a deliberately "high-touch" customer service. It has two full-time agents who are on the phone nonstop throughout the workday helping users set up fundraisers, receive contributions, access and share the ledger of donations, communicate appeals and progress through SMS notifications, verify the fundraiser by accepting and posting medical bills and certificates, link a fundraiser to Facebook, Twitter, and WhatsApp, and cash-out fundraisers. The agents encourage people to communicate about fundraisers through online and offline channels and to plan face-to-face events that can coordinate with the online appeal. Crowdfunding is a complicated process that requires social and technological knowledge, and unfortunately the technological interactions can be clumsy. In my own attempts to start a fundraiser, the name I chose was already taken, and the program responded by giving me personal medical data and other information about an already existing campaign.

One of M-Changa's most important customer services involves helping to create a compelling website with photographs and stories. Stories are short paragraphs that appear on a fundraising page and are meant to spur admiration, compassion, and giving.[6] The following heartrending story from one such page was crafted with assistance from the M-Changa team:

> For Methuselah Oturu, the sky is the limit to what one can achieve regardless of their background or environment. . . . In a family that barely survives on a single meal a day, Oturu defied all odds to post 400 marks in KCPE [Kenya Certificate of Primary Education, a national exam for eighth graders]. Despite the immense talent, ability, and passion to learn, his dreams of joining the prestigious academic giant, Friends School, Kamusinga, are hanging on a thread awaiting fate to hold on or snap. Missing out on Equity Foundation's Wings to Fly Program was a great setback to the ambitious Oturu. . . . Despite applying to the various organizations for support, the father has received no feedback. The wings have been clipped but Oturu must fly! We are calling upon well-wishers to help

support the immensely gifted boy. Any help will be highly appreciated as a little
from the many pockets will bring forth something significant and sustainable.

Methuselah's story emphasizes his ability and work ethic in the face of in-
tractable circumstances, including specific evidence such as exam scores and
unsuccessful scholarship tries. According to the M-Changa team, this evidence
of excellent scores proves to funders that Methuselah is deserving of the support. A good story should provoke "the charitable impulse" toward a specific
need,[7] but importantly, it should show deservingness. Some scholarship has
been critical of crowdfunding, saying that it exposes the inadequacies of public
funding and displaces onto individuals or family groups the responsibilities for
health, education, and so on that institutions should provide.[8] In this critical
view, provoking a charitable impulse emphasizes the individual's merit, rather
than the social problems and structural inequalities that create circumstances
of want.[9]

Indeed, Kenyan people commonly speak of people's negative circumstances
as a result of their moral choices. To take the example of limited school funding, many Kenyan children are put through grueling prep for national exams
on weekends and during vacations. High-scoring children from limited circumstances, like Methuselah, are widely admired and featured in the media.
National exam results are listed by province in newspapers, fueling debates
around government opportunity rationing to the various ethnic groups.

These critiques of crowdfunding may also miss its possible benefits. As-
sembling new crowds around the needy and underserved can make important critiques and produce new communities of care and social goals. One area
that crowdfunding activity could strengthen is philanthropic giving. In the
South, philanthropy often bears the imprint of colonial histories. In India, for
example, applications of British trust law in the late nineteenth century dis-
tinguished charity—as a private sphere of religious and family giving—from
philanthropy—as giving to public social institutions with objectives such as
poverty eradication. Because practices of religious charity and obligation in
India often shored up caste and class differences, many public and state organizations here sought to redefine philanthropy around rationalizing goals like
addressing poverty.[10] But the distinctions between public and private giving,
which may also assume a distinction between self-interest and the public good,
are actually difficult to discern wherever giving also entangles existing ties and
commitments.

Figure 10.2. Wedding fundraiser from M-Changa, 2018.
SOURCE: M-Changa.

M-Changa's platform brings together philanthropic foundations as well as informal groups like and family and village welfare groups. In fact, a variety of faith-based and other NGOs fundraise locally and internationally on M-Changa for schools, hospitals, and missions. The website involves fundraising across personal networks for family needs, but also brings community organizations to the platform, blurring the lines between charity, philanthropy, and informal finance. Philanthropic organizations are also beginning partnerships with M-Changa. These new institutions of distribution can draw on and strengthen local institutions of mutual aid or "horizontal philanthropy," and work toward decolonizing philanthropic institutions in Africa.[11]

The Gates Foundation Grant: Rationale

The successful grant proposal to fund a scale-up of M-Changa sought to explore the potential of crowdfunding for financial inclusion, especially as grounded in local cultures of giving: "We believe that the centuries old practice of mutual philanthropy in African societies has an important role in enhancing and encouraging access to digital financial services. These practices are disproportionately important to the poor . . . this investment seeks to answer key questions about enhancing social network engagement, mitigating fundraising shortfalls, and the potential for mobile fundraising to be a locally led driver of financial inclusion."[12]

However, the proposal argued that social networks were not by themselves working in the right ways to address poverty. It found that "social networks tend to be imperfect sources of money. All too often, there are issues with timing (not getting the money when you need it) and value (not getting enough money) when requesting funds from your social network. Additionally, the size of the requested funds exceeds the social network's capacity."[13]

In other words, then, the M-Changa project sought to address poverty by using digital technology to amplify the size, speed, and economic value of social network money flows. Through a redesign of the M-Changa platform using a mobile phone, crowdfunding would bring together donations for various needs and offer an improved means of circulating and amassing funds in social networks. The grant effort prioritized poverty alleviation, technology design, leveraging local practices, and a market-based or bottom-of-the-pyramid[14] approach, typical of many technology-for-development efforts.[15]

Cultures of Finance and Giving

Gabriel Kunyu, Nanjulula Musombi, and I interviewed 31 urban and 30 rural men and women who gave and received to others through digital and other means. Our goal was to understand local practices of digital finance such as giving, receiving, and fundraising. We were able to describe the myriad ways that e-money gifts express caring, presence, belonging and intimate relations. We described local cultures of giving, family money pooling, community self-help, savings groups, and informal finance and money pooling, already going digital with M-Pesa and WhatsApp.

We also found that M-Pesa is already a medium for organized charitable giving through televangelists. For example, Tabitha, a Nairobi woman in her twenties, watches GBS TV, a Christian TV station, and is frequently moved by its profiles of cases of chronic illness, disability, and hunger. She sends money via M-Pesa to the to the Paybill number that runs at the bottom of the screen as the stories are told. Tabitha's church has a Paybill number through which she pays her tithes and offerings and contributes toward church projects.

Figure 10.3. Political cartoon by Gado. Politicians use *harambee*, the call for community self-help, to extort money from internally displaced persons who have been victims of political violence. To make things even more convenient, please contribute via M-Pesa! SOURCE: Godfrey Mwampembwa (Gado), gadocartoons.com. Reprinted with permission.

Another local culture of giving providing a model for M-Changa is *harambee* ("Let's pull together"), or community self-help. *Harambee* became a national motto under Kenya's first president, Jomo Kenyatta, who mobilized community development projects like schools and roads. *Harambee* sought to harness ideas of African community and self-reliance to build a modern nation. But *harambee* became stigmatized in subsequent decades. By the 1980s it was associated with political corruption, patronage, and conspicuous consumption and schooling abroad. The term is still sometimes associated with patronage, elite capture, and the value-generating practices of the well-off, who gather contributions for schooling, life cycle rituals, and foreign travel (Figure 10.3). A lot of debate surrounds what kinds of needs can be pursued with *harambee* without being viewed as status-seeking. For example, if public school is affordable, should a family hold a *harambee* to fundraise for tuition at a better, private school? Should someone fundraise for school fees if they have an asset that they can liquidate? Will funds really go to stated needs, and how will we know? Should a more responsible person get a digital loan over the mobile phone, rather than burden others? These moral questions swirl around asking and giving.

This blemished reputation notwithstanding, fundraising is still a ubiquitous practice. Networks based on friendship, community, church, and family spread the word using smartphones, particularly WhatsApp groups. Digital fundraising uses money transfer, WhatsApp, and Safaricom's digital payment till to pool money in families, friendship groups, and savings clubs. On the basis of this pervasive evidence of giving, I predicted that the M-Changa scaling project, as a means to amass large numbers of donations more quickly in these everyday contexts, would find fertile ground.

Reimagining M-Changa: Behavioral Economics

Gabriel, Nanjulula, and I joined the M-Changa team armed with the interview study and with IMTFI's design principles,[16] along with two Nairobi design and business consulting firms. The first, the Busara Center, designed for Nairobi business using the principles of behavioral economics. Epitomized by the book *Nudge*,[17] behavioral economics (BE) is the dominant rationality of financial inclusion initiatives. BE is itself a critique of mainstream economics' assumption of rational self-interest; it seeks to design convenience, affordability, and individual-device interactions that encourage inherently quirky and changeable humans to choose more efficient actions and temporalities such as savings, willpower, and self-control.

Nikhil Ravichandar is an economist at Busara who explained to me that his design process works like this: "I identify 'action-intention gaps'—a strong preference to do a particular behavior, which for some (fairly easy to fix) reason, does not happen (usually this is because people are lazy or forgetful). Where there is already an intention to do a particular behavior, design interventions and nudges can render the process easier and more behaviorally informed with reminders, reward incentives, or making things more social."[18] Technology nudges have many applications in personal finance apps. For example, they can reward people for progress toward savings targets or create reminders; they can show what others are giving to spur more giving.

As an anthropologist, attuned to people's experiences and circumstances, I struggled to make sense of the BE view. I thought of research participants who survive by cobbling together digital loans with the ties of their social network. Is a rural woman like Praxides really in need of impulse control or more reminders? Can behavioral economics interventions that help people manage money on an app really impact the historical, embedded conditions of poverty? Querying the Busara team on this issue, I learned the hard way that to adherents of behavioral economics, bringing up the structural dimensions of poverty simply "throws a stink-bomb." To behavioral economists, nudges give people agency. Furthermore, poor people need design nudges even more, as they often fall victim to tunneling, an excessive focus on certain unmet needs.[19]

Busara conducted surveys and focus groups with existing and target customers and used machine learning algorithms to help M-Changa capture customer data to understand what made fundraisers successful. Busara's behavioral economics approach designed and administered surveys of low-income people's money management techniques and probed their processes of mental accounting, such as budgeting, awareness of concepts like interest and interest rates, and evidence of tunneling practices, drawing from banks of validity-tested questions.

Second, in an effort to understand why people give, Busara conducted a set of behavioral economics–based games with 664 volunteers from a low-income area of Nairobi. In the dictator game experiment, people give money to a partner knowing they will not get any back, demonstrating altruistic giving without any possibility of self-interest. The trust game also involves giving; this time the partner can choose to return some of the money. The experiments also simulated a sense of group belonging or membership by having volunteers either wear similar T-shirts or sort colored paper clips as a group-bonding exercise. Experimenters measured the sense of closeness two people shared after sorting a pile of paper clips together by asking them to represent themselves as overlapping circles on a piece of paper, measuring a scale known as inclusion of the other in the self.[20]

Games were played in a series by partners who had either sorted paper clips together or worn the same color T-shirt. The point was to isolate the effects of altruism, reciprocity, and trust under different levels of interpersonal or group bonding. It was a bit of a head-scratcher at first—what the game called "trust"—returning value to someone who had given value to you in a previous game—is what an anthropologist might call delayed reciprocity. The T-shirts, paper clips, and games showed that group membership and an expectation of reciprocity encouraged more delayed giving behavior. The games also *measured* the effects of reward size and the extent of group feeling (T-shirt group versus paper clip group), which the BE perspective values.

The games methodology is a stark contrast to the ethnographic immersion of anthropology. But like ethnography and in their own way, the BE games attempted to get to the gray area at the heart of successful fundraising, which is not exactly about pure altruism on the one hand nor strictly about self-benefit on the other. The idea of trust describes the hopeful expectation that another person will act to one's benefit. Trust is a willingness to take a risk and a willingness to show vulnerability, by potentially losing something of value if others do not also give.[21] No wonder trust is so much harder to observe in real life.

Although behavioral economics seeks to correct the understanding of classical economics that human behavior is purely rational, the assumptions of the economic perspective were still evident in the games setup. First of all, the games approach still assumed that strategies of self-interest could be isolated from strategies of giving, making altruism a problem that needs to be explained. After all, the mythic, purely rational human "would be perplexed by the idea of gifts."[22] Furthermore the games seemed to confuse trust and reciprocity, therefore leaving the question of why people give a black box, and reducing it to a delayed form of self-interest. But what if altruism is a feature of humanity, not a bug in it? The games setup forecloses on interdependency and makes all the participants equal and identical, removing the social identities, moral obligations, and asymmetries that give networks their shape. In real life, relationships make all the difference to giving.

Reimagining M-Changa: Human-Centered Design

Behavioral economics was not the only voice on the project. A contrasting research approach came from ThinkPlace, an amazing human-centered design (HCD) firm headquartered in Australia with a Nairobi office. HCD is an inductive approach that seeks to develop empathy for users and to co-create collaborative designs.[23] ThinkPlace planned to use interviews and participant observation to collect qualitative information about local giving cultures. In its work for M-Changa, ThinkPlace asked, "Knowing that there is strength in numbers, how can we expand existing networks and forge new ones?" ThinkPlace's approach was not to nudge toward rationality, but to work with users to co-design. I found myself at home with this approach.

The HCD team shunned experimental contrivances like games and paper clip sorting. HCD emphasized context, empathy, and engagement with a variety of users and informants. ThinkPlace held a workshop on social network mapping and conducted ethnographic visits, including rural Kisii in the locations where design sprints were conducted. ThinkPlace's design sprints, which combined ethnographic visits and interviews, visited and described different kinds of fundraising events and their associated material culture, costs, location, and guests. These events vary greatly in form, from disco *matangas* (impromptu dances, often in very low-income areas, to collect small amounts of money for a burial), to the more formal *harambee*, to smaller goat-eating and tea party events. People of different social classes and access to technology were interviewed and profiled with regard to their fundraising practices, to suggest what diverse potential users might want from a fundraising platform. Interviews with current users produced journey narratives to show how customers fundraise with M-Changa and through other means. The team's work also tried to show important differences in the potential market across a variety of local settings, highlighting the near absence of smartphones in rural Kisii. We recorded a variety of phenomena such as the material culture of existing fundraising technologies and the emotions and feelings people expressed around fundraising.

HCD puts a priority on empathy to user experience and grounded understandings. In particular, the user engagements and design sprints allowed ThinkPlace to profile people of varying degrees of social connectedness, which were portrayed as diverse user personas to represent the needs, goals, values, and behaviors of customer segments (Figure 10.4).[24] The goal was to show the diversity of potential users for the M-Changa site in terms of their ability to participate and contribute to fundraisers.

Social positioning and ability to use technology vary greatly across the user personas. For example take the *overwhelmed supernode* persona. Charles (Figure 10.4) is a farmer in the Kisii region of Kenya who contributes often to several savings groups and welfare associations and is a member of the county assembly. He started a group to help people fundraise school fees with four other families and has "grown it into a stable structure" with more than 100 families contributing regularly; he is also a member of an executive committee that screens and accepts families and students into the fundraising group. He has organized numerous *harambees* for this group, to which he invites local politicians and religious leaders to be guests of honor. He is well known in the community and uses his feature phone frequently to talk and text with people in the area. He also is an avid radio listener.

Supernodes like Charles make good fundraisers, but many others are not well positioned in their networks. As an example, take the disengaged persona (Figure 10.4) which describes people without abundant social ties. In an

Figure 10.4. Personas from ThinkPlace's User Insights Brief.

example from our interviews, Sarah is a woman in her forties in the Banana Hill region, about 20 kilometers outside of Nairobi. Sarah is speech- and hearing-impaired. She is a tailor and repairs and alters clothing and school uniforms for a living. Her income is very irregular but might be $15 per month. She lives in a house with her father and her two small children; she asked her husband to leave after he was unfaithful. Sarah's social network is limited to her parents and a women's group of eight people at a local church that provides her with occasional food and moral support; she does not contribute money to it. She had been a member of a savings club that the same church tried to initiate for people with disabilities, but the group disbanded when its treasurers absconded with the money. She never uses her bank account and rarely uses M-Pesa; her phone has been broken for some time.

These personas highlighted important differences in access to technology and position in social networks of a potential M-Changa user. Creating personas like Sarah and Charles is important to the HCD process in order to build empathy with different kinds of users. This empathy is the basis of design thinking: "Rather than presuming to know what people need, humanitarian

Table 10.1. A summary of ThinkPlace's findings using a human-centered design approach and their implications for M-Changa's design, based on team conversations and meetings and the ThinkPlace User Insights Brief

People Value . . .	Designs Should . . .
Appreciation and reward	Recognize, show one's ability to mobilize others
Contributions beyond money	Include material goods, farm animals, and time
Charity and helping	Highlight emotive, relatable stories
Digital media	Allow alternative currencies, points, or emojis; always on/intermittent engagement
Debts to others	Keep relationships open
Group membership and belonging	Reinforce solidarity
Existing social practices	Combine new designs with existing savings groups, visiting, *harambee*, and WhatsApp
People Fear. . .	*Designs Should . . .*
Being seen as poor	Allow anonymity for small donations
Being seen as selfish, unworthy, or alone	Emphasize recipient's value and merit
Fundraiser failure, rejection, unfulfilled pledges	Allow anonymity, repeat requests
Scams, conmen, and corruption	Verify fundraisers

designers wonder if they are even asking the right questions. They learn what people value through collaborative practice. [Design] seeks to embrace indigenous and collective ways of knowing and living."[25]

On the basis of the collaborative design sprints, ThinkPlace produced an abundance of findings, summarized in Table 10.1. Our approach emphasized the social value of giving—belonging, solidarity, and being recognized for one's contributions. At the same time, we uncovered important information about barriers to giving and a reluctance to get involved in it, whether in the organized form of a *harambee* or in everyday appeals and requests.

There is widespread suspicion of the M-Changa platform among potential users due to the large number of scams using digital media in Kenya. We realized that design for low-income customers would require grappling with their lack of technological access and their much higher sense of mistrust. Importantly, the personas approach showed that the wealth-in-people of potential clients varies greatly. The act of asking tests one's value in the eyes of others and exposes one's limited means. Several informants were more aware of the potential failure of fundraising and spoke of unfulfilled promises and the shame of "chasing after contributions." Many feared the risks to reputation in being exposed as poor or undeserving, and many of our interlocutors associated fundraising with the wealthy, the well connected, or people from other, better-positioned ethnic groups—ironically a set of associations that are also often attached to the banking industry, whose barriers this initiative sought to bring down. Low-income users often mentioned that if they were to have a fundraiser, they would persuade a guest of honor, Member of Parliament, or religious leader to attend the event, bundle contributions, and legitimate the fundraiser. Their participation was guarded and in need of information. When giving they wanted to know how much others were giving—so as not to "spoil the pattern," as one lady put it. Some participants professed to have little in the way of social or financial ties. Many research participants expressed a preference for anonymous giving, and especially for the giving of non-monetary contributions, such as cooked food, animals, or one's time or labor. Here I realized I was confronting the barrier of shame and reputational risk—strategic ignorance.

Distributing Trust: The Ledger

As it turns out, M-Changa users are already highly attuned to the risks of giving. Getting back to my conversation with Mary that opened this chapter will elaborate. Mary noted that she has several strategies to ensure a successful fundraiser. First of all, she is motivated by her love for God and for following Jesus's example of thinking of others. More concretely, she values being trust-worthy in the eyes of others, by showing them that the money will be used for its stated purpose and that she is not hiding any funds. As a fundraiser leader on M-Changa, Mary can choose up to four other people to share the progress link with. This committee is the same group that spreads the word, brings in others, organizes fundraising events, and cashes out the fundraiser. The com-mittee can see a list of donors online and monitor their contributions as they are coming in. Second, she noted that M-Changa verifies fundraisers by post-ing documents like hospital bills. Verification and ledger-sharing are why Mary uses online fundraising with M-Changa rather than using, say, the Safaricom Paybill number that is widely used to collect contributions solicited via SMS. To her, M-Changa's 4.25% fee, deducted from the amount collected, is worth it.

As an M-Changa user, Mary said, she was mobilizing more and more peo-ple and money with each fundraiser and involving more people on leadership committees. She attributed her growing success to distributing the fundrais-ing ledger to other participants.[26] As she shares the link to the fund account, she "shows the process is transparent and trustworthy . . . it reflects on me positively and makes me trustworthy to the committee. Sharing the link is the buffer between me and the process." As a result, when her father died people were mobilized. "My trustworthiness meant now more people." As Mary and I discussed her growing reputation, she said she was developing "prestige and recognition" in her social network. She took a new marker and added a new medium of exchange, writing "prestige and recognition" on her graph next to the M-Changa line, and adding, "I am realizing more and more who I can be to people through fundraising." She mentioned that she wished to soon support her preferred candidate for Parliament.

Dr. Andrew Mullei is another proponent of M-Changa's distributed led-ger. In an interview, he argued that M-Changa and other digital money forms could redeem African money relations and revive precolonial communalism.[27] To elaborate, recalled M-Changa's genesis in an extended family fund that he and Kyai managed. The fund included Dr. Mullei's other children and more than 30 grandchildren to pool money for education and other needs. Dr. Mul-lei showed me this ledger and his family tree, which included 75 individuals from seven generations of Mulleis. He stressed not only the logistical improve-ments of bringing the many different payment tills and channels together in one ledger, but also explained that the format gives greater transparency. Kyai and Dave Mark also used the word "transparency" to describe the value-add, as they put it, of M-Changa's ability to share the ledger with up to three treasurers. M-Changa also provides SMS notifications of donations and fundraiser progress, verifies fundraisers by authenticating required documents such as medical bills, and detects fraud by flagging suspicious SMS.

M-Changa is not the only animal on the Silicon Savanna appealing to digital transparency. Using digital media against corruption is one of the main goals of digital media initiatives. For example, Muntuyu Waigi, CEO of Umati Capital, writes: "The overarching goal should be to achieve transparency through technology. . . . By digitizing, you will eradicate most of the daily corruption in the system . . . by introducing new, transparent processes together with government leaders who own the process."[28] It is often assumed, as Dr. Mullei does, that revealing more information automatically creates more information sharing and therefore more transparency.[29] However, efforts to create transparency almost always decide what should be revealed and what should remain hidden. Transparency is thus bound up with social power and position.[30]

To illustrate transparency, Dr. Mullei showed me three family fundraiser spreadsheets that indicated his children's and grandchildren's names, ages, phone numbers, most recent contributions, and total contributions. He told me he keeps track of the fund and expects more contributions from grandchildren who are older or earning more steadily, sometimes calling them if he feels it is right. I immediately recalled the experiences of Emmanuel and his overbearing uncles and the many other cases I knew of fathers, uncles, and older siblings who set targets for family fundraisers. Crowdfunding is a paradox of tradition. The rationality of transparency seemed in Dr. Mullei's family to rely on the long-standing nudging mechanism of elder power—which, in a double irony, works very much behind the scenes of a digital ledger.[31]

Gender and M-Changa

M-Changa's entrepreneurs articulate an ambitious desire to reengineer money and society. Its users, however, are building the strength of their personal networks to serve family and community needs and to mobilize the charitable impulse for concerns they care about. They were looking for M-Changa's technical infrastructures to help them build trust, communication, and connections and for its customer service staff to assist with the relational work of an online story that can inspire giving.

M-Changa users relied on healthy social networks of friends and family; they were experienced with linking M-Changa to WhatsApp and Facebook pages and appeals. Users like Mary attribute their skill to the distributed ledger and to their ability to reach large numbers of their contacts quickly through digital technology. Initial customer surveys indicated that M-Changa's most successful fundraisers—those that raised the most money, from the most contributors, and in the shortest amount of time—were more than twice as likely to be run by women.[32] Furthermore, these women fundraising leaders build fundraising momentum by connecting first to other women, who in turn connect to others to drive more fundraising. They are skilled in moving between platforms and apps, in particular WhatsApp and Facebook.

I asked Mary, "Why are women better at fundraising?" She responded immediately: "It is easy for women to ask!" Her friends have difficulties, for example, in marriage. She related a recent incident of marital conflict where "we wives had to get involved and solve the problem." She noted that when women face problems, they tell each other, talk it out, and fundraise together. But . . . "men do not want to appear weak. Their way of dealing with it is to have a drink." Mary explained that women have a habitus of connections, a sharing of vulnerability and mutual concern through which they solve problems and build ties that bind. Indeed, many theories of interpersonal trust emphasize vulnerability.[33] Women turn strategic ignorance on its head. Their ability to *ask* without shame is to Mary an advantage.

Women view themselves, and are widely viewed in Kenyan society, as more engaged in financial activities than men. After decades of microfinance interventions, women now engage in group borrowing and lending at all income levels and are often members of multiple groups for saving, investing, and lending. Similarly WhatsApp groups are often driven by women. "What kind of Kenyan woman is not a member of many groups on her phone?" baker Annette asked me. Women are widely viewed as more trustworthy and honest, as more committed to reciprocating exchanges and as more caring of others. These are new understandings of gender but also new understandings of what it means to be financial.

Women's facility with M-Changa fundraisers builds on their roles in personal and family networks. They leverage their roles as mothers and grandmothers, the same roles that make them trusted brokers of family funds in

M-Pesa circulations. This interconnected way of being is also valued by rural women who wish to be good mothers, sisters, and friends. For women like Mary, it can bring "prestige and recognition."

Changes to the M-Changa Platform

The M-Changa product explored the customer as a network member, rather than as an individual, which led to new ideas and design improvements. The company took special interest in central, powerful nodes and bundlers—thinking about its customers in a networked way rather than as just individuals and considering how customer choices might be shaped by their network roles. One way to bring out these networked users was to give them ways to mobilize others and see evidence of this process—both in the number of contributors they could inspire and in the amount of money they could amass. The M-Changa team looked for ways to make giving visible, with scrolling fundraiser updates and gold medal icons. It made linking to Facebook and WhatsApp easier so that people could tie into social networks on these platforms. For example, in one case a young woman fundraising for her grandfather's funeral set up a fundraiser with $10, and inspired donations of more than $1,000 within a week. The WhatsApp donations tied to her activity were shown to her with a unique code tag. More changes included a redesign of the website to emphasize the distributed ledger, the awards icons, the social media links, and the progress alerts that reward contributors. Machine-learning studies showed that building momentum early is a necessity for fundraiser success, so nudging bundlers to bring donations early can bode well for the success of the entire project.

When Dave Mark expressed concern that his customers wanted the company to become a part of their networks, I suggested that he run with that idea. Could the design team reimagine M-Changa not as a provider but as a participant in clients' social/financial networks? We discussed grouping a set of clients into a network on the platform and seeding this network with money or reward points that the network would circulate, eventually returning the funds to M-Changa. Our team made several mockups in which M-Changa would become a part of the impromptu fundraising typical of rural users dealing with emergencies, such as when a carpenter's son swallows a nail. Clients could receive a small up-front sum for M-Changa, then fundraise the rest in their social network, earning points at the same time. With another new feature called "Build

My Network," users display and build their social networks online. They donate in-kind gifts, say a goat or their time, to fundraisers—true financial inclusion based on non-monetary value. Members of the M-Changa team designed ways that a fundraiser could accept non-monetary contributions in labor, time, or farm animals. However, all of these ideas, based on the design sprints, would mean changing a business model, a risky and time-consuming process for a small company.

Evaluating the Project: Barriers to Scale

I returned to M-Changa for my last visit of the project in 2017. At that time Dave Mark expressed disappointment with the effort to scale to the bottom-of-the-pyramid demographic. "Sibel, here we are two years into the Gates project, and M-Changa is still a bougie product!" Numerous sprints, visits to low-income areas, and incentivized marketing efforts had failed to drive up adoption with the low-income segment. The project faced an inability to scale, to distribute fundraising finance as inclusion to poor customers. This failure suggested that the wealth-in-people network model was either seriously flawed or for some other reason extremely limited as a framework for inclusive finance interventions. I decided to take the setback as an opportunity to understand the barriers to scaling on the African fintech scene.

Urban spaces afford easy access to a technological infrastructure. Internet and Wi-Fi are common in Nairobi's public spaces. A majority of M-Changa customers also had smartphones and in-home Internet and personal computers. The technological advantage is important for M-Changa users, who begin fundraisers on desktop computers of their own or at Internet cafes. Users access the site and contribute through desktops. Facebook and WhatsApp are widely accessed through links on fundraiser pages. Being always on and connected has become an important part of urban and middle-class identity in East Africa's most connected country, and such a habitus of intermittent and frequent digital media connection is frequently alluded to as marking various identities, as Anne did when she referenced "women who are part of many groups on their phones." M-Changa users appreciate the speed and immediacy of digital connection to others and the ability to check fundraiser progress frequently. The most skilled with media also understood the limits of the Internet to expand their networks—they relied on people they already knew as a way to expand network size. Customer journeys highlighted that successful fundraisers integrate to face-to-face meetings, goat eating or tea parties, church and savings group connections, and other events into an online fundraiser. Mary's network drawing (Figure 10.1) maps the multiple platforms she uses, from What's App, to M-Changa, to SMS.

The technological infrastructure in Kenya's rural areas continues to lag far behind the urban. Access to the Internet, phone service, and electricity remain important issues in rural areas. During our effort to onboard rural grandmother Robai from Western Kenya to fundraise for her potting guild, her network cut out several times. We finally gave up and decided to run a brief fundraiser in her name from Nairobi. Because of the lack of Internet service, customers are reached on basic and feature phones using USSD protocols for communicating with customers along with its limitations. In negotiating this foregrounded and often frustrating technological process, M-Changa's two-person customer care team works personally over the phone with every fundraiser in its early stages, to make sure they are properly initiated, and that fundraising momentum builds early. Fundraising is both a social and a technological process; the M-Changa care team is a social infrastructure, and its user support is key.

Another type of technological access that is important to using M-Changa is scanners, which most urban users find at an Internet café or their place of work. Scanners are used to copy documents that M-Changa requires for verification. These are the services that users like Mary appreciate the most, but in rural areas such scanning devices are rare and expensive. Our meetings discussed the likelihood that a rural person would find the money and time to access one of these devices to e-mail a scan of a bill or document to the M-Changa headquarters. Even more importantly, however, many Kenyans have little familiarity with the institutions that produce these documents, and they may mistrust them or feel they are for the wealthy or for others. M-Changa's existing users knew these institutions and how to examine a certificate or bill and know, based on familiarity with its logo or symbols, that the document was legitimate.

Many low-income people produce trust and verification in different ways that the digital financial services industry struggles to capture. Also confronting this problem, Bankable Frontier Associates (BFA) Kenya tested a digital school fees payment system.[34] Children lose instruction when schools send them home for fees. BFA partnered with a school to test a mobile money Paybill for school fees that would connect to parents and to helpers from the social network. It was assumed that with a convenient payment channel and SMS notifications of low balance, parents "would pay faster and pay more," keeping students in class more often.

This study found that adding an M-Pesa payment channel and SMS warnings only modestly increased payments and attendance. Sending children home remained the most effective way to spur payment. A child at home is a verification, a visible sign to the network that the situation is legitimate and urgent. Established rituals of verification and networked negotiation are not easily digitized.

Finally, M-Changa's insistence that it was a legitimate financial company that could protect and support their contributions was unconvincing. Documents designed to endorse and validate fundraisers may have little meaning for people unfamiliar with the institutions being documented. Transparency can create accountability, but only if people understand and contextualize the information that transparency reveals.

Crowdfunding and Social Finance

In evidence-based development, Africa is a laboratory for invention, in synthesis with local knowledge.[35] The M-Changa approach combined behavioral economics with human-centered design into a "hybrid . . . that seeks to enable the coexistence of calculative and cultural rationalities."[36] Despite radically different methods, the behavioral and human-centered approaches also intersected. How can giving be nudged or encouraged? The behavioral economics team tended to emphasize devices and technology, while the HCD team focused on social and cultural obligations and reciprocities. But in my view, the behavioral economics approach was too individual-centric to appreciate the paradoxes of crowdfunding as relational finance. The project was also a hybrid of development funding and a market approach. Indeed, development funding is providing important support to many of the Silicon Savanna's technology start-ups. These stakeholders often measure success through scaling—as one tech entrepreneur in Nairobi put it, "You've got to hit as many poor people in the slums as possible."[37]

Technological divides aside, the social infrastructures of fundraising were the more profound reason why the crowdfunding model did not catch on with the low-income customer segment. Perhaps the biggest mistake came in the beginning with the project's assumptions that technology could nudge the speed and volume of material value flowing in social networks. But these assumptions of the grant—that social networks could be revved up by a technological boost—ended up colliding with the logic and the practices of wealth-in-people.

Many user personas did not feel they had the status and power to fundraise. Instead, they protect their fragile ties through strategic ignorance—to avoid the risks of asking. On the other hand, they would like their own giving to be anonymous, as they negotiate the risks of participation through strategic ignorance. Wealth-in-people is grounded in the long term, and in social power and hierarchies of status and reputation.

Rituals of the life cycle make these asymmetries explicit. Among the urban classes graduations, funerals, coming-of-age rituals, and weddings are becoming more important and expensive, not less. I have attended several of these events over the years. They feature speeches given by sets of siblings and relatives introduced by birth order and generation, ending with the words of matriarchs and patriarchs. At one event I attended in 2017, a brother pledged loyalty and protection to his sister, who had just received a law degree; she responded that her achievement was to be shared with him, and the two then fed each other cake to the cheers of the guests. Extended-family fundraisers provide a moral and temporal framework that powerfully inspires giving, and they reinforce who owes what to whom. Fundraisers for institutions like schools also build the reputation and social identity of alumni. Put simply, there are limits to distributive labors. Wealth-in-people is ever a mode of accumulation, with other meanings, motivations, and time frames beyond the short-term horizons of household finance.[38]

Dr. Mullei's vision, that the original communalism of African money can be recaptured on the Silicon Savanna, catalyzed a crowdfunding platform that umbrellas diverse goals. Some activities might be called philanthropy—humanitarian goals for the public sphere—for example, organizations who fundraise for schools and hospitals. Other activities, such as calls to support worthy individuals with medical or schooling needs, call on the impulse to charity. Other fundraisers among equals—say, groups of siblings or friends who agree to help one another with schooling needs—suggest a savings group model. Fundraising for school fees and medical care could be framed as a kind of informal finance. Finally, family fundraising for rituals of the life cycle and elite schools define identity and status.

M-Changa crowdfunding provokes thought about new institutions and commitments that the circuits of digital money could one day produce. The potential in crowdfunding lies in its ability to distribute new forms of commitment and action, and potentially build local civic associations and institution-alize grounded forms of mutual aid.[39] In the fintech boom, peer-to-peer lend-ing, insurance, and crowdfunding products are promising to reform money around "social finance."[40] Indeed social finance can make morality, ethics, re-ligious obligation, and care financial.[41] M-Changa users create new solidarities around these goals. However, their fundraising might end up creating finance "for just us,"[42] and like charitable giving, reproduce social class, family, and eth-nic boundaries.[43]

Making a market solution scale is much harder than I had ever imagined. It means facing down the predators that prowl the Silicon Savanna. Social in-equalities, mistrust of a sector rife with fraud, the costs and fees that are foisted on the bottom-of-the-pyramid customer because scaling up requires an absent infrastructure—all would prove to be too fierce. Scaling was not the place to find the value of M-Changa. Instead, it lies in the success of novel financial performances like Mary's. She adeptly shares information across diverse apps and platforms, brings collateral, commitment, and caring to group projects of mutual concern, and builds her "prestige and recognition" through her own relational work over time.

Designs for Wealth-in-People

11

The Failure of Financial Inclusion

On March 6, 2020, Kenya made public its first case of COVID-19, in a college student returning home from the United States. Soon drastic measures were put in place to contain the virus, including curfews, social distancing, and the closing of roads. For many, the coronavirus pandemic was just the latest crisis in a world of precarity and uncertainty. In this world, people's fates are increasingly tied to their participation in the social networks of mobile money. Participation in networks that borrow, lend, fundraise, and invest money has become necessary for economic life and social belonging.

Among the poorest, these networks distribute risk and enable people to survive. Wealthier networks are able to reach new members and sources of money to fundraise for the unexpected or make investments for the future. The productivity of these ties varies greatly, and the networks themselves comprise different kinds of people with different resources to offer, who create different roles, ranging from distributive hubs to receivers. The social networks of mobile money have been praised for building resilience and reducing poverty,[1] but these claims prove true for only some networks. We know little of how these networks will affect poverty, prosperity, empowerment, or exclusion, or how new monetary technologies will shape the outcomes. Such informal arrangements and networks, built from the ground up, will determine the success of financial inclusion. Taken as a whole, the picture suggests a future of greater, not lesser, inequality.

The 2020 crisis around the arrival of coronavirus echoes the post-election violence of 2007–8, which happened just months after M-Pesa was launched. Back then, anthropologist Olga Morawczynski witnessed roads, stores, and banks closed amid post-election unrest and described how people turned to M-Pesa to reach friends and family in need.[2] It was a turning point for scaling digital money transfer.

The 2020 crisis created similar circumstances. On March 9 President Kenyatta announced the government response to COVID-19, including a nightly curfew, closing of all major roads, and social distancing. His edict also addressed money—and encouraged Kenyans to use electronic payment such as mobile money or credit and debit cards, warning that passing cash from hand to hand could hasten the spread of coronavirus. In sync with his directive, e-money transfer providers in Kenya and Uganda cut or lifted their fees. Would another crisis push Kenya further toward a cashless future?

In the days that followed, transportation and movement were curtailed, and major roads were closed. Under curfew, informal workers—barbers, hairdressers, shopkeepers, mechanics, and others—had to make money during shortened daylight hours. The commercial activity they depended on had plummeted. Kenyans experienced dramatic loss of jobs and income and rising prices of scarce food and goods.

In 2007–8, there was an uptake in the use of a new service—mobile money. This time, the 2020 crisis revealed the social inequality of money, as shaped by diverse media and users. Here the well-off shopped at grocery stores and avoided cash, instead using credit and debit cards and *Lipa na M-Pesa* (merchant payment for mobile money). Customers with cash elicited disapproving looks from other customers and from cashiers, who nervously disinfected their workspaces after handling it.

One might expect that low-income users would rely on money transfer to help and share within their networks. But this time, the social networks of mobile money were depleted. Our team members Gabriel Kunyu and Chap Kusimba were in Kenya at the time. Gabriel was living in the town of Machakos during May 2020. Located 60 kilometers southeast of Nairobi in Central Kenya, Machakos has been a hub of trade in and out of Kenya's capital since colonial times and before.[3] Nairobi and the port town of Mombasa were closed, and the cost of foodstuffs and tradeable goods such as secondhand clothes doubled or tripled. With Nairobi closing off, many left the city for their rural homes; shops had little business as people feared the virus; gatherings and celebrations were forbidden.

Agents in Machakos and Western Kenya[4] reported that despite the reduction in fees, their customers were no longer coming, as they had no money. As M-Pesa agent Millicent put it: "I saw people rejoice when it was announced that there would be no transaction fees for any amount sent below 1,000 ($10). But now there is no money, so people do not send." People used to wait in the queue at Millicent's shop before COVID-19, but during the crisis she was seeing at most two or three people in a whole day. She reflected that a lot of people had sent money in the week before the restrictions. Itinerant urban workers were sending money to their rural families. Although Millicent used to send money to friends and family before the virus came, nowadays she has no money to send.

During this crisis, Gabriel and Chap found that people were not sending money, because there was nothing to send. Men who balanced payments to their wives and their mothers had to choose whom to support. The poorest, who often depended on others for remittances, were left on their own. A tailor said that the poor still come to her with a few coins to repair their torn clothes. And Millicent added that people have so many Fuliza loans (the Safaricom overdraft service), that they have gone back to using cash to avoid the wallet balance being garnished. Some lucky few were trying to help: one seller of movie DVDs had more business in the lockdown. He was sending money to the hungry and the stranded. Many were relying on Fuliza loans for airtime and on digital M-Shwari loans. Agent Millicent is using M-Shwari loans to feed her family. "Any money I get goes to paying these loans and for food. I cannot send to my friends anymore."

As in 2007–8, brave agents were staying open. But COVID-19 and public health efforts to contain it put the social networks of mobile money under tremendous strain. In spite of the suspension of fees, the increasing use of digital payment was concentrated among wealthier people who shopped in supermarkets and spent more money. The poor were focusing on cash and paying in small amounts. Cash was also a way to keep value safe in uncertain times and a form of strategic ignorance to protect funds from the Fuliza overdraft service. In response to Kenyatta's anti-cash push, an M-Pesa agent devised a motorized "cash sanitizer" using paint rollers and a plastic squeeze bottle. This bricolage made him a social media star.[5]

Distribution

Money transfer has become a deep part of Kenyan national identity and cultural wealth, and a medium of everyday relations of friendship and intimacy. Remittances are bringing more money into rural areas through family networks, shaped by distributional labors of grandmothers, young men, and others. Innovative group finance models such as family networks, cooperatives, savings clubs, solidarity entrepreneurialism, and fundraising are capturing aspirations for success. Networks of wealth-in-people have enabled survival and thriving over the years. But these networks cannot circulate value they do not have. Furthermore, they are being depleted by debt rather than seeded with credit. Many are left out of the resilience that mobile money should have brought.

Because of the commercial success and cultural importance of digital finance in Kenya, its divides and exclusions are often left out of the picture. Without the distributive labors of people in networks, failures of inclusion and access would be far greater. Distribution is the basic act of the repertoire. Airtime gifting—still known by its Safaricom menu name, *sambaza* (Swahili for "distribute")—was the origin story for the whole narrative, for the cultural wealth of innovators, regulators, entrepreneurs, and start-up hubs. Distributive labors with money transfer sustain people in poverty, and they nurture, educate, and invest in the future. Women bring their distributive goals to hearthhold networks and crowdfunding websites. Distributed identities involve SIM cards, handsets, and PIN numbers. Agents and users take on others' fees to enable their access. The costs, risks, debts, and identities of digital money become a distributed process in which agency and action are a product of relationships between people and material systems and even supernatural forces, which are also agents in these networks.[6] Digital divides and digital inequalities are often thought of as a material issue, a problem of rurality or a technological barrier. Sometimes culture and social norms are blamed.[7] But these barriers are already mediated by social relationships with agents and other users, and the cultural setting that values mutual aid and reciprocity.

In 2020 social inequality and financial health appear to be worsening.[8] Costs, fees, penalties, and debt are reaching further into the lives of the poorest people, into the circuits of the economy of affection. Weighty expectations lead to jealousy and conflict. People then retreat from their networks, leading to strategies of non-use. The ethnographic approach to social network roles shows how the effects of digital finance vary. They accrue to those who are socially positioned to build their wealth-in-people—like successful users of a crowdfunding website. But they may be more elusive to people without a central network position. How many grandmothers can meet the distributive challenges of their network roles?

To answer this question requires a shift to an interdisciplinary perspective that fully incorporates the social meaning of money. Consider the dominant design approach from behavioral economics. Following this view, financial designs want to enable rational choices to optimize how people save, spend, and use money.[9] To build these tools, financial diaries have become an important research method. Financial diaries model a household as a firm and quantify money brought in and spent over weeks or months.[10] The emphasis is on measuring transfers in and out of the household.

The use of diary methods began in Africa in the 1950s as part of the colonial imposition of nuclear family life onto the flexible and multi-sited African corporate group.[11] Depending on how they are interpreted, they may impose a narrow view in which a social network is appreciated only in its economic dimension. For example, the Kenya diaries found that funeral calls can very quickly amass large amounts of money donations—as much as $600. A vignette from one of the families describes how a call for medical help failed to bring in donations, but that after the individual died money transfers came in abundance: "Shortly before Christmas, Isaac's wife became ill and had trouble swallowing. After review, the hospital informed her that she had a tumor in her throat that would need to be removed. It would cost KSh23,000 . . . they could not raise the full KSh23,000 fast enough and his wife died. Immediately, Isaac was flooded with contributions in cash and in-kind worth more than KSh33,000. The social network worked but, in this case, too late to save a life."[12]

The study described the social network's slowness as a "flaw in the social network." The authors further suggested that although "cultural norms" might make funeral fundraising "efficient . . . faster-acting financial devices" should be developed, which would somehow compel people to donate "in time"[13] so that medical care could be sought. The study recommended a faster monetary device that could accelerate donations and prevent people from dying in the first place, turning funeral donations into medical care that would save the life in question. In this view, each money transaction of a household is like any other, and a funeral donation can be transformed into a hospital stay through a technological nudge.

The M-Changa study followed this lead. Our design team wanted to make fundraising more efficient. We wanted social networks to raise more money in a shorter amount of time. But in the end, efficiencies get you only so far. The inflows and outflows of financial diaries are more properly viewed as instances of earmarking[14] associated with specific social relationships, meanings, and temporalities. Financial diaries, in other words, record the social meanings of money. In Kenya, the social meaning of money is wealth-in-people. Money strategies and commitments that involve giving, and even *not* giving, from money transfer to airtime sending to drawing on digital debt to fundraising, are aimed at generating and protecting wealth-in-people. Wealth-in-people seeks rights to others through transfers of material value that account for and share a record of money relationships. Like relational work it is both social and material. Digital finance and loans become a part of these networks. An approach that combines the social meaning of money and quantitative data could make clear what money technologies can and cannot offer to improve the financial health of people holding different network roles and positions.

Designs for Wealth-in-People

Some design points emerged from the drawings that research participants made of the social meanings of money. Designs can take some inspiration from the network self-portrait drawings: the boat (Figure 6.5b), the lockbox (Figure 6.4b), the rat (Figure 9.1b), the eye (Figure 9.3b), and finally the airplane (Figure 9.3c).

The Boat (Figure 6.5b). Consolata's boat is a financial relationship in which one person assumes another's risks and vulnerability and provides the other person with protection and mobility.[15] Pursuing wealth-in-people means combining your own agency and fate with that of others. This is not a zero-sum game. Rather the goal is to be a part of a constellation of ties, toward a collective upliftment.[16] Forms of group finance are burgeoning across the formal/informal spectrum, such as hearthholds, saving clubs, solidarity entrepreneurs, investment groups, cooperatives, WhatsApp groups, coming-of-age rituals, and crowdfunding platforms. These groups are journeying across the waters together, to build durable and bequeathable assets. All of this goes back to wealth-in-people as an investment across the life cycle that brings together short- and long-term intentions.

The movement of digital money is enabled by central figures in networks of wealth-in-people—a maternal uncle with a distributive role, a niece who collects gifts from aunts and uncles. Those who give out build productive economic ties in their communities and find positions of prestige and security. Money relationships are group-oriented, but not egalitarian. The boat has agency, but it also has the responsibility to care for and to provide mobility for its passengers. Similar asymmetrical relationships of creditor to debtor involve seniors and juniors or gendered relationships. Through these connections, subordinates make important financial claims. Gender norms are significant ways that women and men gain from digital finance and enhance and deepen the meaning of their relationships.[17] Furthermore, these roles shift with the passage of time. The passenger today may tomorrow be the boat who carries others.

Consistent with the relations depicted by the boat, money designs should be embedded in talk and text, and give users ways of expressing their emotions and social and gender identities. Financial service providers could model themselves as members of networks in different ways. For example, a provider might seed liquidity into a network, which could circulate it and build it before it returns to the provider, thus incorporating flexibility, lowering fees, and distributing the benefit. A positive credit score should be given not just to someone who builds value over time, but also to someone who gives to others. Distributive labors of all kinds—such as paying for other people's fees—should earn positive credit scores. Maintaining a low savings balance in favor of sending to others is a mark of relational financial strength.

The Lockbox (Figure 6.4b). I might draw a savings vehicle as a piggy bank. Consolata drew the M-Shwari digital bank/loan product as a box with three locks on it. The box depicts security and storage as important parts of financial agency, which can allow for calculation, deliberation, juggling, value-building, and control. Where do these understandings of saving and money accounting come from? The origin of this three-keyed lockbox is in a savings club methodology developed by Care International for Niger, which became rapidly adopted across East Africa. Three different elected group members have keys, and all three must be present to open the box. Meetings are structured around a ritualized locking and unlocking of the box, as "a public performance of accountability."[18] The savings group has predictable rules but can also negotiate flexibility.[19] Its temporality can vary, and its commitments can end after a set period, or continue. Interestingly the lockbox connects the activity of saving and money accounting not to a private and individuated context such as a piggy bank, but rather to a group setting. Like the "contingency fund" on the mobile wallet, digital tools aimed at individual control and safekeeping will eventually be integrated into a network of money relationships. People want both the lockbox *and* the boat.[20]

The Rat (Figure 9.1b). The rat on Brendah's drawing represents shame. Strategic ignorance is a heretofore unrecognized barrier to scaling, which hindered the growth of the crowdfunding website M-Changa. Digital loans and crowd-funding platforms can build wealth-in-people for those who can bring suffi-cient collateral to a group, secure repayment, or compel others to give. Others may shy away from the reputational risks of exposure—the rat. Precarity of wealth-in-people leads people to protect it—withdrawing from networks to a safer stance of non-use. While digital finance can increase the potential ties and pathways of distribution, the productivity of these ties is never certain.[21] People should have the freedom to form financial relationships informally and of their own choosing. They may seek out superiors or subordinates, and in group set-tings they prefer to save with people who are similar to themselves to avoid facing unfulfillable expectations and standards.

The Eye (Figure 9.3b). The eye expresses the power of debt, charges, and fees in people's lives. The reliance on digital debt has led to stress, juggling, and social risks for people like Praxides.[22] But people in poverty need liquidity, not debt.[23] The Givedirectly organization gives poor people money, which has for the most part benefited them economically and psychologically.[24] Such cash transfers might be what many people taking this debt really need. Compari-sons of the effects of digital debt versus money gifts could reveal what kinds of people, if any, would benefit from digital debt.

Furthermore, the terms of these loans should be not only more transparent but much more flexible. As in the informal sphere, could a loan in time become a gift? A pro–poor consumer financial system should not charge fees. The costs of digital financial services are excessive, forcing the poor into distributive la-bors around money for fees, fines, government taxes, and penalties, and access to handsets and SIM cards—all hindering inclusion. Is a private sector, fee-for-service, bottom-of-the-pyramid model really the only successful approach to providing digital finance? Like cash money, money transfer could and should be a fare-free channel and a public good.[25] Given that digital payment is cel-ebrated as part of Kenya's national identity and cultural wealth, and widely viewed as a quasi-public service, the Kenyan government could once again lead the way in providing digital money transfer as a public infrastructure. A joint partnership between Safaricom and other mobile network operators and the Central Bank of Kenya could work to create a fare-free digital money trans-fer network, possibly with the contribution of the numerous development, technology-sector, and finance interests that have already invested billions of dollars promoting money transfer and debt that poor people have to pay for. An analogous design lesson might come from fare-free public transportation, which in more than 100 global cities has been supported by the investment of local stakeholders and has brought increases in commercial and retail activity, ridership, air quality, and traffic control, among many other benefits.[26]

The Airplane (Figure 9.3c). Praxides's airplane depicts the importance of speed and immediacy. Crises around health, school fees, food, and transportation drive money transfer in response to the emergencies that people in poverty face daily. The airplane represents the precarity and unpredictability of people's lives and the urgency of their needs. Even financial diary studies in the United States have shown that income volatility is greater than previously believed, and that saving and smoothing as a kind of intertemporal redistribution cannot bring long-term security to people living in persistent instability.[27]

The airplane, as a symbol of precarity, points to the limits of design. Tailored to the vulnerable as economic rationality (income smoothing), digital debt often meets urgent needs instead. Digital debt and money transfer, in their immediacy, support mutuality (for a fee) as a coping strategy for people who move from crisis to crisis in the face of the loss of a farming way of life with nothing certain to replace the land they cherish. Does designing the individual's ability to endure circumstance shift attention and responsibility away from ameliorating these circumstances? Financial services design as a collective, social, and public process[28] should go beyond the individual's needs and wants. As it stands now, digital finance designed for the poor falls far short of the living, breathing, and naturally reproducing money that shaped the political economy of wealth-in-people. This money compelled those who shepherded and husbanded it to distribute it, to incorporate and include others. This too was nudging.

The next chapter for the M-Pesa story is beyond the frame of this book. The canceling and reducing of money transfer fees during the COVID pandemic could catalyze a free public infrastructure for digital payments. New forms of payment and new forms of tracking and identifying people will follow and create lasting financial relations. Who will benefit?

Notes

Chapter 1: A Central Banker Talks Money

1. Real-time gross settlement allows interbank transfers to be settled individually and without a waiting period, potentially increasing the oversight of the Central Bank and reducing the risk of error and fraud.

2. Maurer 2015.

3. Tilley 2011.

4. Ndemo and Weiss 2017.

5. Sen 2010.

6. CGAP 2019a.

7. Fine 2010 ; Roodman 2011; Roy 2010.

8. Klapper 2019.

9. For example, see Loizos 2018.

10. Jack, Ray, and Suri 2013; Kikulwe, Fischer, and Qaim 2014; ApplePay, Venmo, and WeChat Pay.

11. Suri and Jack 2016.

12. Rhyne and Kelly 2018.

13. Duvendack and Mader 2019.

14. Duvendack and Mader 2019; Mader 2017; Rhyne and Kelly 2018.

15. Wyche and Olson 2018; Roessler 2018.

16. Smart Campaign 2017; Microsave 2019.

17. Dalinghaus 2019; Jenkins 2018; Jeong 2016.

18. Susan Johnson 2004; Susan Johnson 2012; Susan Johnson 2017; Susan Johnson and Frichte Krijtenburg 2018; Maurer 2015; Zelizer 2017.

19. Geertz 1998, 70–71. What he calls here "localized, long-term, close-in, vernacular field research" is the model for anthropology.

20. Bohannon 1959; Guyer 2011; Maurer 2015.

21. Zelizer 2017, 42–44.

22. Zelizer 2005, 37

23. Morduch 2017.

24. Radcliffe-Brown 1952.

25. Bledsoe 1980, chapter 3; Cooper 2017; Guyer 1995; Guyer and Belinga 1995; Kopytoff and Miers 1977; Kusimba 2020; Makhulu 2017.

26. Zelizer 2005, 37.

27. Gershon 2000.

28. Baumer et al. 2015.

Chapter 2: Airtime Money

1. Maurer 2015.

2. GSMA 2012.

3. The national currency is the Kenya shilling. One hundred Kenya shillings are equal to US$1.

4. Donner 2009.

5. Heald 1990; Radcliffe-Brown 1940. Avoidance and joking are often expressed in everyday family life in East Africa.

6. Zelizer 2005, 37.

7. Ingham 2004, 24.

8. Hart 2001, 258.

9. Hart 2007.

10. Senders and Truitt 2007.

11. LeVine 1973, 133–34.

12. Senders and Truitt 2007.

13. Okoudjou 2019; see also Maurer 2015, Chapter 8.

14. Connolly 2014.

15. Akrich 1992.

16. Maurer 2012, 591.

17. Omwansa and Sullivan 2012.

18. Camner, Pulver, and Sjöblom 2009.

19. Camner, Pulver, and Sjöblom 2009; Kuriyan, Nafus, and Mainwaring 2012.

20. Morawczynski 2009.

21. Morawczynski 2009.

22. Zelizer 2000, 385.

23. Guyer 2011.

24. The Kenyan Telecommunications Commission estimates that in 2018 about one-third of Kenyans had more than one registered line. The actual number of individuals with at least one registration is lower but is rarely estimated in official reports.

25. Hanlon, Barrientos, and Hulme 2010.

26. Larkin 2013, 327.

27. Maurer, Nelms, and Rea 2013; Mas 2013.

28. Latour 2005, 221.

29. Blumenstock et al. 2016.

Chapter 3: Money Leapfroggers

1. Mann and Nzayisenga 2015.

2. Manuel 2019.

3. CGAP 2019a.

4. Juma 2017.

5. Aker and Mbiti 2010.

6. Kaberuka 2015.

7. Graham and Mann 2013; Poggiali 2016.

8. Mureithi 2017.

9. Oranye 2017, 33.

10. Ndemo 2017, 7.

11. Weiss 2017.

12. Drouillard 2017, 101.

13. https://www.cellulant.com/.

14. Iazzolino and Wasike 2015; FSD Kenya 2014.

15. CGAP 2013.

16. Blumenstock and Eagle 2012; Kiiti and Mutinda 2018; Roessler 2018; Wyche and Olson 2018.

17. Burrell 2010.

18. Matthews and Nyasenga 2016; Woldmariam et al. 2016; Wyche and Olson 2018.

19. FSD Kenya 2016, 19.

20. Iazzolino and Mann 2019.

21. https://mercycorpsagrifin.org/wp-content/uploads/2019/05/DigiFarm-Platform -Case_Final.pdf.

22. I am grateful to John Sharp for fleshing out this point in discussions about MFS Africa and its API. See also Okoudjou 2019; https://mfsafrica.com/about/.

23. https://soundcloud.com/african-tech-round-up/a-chat-with-dare-okoudjou-of -mfs-africa/.

24. https://soundcloud.com/african-tech-round-up/a-chat-with-dare-okoudjou-of -mfs-africa/.

25. [Automated regulatory checks on customer identification: KYC is "know your customer," and AML is "anti-money laundering."].

26. Internet satellite connection for remote areas.

27. Okoudjou 2019. He added that customers often memorize numerical codes for airtime topups or other services. Changing these codes creates difficulties for customers.

28. Kottack 1999, 33.

29. Morawczynski 2009.

30. Nafus 2017, 170.

31. http://qz.com/425242/we-need-to-stop-talking-about-how-mobile-phones-will -save-africa-and-think-bigger/.

32. Poggiali 2016.

33. Toyama 2015.

34. Prahalad 2005.

35. Johnson 2011.

36. Simone 2004.

Chapter 4: Whose Money Is This?

1. https://bizextras.wordpress.com/2011/05/23/so-who-invented-m-pesa/.

2. http://www.humanipo.com/news/2484/full-safaricom-ltd-response-on-the-m
-pesa-series/.

3. http://www.humanipo.com/news/2484/full-safaricom-ltd-response-on-the-m
-pesa-series/.

4. Bandelj and Wherry 2011.

5. Bandelj and Wherry 2011.

6. See Muthiora 2015.

7. Riley and Kulathunga 2015, 41.

8. https://www.safaricom.co.ke/images/Downloads/Terms_and_Conditions/M
-PESA_Trust_Deed_23.02.2007.pdf/.

9. Burns 2018.

10. Personal communication, November 2018.

11. Riley and Kulathunga 2015, 69.

12. Muthiora 2015.

13. Sunderland and Denny 2016, 14.

14. Maurer 2012.

15. http://www.bankingtech.com/2017/02/kenya-bankers-association-unveils-real
-time-interbank-switch/.

16. Kuriyan, Nafus, and Mainwaring 2012.

17. Park and Donovan 2016.

18. Park and Donovan 2016.

19. Kuriyan, Nafus, and Mainwaring 2012, 9.

20. Gajjala and Tetteh 2014.

21. Morawczynski 2009.

22. Malingha 2019.

23. Here and throughout the text, I have used pseudonyms for my interlocutors.

24. Johnson 2012.

25. https://www.youtube.com/watch?v=_FAjSmSvKSI.

26. Many of my interlocutors in Kimilili have wondered why one should pay more when the act of money sending is in effect just a text message. After all, this is not physical money, which would naturally be harder to move in large amounts. Text-message money, they reason, being just tiny lights on the phone screen, should require the same sending effort, regardless of size. Physical cash *is* moved, of course, across the network of agents and the distribution system of cash float.

27. *The Standard* 2017.

28. Innovations for Poverty Action 2017.

29. Loizos 2018.

30. FSD Kenya 2014.

31. Malingha 2019.

32. FSD Kenya 2016; FSD Kenya 2019a; FSD Kenya 2019b; Microsave 2017; Microsave 2019.

33. Microsave 2019; FSD Kenya 2019a.

34. Microsave 2017.

35. https://www.nation.co.ke/oped/opinion/SIM-swap-fraud-threatens-online-banking/440808-4938344-skas5jz/index.html/.

36. Smart Campaign 2017; Microsave 2019.

37. CGAP 2016a; CGAP 2016c; CGAP 2016b; Microsave 2019; Microsave 2017.

38. Microsave 2019.

39. Microsave 2019.

40. Mahoney 2017, 150–53.

41. *The Economist* 2018. It is not quite clear what kind of loans the 2015 Findex refers to here, but a substantial number of these loans seem to be digital credit over the mobile phone.

42. Seamster and Charron-Chenier 2017.

43. Williams 2005.

44. Baradaran 2015; Servon 2017; Wherry, Seefeldt, and Alvarez 2019.

45. Financial Health Network 2019.

46. James 2015.

47. Gronbach 2019; Torkelson 2020.

48. James 2015, 37–38, 41, 95–97, 229–31.

49. FSD Kenya 2019a.

50. Baradaran 2015; Deville 2020; Fergus 2018; James 2015; Lauer 2020; Torkelson 2020; Wherry, Seefeldt, and Alvarez 2018.

51. Omwansa and Sullivan 2012.

52. http://www.humanipo.com/news/2484/full-safaricom-ltd-response-on-the-m-pesa-series/.

Chapter 5: Money and Wealth-in-People

1. Bledsoe 1980; Daloz 2003; Mair 1961; Kopytoff and Miers 1977; Smith 2017.

2. Bledsoe 1980, Chapter 3; Guyer 1993; Guyer 1995; Guyer and Belinga 1995.

3. Schneider 1981, 217.

4. Kopytoff and Miers 1977.

5. Cooper 2017, 136.

6. Guyer 1995.

7. See Portes 1998 for many definitions of this term.

8. Bourdieu 1985, 21.

9. Zelizer 2012, 148.

10. Zelizer 2005, 37, 56, 57.

11. Penwill 1951.

12. Schneider 1968, 394.

13. Hakansson 1989.

14. Evans-Pritchard 1940; Hakansson 1989; Hutchinson 1992; Schneider 1968.

15. Cooper 1995.

16. Wagner 1949, 1:79.

17. Oboler 1996.

18. Wagner 1975, 1 and 2:84. Detailed examples of ongoing wedding gifts and obligations between in-laws are found on 83–86 and 429–32.

19. Evans-Pritchard 1940, 18.

20. Kusimba 2018b.

21. Wagner 1949, 1:131.

22. Galaty 2014.

23. Nangendo 1998.

24. Wagner 1975, 2:536.

25. Walsh 1983, 647.

26. Lonsdale 1978, 288.

27. Pallaver 2015.

28. Pallaver 2015.

29. Wynne-Jones and Fleisher 2012.

30. Comaroff and Comaroff 2017, 35; Pallaver 2015, 499.

31. Shipton 1989.

32. Hutchinson 1992.

33. Adebanwi 2017; Mukhulu 2017, 228.

34. Ndambuki and Robertson, 2000.

35. White 1990.

36. King 1996; Kinyanjui 2014; Macharia 1997; Morange 2015; Oka 2011. See Meagher 2010 for a theoretical discussion on the relationship between the concepts of informal economy and social networks in African studies.

37. Adebanwi 2017, 1.

38. Hart 2006, cited in Meagher 2010, 14.

39. Ojong 2020; Owen 2015.

40. Green et al. 2012.

41. Schmidt 2017a; Schmidt 2017b.

42. Meiu 2017, 202–6.

43. Kusimba 2018b; MacIntosh 2001.

44. Kusimba 2018b.

45. Wandibba 1985.

46. Wagner 1975, 1 and 2: plate I.

47. Scully 1974; Wandibba 1997.

48. Shipton 2010, 32, 62.

49. Kusimba and Wilson 2007.

50. Ling and Yttri 2002.

51. Kusimba 2018b.

52. Parry and Bloch 1989, 2.

53. Guyer 2011, 2214.

54. Parry and Bloch 1989, 2.

55. Guyer 2011, 2214.

56. Iazzolino and Wasike 2015, 230.

57. Kusimba 2018b.

58. Guyer 2018, 446.

59. Wu 2018.

60. Mbembe 2001, 16.

61. Rodima-Taylor and Bähre 2014, 508.

Chapter 6: Hearthholds of Mobile Money

1. For a color version of maps for 12 families, see the online open access version of Kusimba, Yang, and Chawla 2015; Kusimba, Yang, and Chawla 2016. For a video about these networks, see https://sibelkusimba.com/presentations/.

2. Ferguson 2015, 90–91.

3. Atieno-Odhiambo and Cohen 1989.

4. Atieno-Odhiambo and Cohen 1989; Wandibba 1997; Weisner, Bradley, and Kilbride 1997.

5. Whyte and Kariuki 1997.

6. Whyte 1997, 126.

7. Whyte and Kariuki 1997.

8. Ramisch 2015.

9. Ross and Weisner 1977.

10. Atieno-Odhiambo and Cohen 1989, 55; Kitching 1980.

11. Bryceson 2002; Ramisch 2015.

12. International remittances are not common among Kenyan households, but working with families who received abundant remittances allowed me to see what happens to money in such circumstances—and to reveal the redistributive practices and norms of generosity that the more affluent are able to express.

13. Stovel and Shaw 2012.

14. Lijembe, Apoko, and Nzioki 1967.

15. Ekejiuba 2005. Accounts from East Africa have described how this "house-property complex" gave women significant property and inheritance rights; see Oboler 1996.

16. de Bruijn 1997, 636.

17. de Bruijn 1997, 625.

18. An ethnographically grounded study of networks can also provide more context for the differences in remittance sending and receiving that more-common research instruments such as household surveys and financial diaries call gender differences. FSD Kenya (2014, 41) highlighted the advantages that women have as e-money receivers—on average 33% of their income comes from digital money transfers, whereas men receive

only 4% of their income from such transactions. Furthermore, women, as compared to men, were "more likely to receive help when they need it."

19. Green 2019.

20. See Chapter 11 for more on the lockbox.

21. Wherry 2012, 204.

22. Zelizer 2000, 385.

23. Zelizer 2000, 388; Zeliger 2005, 37.

24. Stovel and Shaw 2012.

25. Lipset 2014.

26. Gell 1998, 21.

27. Gell 1998, 139.

28. Tronto 1993, 107.

29. Kilbride and Kilbride 1997.

30. See Chapter 5.

31. Whyte and Kariuki 1997.

32. Collier 1988, 125.

33. Ramisch 2015.

Chapter 7: Distributive Labors

1. Ferguson 2015, 90–91, 98–102.

2. Durham and Solway 2017.

3. Geschiere 2009, 196.

4. Jindra and Noret 2011.

5. Hyden 1980.

6. Ross and Weisner 1977.

7. See also Smith 2004.

8. Atieno-Odhiambo and Cohen 1989.

9. The new status marker; see also Green 2014, 165–71.

10. See also Cooper 2018.

11. Geschiere 2009, 30.

12. Bouman 1994; Develtere, Pollet, and Wanyama 2008; Green 2019; Kinyanjui 2014; Kusimba, Kunyu, and Gross 2018; Ledgerwood and Jethani 2013; Mahoney 2017; Rodima-Taylor 2013; Rodima-Taylor and Bähre 2014. See Chapter 10 for more on crowdfunding platforms.

13. Iazzolino and Wasike 2015.

14. Kinyanjui 2014, 96.

15. See the video at https://www.youtube.com/watch?v=q_uxYnijYXc/.

16. Ferguson 2015, 90–91.

Chapter 8: Strategic Ignorance

1. Gershon 2000; Wherry, Seefeldt, and Alvarez 2018.

2. Baumer et al. 2015; Latour 1999.

3. Mauss 2016, 71.

4. Shipton 2007, 30.

5. FSD Kenya 2014, 41.

6. Bandelj 2012, 180.

7. Burrell 2016; Enfield 2017; Muniesa, Millo, and Callon 2007.

8. Ling 2004, 184.

9. See Chapter 5.

10. In a survey in Central Kenya, about 34% of people kept money on their phones for emergencies in their social networks; see Johnson 2012.

11. Kusimba, Yang, and Chawla 2015.

12. See also Archambault 2011.

13. Latour 1999; Tronto 1993; Waelbers 2009.

14. Gershon 2000, 99.

15. Sahlins 1965, 147–48.

16. Kitching 1980.

17. Hart 1988.

18. Green 2019.

19. Neumark 2017.

20. Microsave 2019.

Chapter 9: Reimagining Debt

1. Hayes 2017; Schuster 2015, 138–40.

2. Zelizer 2005, 37.

3. Cull, Demirguc-Kunt, and Morduch 2012, 3.

4. Fouillet et al. 2013; Garikipati 2013; Banerjee et al. 2015; Garikipati et al. 2017.

5. Hickel 2015; Kar 2018, 18; Roodman 2011.

6. Bylander 2014; Stoll 2012.

7. Elyachar 2010; Schuster 2015, 138–39.

8. Karim 2011; Guérin 2014; Guérin, Morvant-Roux, and Villarreal 2013.

9. See also Kar 2018, 203.

10. Innovations for Poverty Action webinar, March 24, 2017.

11. CGAP 2017a; CGAP 2017b.

12. Gates Foundation 2015, 2.

13. Green 2019.

14. See a review in Chapter 4.

15. CGAP 2016a; Microsave 2019; Microsave 2017.

16. CGAP 2019b.

17. CGAP 2019b.

18. Roy 2010, 54.

19. Guérin 2014.

20. Guérin, Kumar, and Venkatasubramanian 2017.

21. Zelizer 2000, 388.

22. Maurer 2015, 70–71.

23. Tuwei 2018, 129, 131.

24. See a review in Bahre 2020; Guérin, Kumar, and Agier 2013.

Chapter 10: Reimagining Giving

1. Tooker and Clarke 2018.

2. https://blog.fundly.com/crowdfunding-statistics/#general/.

3. Interview with Ma Boyang and Gong Chen of Drop of Water, July 28, 2018.

4. Ndemo and Weiss 2017.

5. Personal vehicles are quite rare in Kenya, where, according to the World Bank, there are only 29 vehicles (including public vehicles) per 1,000 people.

6. Johnson, Stevenson, and Letwin 2018; Kneese 2018.

7. Bornstein 2009.

8. Cox et al. 2018; Farnel 2015; Paulus and Roberts 2017.

9. Berliner and Kenworthy 2017; Kenworthy 2019.

10. Bornstein 2009.

11. Aina and Moyo 2013.

12. Changa Labs 2015, 1.

13. Changa Labs 2015, 1.

14. Prahalad 2005.

15. Kuriyan, Nafus, and Mainwaring 2012; Schwittay 2011; Toyama 2015.

16. IMTFI 2010.

17. Thaler and Sunstein 2009.

18. Johnson 2016, 84.

19. Mullainathan and Shafir 2013.

20. Aron, Aron and Smollan 1992.

21. Hart 1988; Mayer, Davis, and Schoorman 1995.

22. Thaler 2015.

23. Schwittay 2014.

24. Thinkplace 2016.

25. Schwittay 2014, 43.

26. Maurer 2017.

27. Dr. Mullei's story of the evolution of money is featured in Chapters 1 and 5.

28. Waigi 2017, 222–23.

29. But see Jimenez 2011; Strathern 2000.

30. Poggiali 2016; Mahoney 2017.

31. Mahoney (2017, 154–57) discusses the irony of transparency, in particular how hiding and obfuscating information is important to practices of "transparency" with digital media in Kenya.

32. Kusimba, Kunyu, and Mark 2016. A study of U.S. crowdfunding on Kickstarter found that women entrepreneurs also benefited from the stereotype that they were more trustworthy. See Johnson, Stevenson, and Letwin 2018.

33. Mayer, Davis, and Schoorman 1995.

34. FSD Kenya and Bankable Frontier Associates 2017.
35. Tilley 2011.
36. Schwittay 2014, 41–42.
37. La Chaux and Okune 2017, 278.
38. Guyer and Belinga 1995, 106.
39. Aina and Moyo 2013.
40. Tooker and Clarke 2018, 58.
41. Schwittay 2015; Tooker and Clarke 2018.
42. Nelms et al. 2018.
43. Bornstein 2012; Hanson 2015.

Chapter 11: Designs for Wealth-in-People

1. Jack, Ray, and Suri 2013; Suri and Jack 2016.
2. Morawczynski 2009.
3. Traders, including women traders, from the region around Machakos were instrumental in building networks connecting the colonial capital with supplies of foodstuffs and other goods. See Robertson 1997.
4. Kusimba, Kusimba, and Kunyu 2020.
5. https://twitter.com/iam_bett/status/1260933959178784768/.
6. Latour 2005, 48.
7. CGAP 2017b.
8. FSD Kenya, 2019a.
9. Johnson 2016.
10. FSD Kenya 2014, "The Kenya Financial Diaries."
11. Guyer 1981; Guyer 2017; Guyer 2018.
12. FSD Kenya 2014, 29.
13. FSD Kenya 2014, 30.
14. Zelizer 2017, 225.
15. A financial relationship called liability—Schuster 2015, 15.
16. Johnson and Krijtenburg 2018.
17. Kusimba 2018a.
18. Green 2019, 111.
19. Bouman 1995; Ledgerwood and Jethani 2013.
20. Woldmariam et al. (2016) present a set of design principles that allow money to shift back and forth from "segregated and aggregate [to] disclosed and secret" (473).
21. Mahoney 2017, 126–53.
22. Mader 2017; Seamster and Charron-Chenier 2017.
23. Hanlon, Barrientos, and Hulme 2010.
24. Haushofer and Shapiro 2016.
25. Dalinghaus 2019.
26. Straub and Jaros 2019.
27. Morduch and Schneider 2017, 168–69; Atkinson 2019.
28. Johnson 2011.

References

Adebanwi, Wale. 2017. "Approaching the Political Economy of Everyday Life: An Introduction." In *The Political Economy of Everyday Life in Africa: Beyond the Margins*, edited by Wale Adebanwi, 1–31. London: Boydell and Brewer.

Aina, Tade Akin, and Bhekinkosi Moyo. 2013. *Giving to Help and Helping to Give: The Context and Politics of African Philanthropy*. Dakar, Senegal: Trust Africa Foundation and Amalion Publishing.

Ainslie, Andrew. 2014. "Harnessing the Ancestors: Mutuality, Uncertainty, and Ritual Practice in the Eastern Cape Province, South Africa." *Africa* 84 (4): 530–52.

Aker, Jenny C., and Isaac M. Mbiti. 2010. "Mobile Phones and Economic Development in Africa." *Journal of Economic Perspectives* 24 (3): 207–32.

Akrich, M. 1992. "The De-Scription of Technical Objects." In *Shaping Technology/ Building Society*, edited by W. Bijker and John Law, 205–24. Cambridge, MA: MIT Press.

Archambault, Julie Soleil. 2011. "Breaking Up 'Because of the Phone' and the Transformative Potential of Information in Southern Mozambique." *New Media and Society* 13 (3): 444–56.

Aron, Arthur, Elaine N. Aron, and Danny Smollan. 1992. "Inclusion of Other in the Self Scale and the Structure of Interpersonal Closeness." *Journal of Personality and Social Psychology* 63 (4): 596–612.

Atieno-Odhiambo, E. S., and William Cohen. 1989. *Siaya: The Historical Anthropology of an African Landscape*. London: James Currey.

Atkinson, Abbye. 2019. "Rethinking Credit as Social Provision." *Stanford Law Review* 71 (5). https://www.stanfordlawreview.org/print/article/re.

Bahre, Erik. 2020. "Financialization, Solidarity, and Conflict." *Economic Anthropology* 7:159–61.

Bandelj, Nina. 2012. "Relational Work and Economic Sociology." *Politics and Society* 40 (2): 175–201.

Bandelj, Nina, and Frederick F. Wherry. 2011. "Introduction: An Inquiry into the Cultural Wealth of Nations." In *The Cultural Wealth of Nations*, 1–22. Stanford, CA: Stanford University Press.

Banerjee, Abhijit, Esther Duflo, Rachel Glennerster, and Cynthia Kinnan. 2015. "The Miracle of Microfinance? Evidence from a Randomized Evaluation." *American Economic Journal: Applied Economics* 7 (1): 22–53.

Baradaran, Mehrsa. 2015. *How the Other Half Banks: Exclusion, Exploitation, and the Threat to Democracy.* Cambridge, MA: Harvard University Press.

Baumer, Eric P. S., Morgan Ames, Jenna Burrell, Jed R. Brubaker, and Paul Dourish. 2015. "Why Study Technology Non-Use?" *First Monday* 20 (11). https://doi.org/10.5210/fm.v20i11.6310.

Berliner, Lauren S., and Nora J. Kenworthy. 2017. "Producing a Worthy Illness: Personal Crowdfunding amidst Financial Crisis." *Social Science and Medicine* 187:233–42.

Bledsoe, Caroline. 1980. *Women and Marriage in Kpelle Society.* Stanford, CA: Stanford University Press.

Blumenstock, Joshua Evan, and Nathan Eagle. 2012. "Divided We Call: Disparities in Access and Use of Mobile Phones." *Information Technologies and International Development* 8 (2): 1–16.

Blumenstock, Joshua Evan, Nathan Eagle, and Marcel Fafchamps. 2016. "Airtime Transfers and Mobile Communications: Evidence in the Aftermath of Disasters." *Journal of Development Economics* 120:157–81.

Bohannon, Paul. 1959. "The Impact of Money on an African Subsistence Economy." *Journal of Economic History* 19 (4): 491–503.

Bornstein, Erica. 2009. "The Impulse of Philanthropy." *Cultural Anthropology* 24 (4): 622–51.

———. 2012. *Disquieting Gifts: Humanitarianism in New Delhi.* Stanford, CA: Stanford University Press.

Bouman, F. J. A. 1994. "ROSCA and ASCRA: Beyond the Financial Landscape." In *Financial Landscapes Reconstructed: The Fine Art of Mapping Development*, edited by F. J. A. Bouman and O. Hospes, 375–94. Westview Press.

———. 1995. "Rotating and Accumulating Savings and Credit Associations: A Development Perspective." *World Development* 23 (3): 371–84.

Bourdieu, Pierre. 1985. "The Forms of Capital." In *Handbook of Theory and Research for the Sociology of Education*, edited by John Richardson, 241–58. New York: Greenwood Press.

Bruijn, Mirjam de. 1997. "The Hearthhold in Pastoral Fulbe Society, Central Mali: Social Relations, Milk, and Drought." *Africa* 67 (4): 625–51.

Bryceson, D. F. 2002. "The Scramble in Africa: Reorientating Rural Livelihoods." *World Development* 30 (5): 725–39.

Burns, Scott. 2018. "M-Pesa and the 'Market-Led' Approach to Financial Inclusion." *Economic Affairs* 38 (3): 406–21.

Burrell, Jenna. 2010. "Evaluating Shared Access: Social Equality and the Circulation of Mobile Phones in Rural Uganda." *Journal of Computer-Mediated Communication* 15 (2): 230–50.

———. 2016. "Material Ecosystems: Theorizing (Digital) Technologies in Socioeconomic Development." *Information Technologies and International Development* 12 (1): 1–13.

Bylander, Maryann. 2014. "Borrowing across Borders: Migration and Microcredit in Rural Cambodia." *Development and Change* 45 (2): 284–307.

Camner, G., C. Pulver, and E. Sjöblom. 2009. *What Makes a Successful Mobile Money Implementation? M-PESA in Kenya and Tanzania.* Nairobi: FSD Kenya.

CGAP. 2013. "Rural versus Urban Mobile Money Use: Insights from Demand-Side Data." *CGAP* (blog). http://www.cgap.org/blog/rural-vs-urban-mobile-money-use-insights-demand-side-data/.

———. 2015. "How M-Shwari Works: The Story So Far." *CGAP* (blog). http://www.cgap.org/publications/how-m-shwari-works-story-so-far/.

———. 2016a. "Digital Credit in Kenya: Time for Celebration or Concern?" *CGAP* (blog). http://www.cgap.org/blog/digital-credit-kenya-time-celebration-or-concern/.

———. 2016b. "The Proliferation of Digital Credit Deployments." *CGAP* (blog). http://www.cgap.org/publications/proliferation-digital-credit-deployments/.

———. 2016c. "Time to Take Data Privacy Concerns Seriously in Digital Lending." *CGAP* (blog). http://www.cgap.org/blog/time-take-data-privacy-concerns-seriously-digital-lending/.

———. 2017a. "How Social Norms Affect Women's Financial Inclusion." *CGAP* (blog).

———. 2017b. "Social Norms Change for Women's Financial Inclusion." Washington, DC.

———. 2019a. "Great Expectations: Fintech and the Poor." *CGAP* blog. https://www.cgap.org/blog/great-expectations-fintech-and-poor/.

———. 2019b. "We Need to Talk about Credit." *CGAP* (blog). https://www.cgap.org/blog/we-need-talk-about-credit/.

Changa Labs. 2015. "Catalyzing Community Fundraising at Scale via Mobile Mobile Money." Nairobi, Kenya.

Chen, Juyie, Zhifie Mao, and Jack Linchuan Qui. 2018. *Super-Sticky WeChat and Chinese Society.* Bradford, UK: Emerald Press.

Clark, Gracia. 2010. *Onions Are My Husband: Survival and Accumulation by West African Market Women.* Chicago: University of Chicago Press.

Collier, Jane Fishburne. 1988. *Marriage and Inequality in Classless Societies.* Stanford, CA: Stanford University Press.

Collier, Paul. 2007. *The Bottom Billion: Why the Poorest Countries Are Failing and What Can Be Done about It.* Oxford: Oxford University Press.

Comaroff, Jean, and John Comaroff. 2017. "Cattle, Currencies, and the Politics of Commensuration on a Colonial Frontier." In *The Political Economy of Everyday Life in Africa: Beyond the Margins,* edited by Wale Adebanwi, 35–71. London: Boydell and Brewer.

Connolly, Chris. 2014. "The Other Digital Currency: Cryptocurrencies Get All the Attention, but Using Airtime as Currency Could Play a Vital Role in Developing the Digital Finance Ecosystem." *Next Billion* (blog). 2014. https://nextbillion.et/the -other-digital-currency/.

Cooper, Barbara M. 1995. "Women's Worth and Wedding Gift Exchange in Maradi, Niger, 1907–89." *Journal of African History* 36 (1): 121–40.

Cooper, Elizabeth. 2018. "Beyond the Everyday: Sustaining Kinship in Western Kenya." *Journal of the Royal Anthropological Institute* 24 (1): 30–46.

Cooper, Frederick. 2017. "From Enslavement to Precarity? The Labour Question in African History." In *The Political Economy of Everyday Life in Africa:Beyond the Margins*, edited by Wale Adebanwi, 136–56. London: Boydell and Brewer.

Couldry, Nick, and Ulises Mejias. 2019. *The Costs of Connection: How Data Is Colonizing Human Life and Appropriating It for Capitalism*. Stanford, CA: Stanford University Press.

Cox, Joe, Thang Nguyen, Andy Thorpe, Alessio Ishizaka, Salem Chakhar, and Liz Meech. 2018. "Being Seen to Care: The Relationship between Self-Presentation and Contributions to Online Pro-Social Crowdfunding Campaigns." *Computers in Human Behavior* 83:45–55.

Cull, Robert, Asli Demirguc-Kunt, and Jonathan Morduch. 2012. Introduction to *Banking the World: Empirical Foundations of Financial Inclusion*, edited by Robert Cull, Asli Demirguc-Kunt, and Jonathan Morduch, 1–16. Cambridge, MA: MIT Press.

Dalinghaus, Ursula. 2019. *Virtually Irreplaceable: Cash as Public Infrastructure*. Irvine, CA: Cashmatters and IMTFI.

Daloz, Jean-Pascal. 2003. "Big Men in Sub-Saharan Africa: How Elites Accumulate Positions and Resources." *International Studies in Sociology and Social Anthropology* 2 (1): 271–85.

Develtere, Patrick, Ignace Pollet, and Frederick O. Wanyama. 2008. *Cooperating Out of Poverty: The Renaissance of the African Cooperative Movement*. Geneva, Switzerland: International Labour Office, World Bank Institute.

Deville, Joe. 2016. "The Matter of Payment." In *The Book of Payments*, edited by B. Batiz-Lazo and L. Efthymiou, 187–99. London: Palgrave Macmillan.

———. 2020. "Digital Subprime: Tracking the Credit Trackers." In *The Sociology of Debt*, edited by Mark Featherstone. Bristol, UK: Policy Press.

Donner, Jonathan. 2009. "Blurring Livelihoods and Lives: The Social Uses of Mobile Phones and Socioeconomic Development." *Innovations: Technology, Governance, Globalization* 4 (1): 91–101.

Drouillard, Marissa. 2017. "Addressing Voids: How Digital Start-ups in Kenya Create Market Infrastructure." In *Digital Kenya: An Entrepreneurial Revolution in the Making*, edited by Bitange Ndemo and Tim Weiss, 97–122. London: Palgrave Macmillan.

Durham, Deborah, and Jacqueline Solway. 2017. *Elusive Adulthoods: The Anthropology of New Maturities*. Bloomington: Indiana University Press.

Duvendack, Maren, and Philip Mader. 2019. "Impact of Financial Inclusion in Low- and Middle-Income Countries: A Systematic Review of Reviews." *Campbell Corporation Reviews*, 1–57.

The Economist. 2018. "In South Africa, More People Have Loans than Jobs: Household Debt Is Hobbling the Black Middle Class." https://www.economist.com/middle-east-and-africa/2.

Ekejiuba, Felicia. 2005. "Down to Fundamentals: Women-Centered Hearth-Holds in Rural West Africa." In *Readings in Gender in Africa*, edited by Andrea Cornwall, 41 46. Bloomington: Indiana University Press.

Elyachar, Julia. 2010. "Phatic Labor, Infrastructure, and the Question of Empowerment in Cairo." *American Ethnologist* 37 (3): 452–64.

Enfield, N. J. 2017. "Distribution of Agency." In *Distributed Agency*, edited by N. J. Enfield and Paul Kockelman, 9–14. Oxford: Oxford University Press.

English-Lueck, J. A. 2017. *Cultures@SiliconValley*. Stanford, CA: Stanford University Press.

Farnel, Megan. 2015. "Kickstarting Trans: The Crowdfunding of Gender/Sexual Reassignment Surgeries." *New Media and Society* 17 (2): 215–30.

Fergus, Devin. 2018. *Land of the Fee: Hidden Costs and the Decline of the American Middle Class*. Oxford, UK: Oxford University Press.

Ferguson, James. 2015. *Give a Man a Fish: Reflections on the New Politics of Distribution*. Durham, NC: Duke University Press.

Financial Health Network. 2019. "U.S. Financial Health Pulse." Chicago.

Fine, Ben. 2010. "Locating Financialisation." *Historical Materialism* 18 (2): 97–116.

Fouillet, Cyril, Marek Hudon, Barbara Harriss-White, and James Copestake. 2013. "Microfinance Studies: Introduction and Overview." Supplement, *Oxford Development Studies*: S1–16.

FSD Kenya. 2014. *Kenya Financial Diaries: Shilingi Kwa Shilingi: Financial Lives of the Poor*. Nairobi: Financial Sector Deepening Kenya.

———. 2016. *2016 FinAccess Household Survey*. Nairobi: Financial Sector Deepening Kenya.

———. 2019a. *2019 FinAccess Household Survey: Access, Usage, Quality, Impact*. Nairobi: Financial Sector Deepening Kenya.

———. 2019b. *Digital Credit Audit Report: Evaluating the Conduct and Practice of Digital Lending in Kenya*. Nairobi: Financial Sector Deepening Kenya.

FSD Kenya and Bankable Frontier Associates. 2017. "Engaging Social Networks for School Fees Payments: Lessons from an Experiment in Kenya." Nairobi.

Gajjala, Radhika, and Dinah Tetteh. 2014. "Relax, You've Got M-PESA: Leisure as Empowerment." *Information Technologies and International Development* 10 (3): 31–46.

Galaty, John G. 2014. "Animal Spirits and Mimetic Affinities: The Semiotics of Intimacy in African Human/Animal Identities." *Critique of Anthropology* 34 (1): 30–47.

Garikipati, Supriya. 2013. "Microcredit and Women's Empowerment: Have We Been Looking at the Wrong Indicators?" Supplement, *Oxford Development Studies*, no. S1: S53–75.

Garikipati, Supriya, Susan Johnson, Isabelle Guérin, and Ariane Szafarz. 2017. "Microfinance and Gender: Issues, Challenges and the Road Ahead." *Journal of Development Studies* 53 (5): 641–48.

Gates Foundation. 2015. "Putting Women and Girls at the Center of Development." http://gcgh.grandchallenges.org/GCGHDocs/WGCD_RFP.

Geertz, Clifford. 1998. "Deep Hanging Out." *New York Review of Books* 45 (16): 69–72.

Gell, Alfred. 1998. *Art and Agency: An Anthropological Theory.* Oxford, UK: Clarendon Press.

Gershon, Ilana. 2000. "How to Know When Not to Know: Strategic Ignorance When Eliciting for Samoan Migrant Exchanges." *Social Analysis: The International Journal of Social and Cultural Practice* 44 (2): 84–105.

Geschiere, Peter. 2009. *The Perils of Belonging: Autochthony, Citizenship, and Exclusion in Africa.* Chicago: University of Chicago Press.

Gluckman, Max. 1972. "Marriage Payments and Social Structure among the Lozi and Zulu." In *Kinship: Selected Readings.* Harmondsworth, UK: Penguin.

Graham, Mark, and Laura Mann. 2013. "Imagining a Silicon Savannah? Technological and Conceptual Connectivity in Kenya's BPO and Software Development Sectors." *Electronic Journal of Information Systems in Developing Countries* 56 (2): 1–19.

Green, Maia. 1999. "Trading on Inequality: Gender and the Drinks Trade in Southern Tanzania." *Africa* 69 (3): 404–25.

———. 2014. *The Development State: Aid, Culture, and Civil Society in Tanzania.* London: James Currey.

———. 2019. "Scripting Development through Formalization: Accounting for the Diffusion of Village Savings and Loans Associations in Tanzania." *Journal of the Royal Anthropological Institute* 25:103–22.

Green, Maia, Uma Kothari, Claire Mercer, and Diana Mitlin. 2012. "Saving, Spending, and Future-Making: Time, Discipline, and Money in Development." *Environment and Planning A* 44 (7): 1641–56.

Gronbach, Lena. 2019. "Financial Inclusion via Social Cash Transfers: The Case of South Africa." In *Digital Finance in Africa's Future,* edited by John Sharp, Lena Gronbach, and Riaan De Villiers, 51–54. Pretoria, South Africa: Human Economy Research Programme, University of Pretoria.

GSMA. 2012. "Sub-Saharan Africa Mobile Observatory 2012." London.

Guérin, Isabelle. 2014. "Juggling with Debt, Social Ties, and Values." *Current Anthropology* 55 (S9): S40–50.

Guérin, Isabelle, Santosh Kumar, and Isabelle Agier. 2013. "Women's Empowerment: Power to Act or Power over Other Women? Lessons from Indian Microfinance." *Oxford Development Studies* 41 (S1): S76–94.

Guérin, Isabelle, Santosh Kumar, and G. Venkatasubramanian. 2017. "The Dangerous Liaisons between Demonetization and the Indian Informal Economy." *IMTFI* (blog). 2017. http://blog.imtfi.uci.edu/2017/02/special-perspectives-series-on.html.

Guérin, Isabelle, Youna Lanos, Sebastien Michiels, Christophe Nordman, and G. Venkatasubramanian. 2017. "Insights on Demonetisation from Rural Tamil Nadu: Understanding Social Networks and Social Protection." *Economic and Political Weekly* 52:44–53.

Guérin, Isabelle, Solène Morvant-Roux, and Magdalena Villarreal. 2013. Introduction to *Microfinance, Debt, and Over-Indebtedness: Juggling with Money*, edited by Isabelle Guérin, Solène Morvant-Roux, and Magdalena Villarreal, 1–23. London: Routledge.

Guyer, Jane. 1981. "Household and Community in African Studies." *African Studies Review* 24 (2/3): 87–137.

——— 1993. "Wealth in People and Self-Realization in Equatorial Africa." *Man*, n.s., 28 (2): 243–65.

———. 1995. "Wealth in People, Wealth in Things: Introduction." *Journal of African History* 36 (1): 83–90.

———. 2004. *Marginal Gains: Monetary Transactions in Atlantic Africa*. Chicago: University of Chicago Press.

———. 2011. "Soft Currencies, Cash Economies, New Monies: Past and Present." *Proceedings of the National Academy of Sciences of the United States of America* 109 (7): 2214–21.

———. 2017. "Survivals as Infrastructure: Twenty-First-Century Struggles with Household and Family in Formal Computations." In *Infrastructures and Social Complexity: A Companion*, edited by Penelope Harvey, Casper Bruun Jensen, and Atsuro Morita, 323–38. New York: Routledge.

———. 2018. "Pauper, Percentile, Precarity: Analytics for Poverty Studies in Africa." *Journal of African History* 59 (3): 437–48.

Guyer, Jane, and Samuel Belinga. 1995. "Wealth in People as Wealth in Knowledge : Accumulation and Composition in Equatorial Africa." *Journal of African History* 36 (1): 91–120.

Hakansson, Thomas. 1989. "Family Structure, Bridewealth, and Environment in Eastern Africa: A Comparative Study." *Ethnology* 28 (2): 117–34.

Hanlon, Joseph, Armando Barrientos, and David Hulme. 2010. *Just Give Money to the Poor: The Development Revolution from the Global South*. Sterling, VA: Kumarian Press.

Hanson, John H. 2015. "The Anthropology of Giving: Toward a Cultural Logic of Charity." *Journal of Cultural Economy* 8 (4): 501–20.

Hart, Keith. 1988. "Kinship, Contract, and Trust: The Economic Organization of Migrants in an African City Slum." In *Trust: Making and Breaking Cooperative Relations*, edited by Diego Gambetta, 176–93. New York: Basil Blackwell.

———. 2001. *Money in an Unequal World: Keith Hart and His Memory Bank*. New York: Texere.

———. 2007. "Money Is Always Personal and Impersonal." *Anthropology Today* 25 (5): 12–16.

Haushofer, Johannes, and Jeremy Shapiro. 2016. "The Short-Term Impact of Unconditional Cash Transfers to the Poor: Experimental Evidence from Kenya." *Quarterly Journal of Economics* 131 (4): 1973–2042.

Hayes, Lauren A. 2017. "The Hidden Labor of Repayment: Women, Credit, and Strategies of Microenterprise in Northern Honduras." *Economic Anthropology* 4 (1): 22–36.

Heald, Suzette. 1990. "Joking and Avoidance, Hostility and Incest: An Essay on Gisu Moral Categories." *Journal of the Royal Anthropological Institute* 25 (3): 377–92.

Hickel, Jason. 2015. "The Microfinance Delusion: Who Really Wins?" *The Guardian*. https://www.theguardian.com/global-development-professionals-network/2015/jun/10/the-microfinance-delusion-who-really-wins/.

Hutchinson, Sharon. 1992. "The Cattle of Money and the Cattle of Girls among the Nuer, 1930–1986." *American Ethnologist* 19 (2): 294–316.

Hyden, Goren. 1980. *Beyond Ujamaa in Tanzania: Underdevelopment and an Uncaptured Peasantry*. Berkeley: University of California Press.

Iazzolino, Gianluca, and Laura Mann. 2019. "Harvesting Data: Who Benefits from Platformization of Agricultural Finance in Kenya?" *Developing Economics: A Critical Perspective on Development Economics*. https://developingeconomics.org/2019/03/29/harvesting-data-who-benefits-from-platformization-of-agricultural-finance-in-kenya/.

Iazzolino, Gianluca, and Nambuwani Wasike. 2015. "The Unbearable Lightness of Digital Money." *Journal of Payments Strategy and Systems* 9 (3): 229–40.

IMTFI. 2010. "Monetary Ecologies and Repertoires: Research from the Institute for Money, Technology, and Financial Inclusion First Annual Report: Design Principles." Irvine, CA.

Ingham, Geoffrey. 2004. *The Nature of Money*. London: Polity Press.

Jack, William, Adam Ray, and Tavneet Suri. 2013. "Transaction Networks: Evidence from Mobile Money in Kenya." *American Economic Review* 103 (3): 356–61.

James, Deborah. 2015. *Money from Nothing: Indebtedness and Aspiration in South Africa*. Stanford, CA: Stanford University Press.

Jenkins, Patrick. 2018. "'We Don't Take Cash': Is This the Future of Money?" *Financial Times Magazine*, May 10, 2018. https://www.ft.com/content/9fc55dda-5316-11e8-b24e-cad6aa67e23e/.

Jeong, Sarah. 2016. "How a Cashless Society Could Embolden Big Brother." *The Atlantic*, April 8. https://www.theatlantic.com/technology/archive/2016/04/cashless-society/477411/.

Jilinskaya-Pandey, Mariya, and Nicolas DeZamaroczy. 2019. "'From That Day Onwards, I Decided I Would Never Again Be in Such a Helpless State': How North Indian Women Safeguard Their Money in Times of Uncertainty." *International Feminist Journal of Politics* 21 (2): 334–42.

Jimenez, Alberto Corsin. 2011. "Trust in Anthropology." *Anthropological Theory* 11 (2): 177–96.

Jindra, Michael, and Joel Noret. 2011. "African Funerals and Sociocultural Change: A Review of Momentous Transformations across a Continent." In *Funerals in Africa: Explorations of a Social Phenomenon*, 11–35. New York: Berghan Books.

Johnson, Cedric G. 2011. "The Urban Precariat, Neoliberalization, and the Soft Power of Humanitarian Design." *Journal of Developing Societies* 27 (3–4): 445–75.

Johnson, Michael A., Regan M. Stevenson, and Chaim R. Letwin. 2018. "A Woman's Place Is in the . . . Startup! Crowdfunder Judgments, Implicit Bias, and the Stereotype Content Model." *Journal of Business Venturing* 33 (6): 813–31.

Johnson, Susan. 2004. "Milking the Elephant: Financial Markets as Real Markets in Kenya." *Development and Change* 35 (2): 249–75.

———. 2012. *The Search for Inclusion in Kenya's Financial Landscape: The Rift Revealed.* Bath, UK, and Nairobi: FSD Kenya and the University of Bath Centre for Development Studies.

———. 2016. "Competing Visions of Financial Inclusion in Kenya: The Rift Revealed by Money Transfer." *Canadian Journal of Development Studies* 37 (1): 83–100.

———. 2017. "We Don't Have This Is Mine and This Is His: Managing Money and the Character of Conjugality in Kenya." *Journal of Development Studies* 53 (5): 755–68.

Johnson, Susan, and Frichte Krijtenburg. 2018. "Upliftment, Friends, and Finance: Everyday Exchange Repertoires and Mobile Money Transfer in Kenya." *Journal of Modern African Studies* 56 (4): 569–94.

Juma, Calestous. 2017. "Leapfrogging Progress: The Misplaced Promise of Africa's Mobile Revolution." *Breakthrough Journal,* Issue 7. https://thebreakthrough.org/index .php/journal/past-issues/issue-7/leapfrogging-progress/.

Kaberuka, David. 2015. "From a Scar on the Conscience of the World to the Most Exciting Continent on the Planet." *The East African.* https://www.theeastafrican.co.ke/ OpEd/comment/AfDB/.

Kar, Sohini. 2018. *Financializing Poverty: Labor and Risk in Indian Microfinance.* Stanford, CA: Stanford University Press.

Karim, Lamia. 2011. *Microfinance and Its Discontents.* Minneapolis: University of Minnesota Press.

Kenworthy, Nora J. 2019. "Crowdfunding and Global Health Disparities: An Exploratory Conceptual and Empirical Analysis." Supplement, *Globalization and Health* 15: S71–84.

Kiiti, Ndunge, and Jane W Mutinda. 2018. "The Use of Mobile-Money Technology among Vulnerable Populations in Kenya: Opportunities and Challenges for Poverty Reduction." In *Money at the Margins: Global Perspectives on Technology, Financial Inclusion, and Design,* edited by Bill Maurer, Smoki Musaraj, and Ivan Small, 66–85. London: Berghahn Books.

Kikulwe, Enoch M., Elisabeth Fischer, and Martin Qaim. 2014. "Mobile Money, Smallholder Farmers, and Household Welfare in Kenya." *PloS One* 9 (10): e109804.

Kilbride, Philip, and Janet Kilbride. 1997. "Stigma, Role Overload, and Delocalization among Contemporary Kenyan Women." In *African Families and the Crisis of Social Change,* edited by Thomas S. Weisner, Candace Bradley, and Philip Kilbride, 208–23. Westport, CT: Bergen and Garvey.

King, Kenneth. 1996. *Jua Kali Kenya: Change and Development in an Informal Economy, 1970–1995.* Columbus: Ohio University Press.

Kinyanjui, Mary Njeri. 2014. *Women and the Informal Economy in Urban Africa: From the Margins to the Centre.* London: Zed Books.

Kitching, Gavin. 1980. *Class and Economic Change in Kenya: The Making of an African Petite Bourgeoisie.* New Haven, CT: Yale University Press.

Klapper, Leora. 2019. "The Global Findex Database Shows We Can't Meet Development Goals without Financial Inclusion." *Next Billion* (blog). https://nextbillion.net/global-findex-sdgs-financial-inclusion/.

Kneese, Tamara. 2018. "Mourning the Commons: Circulating Affect in Crowdfunded Funeral Campaigns." *Social Media and Society* 4 (1): 1–12.

Kopytoff, Igor, and Suzanne Miers. 1977. "African 'Slavery' as an Institution of Marginality." In *Slavery in Africa: Historical and Anthropological Perspectives*, edited by Suzanne Miers and Igor Kopytoff, 3–81. Madison: University of Wisconsin Press.

Kottack, C. 1999. "The New Ecological Anthropology." *American Anthropologist* 101 (1): 23–35.

Kuriyan, Renee, Dawn Nafus, and Scott Mainwaring. 2012. "Consumption, Technology, and Development: The 'Poor' as 'Consumer.'" *Information Technology and International Development* 8 (1): 1–12.

Kusimba, C. M., and C. O. Wilson. 2007. "Contemporary Socio-Economic Dynamics of Bungoma County." Unpublished manuscript.

Kusimba, Sibel. 2018a. "'It Is Easy for Women to Ask!': Gender and Digital Finance in Kenya." *Economic Anthropology* 5 (2): 247–60.

———. 2018b. "Money, Mobile Money, and Rituals in Western Kenya: The Contingency Fund and the Thirteenth Cow." *African Studies Review* 61 (2): 158–82.

———. 2020. "Embodied Value: Wealth-in-People." *Economic Anthropology* 7 (2): 1–10.

Kusimba, Sibel, Gabriel Kunyu, and David Mark. 2016. "Women, Social Capital, and Financial Inclusion: Linking Customer Data with Ethnographic Perspectives." *IMTFI* (blog). http://blog.imtfi.uci.edu/2016/08/women-social-capital-and-financial.html/.

Kusimba, Sibel, Chap Kusimba, and Gabriel Kunyu. 2020. "The War against COVID in Kenya: Will the Social Networks of Mobile Money Survive?" *IMTFI* (blog), May 28. http://blog.imtfi.uci.edu/2020/05/part-2-war-on-covid-in-kenya-will.html?utm_source=feedburner&utm_medium=email&utm_campaign=Feed%3A+ImtfiBlog+%28IMTFI+Blog%29/.

Kusimba, Sibel, Yang Yang, and Nitesh Chawla. 2015. "Family Networks of Mobile Money in Kenya." *Information Technologies and International Development* 11 (3): 1–21.

———. 2016. "Hearthholds of Mobile Money in Western Kenya." *Economic Anthropology* 3 (2): 266–79.

La Chaux, Marlen De, and Angela Okune. 2017. "The Challenges of Technology Entrepreneurship in Emerging Markets: A Case Study in Nairobi." In *Digital Kenya: An Entrepreneurial Revolution in the Making*, edited by Bitange Ndemo and Tim Weiss, 265–89. London: Palgrave Macmillan.

Larkin, Brian. 2013. "The Politics and Poetics of Infrastructure." *Annual Review of Anthropology* 42 (1): 327–43.

Latour, Bruno. 1999. "A Collective of Humans and Non-Humans." In *Pandora's Hope: Essays on the Reality of Science Studies*, 174–93. Cambridge, MA: Harvard University Press.

———. 2005. *Reassembling the Social: An Introduction to Actor-Network Theory*. Oxford: Oxford University Press.

Lauer, Josh. 2020. "Plastic Surveillance: Payment Cards and the History of Transactional Data, 1888 to the Present." *Big Data and Society* (January–June): 1–14.

Ledgerwood, Joanna, and Alyssa Jethani. 2013. "Savings Groups and Financial Inclusion." In *Savings Groups at the Frontier*, edited by Candace Nelson, 13–38. Bourton on Dunsmore, UK: Practical Action Publishing.

LeVine, Robert A. 1973. "Patterns of Personality in Africa." *Ethos* 1 (2): 123–52.

Lijembe, Joseph A., Anna Apoko, and Mutuku Nzioki. 1967. *East African Childhood: Three Versions*. Oxford: Oxford University Press.

Ling, Richard. 2004. *The Mobile Connection: The Cell Phone's Impact on Society*. New York: Morgan Kauffman.

Ling, Richard, and Brigitte Yttri. 2002. "Hyper-Coordination via Mobile Phones in Norway." In *Perpetual Contact: Mobile Communication, Private Talk, Public Performance*, edited by James E. Katz and Mark A. Aakhus, 139–69. Cambridge, UK: Cambridge University Press.

Lipset, David. 2014. "Charon's Boat and Other Vehicles of Moral Imagination." In *Vehicles: Cars, Canoes, and Other Metaphors of Moral Imagination*, 1–17. New York: Berghahn Books.

Loizos, Connie. 2018. "This Young Lending Start-up Just Secured $70 Million to Lend $2 at a Time." *TechCrunch*. March 28, 2018. https://techcrunch.com/2018/03/28/this-young-lending-startup-just-secured-70-million-to-lend-2-at-a-time/.

Lonsdale, John. 1978. "The Economic History of Kenya and Uganda." *Journal of African History* 19 (2): 278–79.

Macharia, Kinuthia. 1997. *Social and Political Dynamics of the Informal Economy in African Cities: Nairobi and Harare*. Ann Arbor, MI: University Press of America.

Mader, Philip. 2017. "Contesting Financial Inclusion." *Development and Change* 49 (2): 461–83.

Mahoney, Dillon. 2017. *The Art of Connection: Risk, Mobility, and the Crafting of Transparency in Coastal Kenya*. Oakland: University of California Press.

Mair, Lucy. 1961. "Clientship in East Africa." *Cahiers d'Etudes Africaines* 6:315–25.

———. 1969. *African Marriage and Social Change*. New York: Routledge.

Malingha, David. 2019. "This Nobel Prize-Winning Idea Is Piling Debt on Millions." *Bloomberg News*. https://www.bloomberg.com/news/articles/2019-08-22.

Mann, Laura, and Elie Nzayisenga. 2015. "Sellers on the Street: The Human Infrastructure of the Mobile Phone Network in Kigali, Rwanda." *Critical African Studies* 7 (1): 26–46.

Manuel, Trevor. 2019. "Keynote Address." 2019. In *Digital Finance in Africa's Future: Innovations and Implications*, edited by J. Sharp, L. Gronbach, and R de Villiers, 13–16. Pretoria, South Africa: Human Economy Research Programme, University of Pretoria.

Mas, Ignacio. 2013. "Better than Cash, or Just Better Cash?" *CGAP* (blog). http://www
.cgap.org/blog/better-cash-or-just-better-cash.

Mas, Ignacio, and Nicholas P. Sullivan. 2011. "Mobile Money as Information Utility
that Touches Everyone." *Innovations: Technology, Governance, Globalization* 6 (4):
17–25.

Matthews, Brett Hudson, and Hawa Nuhu Nyasenga. 2016. "Financial Numeracy in
Tanzania: An Exploratory Study." Toronto, Canada: My Oral Village, Inc. https://
myoralvillage.org/research/publications/.

Maurer, Bill. 2012. "Mobile Money: Communication, Consumption, and Change in the
Payments Space." *Journal of Development Studies* 48 (3): 1–16.

———. 2015. *How Would You Like to Pay?* Durham, NC: Duke University Press.

———. 2017. "Money as Token and Money as Record in Distributed Accounts." In *Distributed Agency*, edited by N. J. Enfield and Paul Kockleman, 110–16. Oxford: Oxford
University Press.

Maurer, Bill, Taylor C. Nelms, and Stephan C. Rea. 2013. "'Bridges to Cash': Channeling Agency in Mobile Money." *Journal of the Royal Anthropological Institute* 19 (1):
52–74.

Mauss, Marcel. 2016. *The Gift*. Chicago: Hau Books.

Mayer, Roger C., James H. Davis, and F. David Schoorman. 1995. "An Integrative Model
of Organizational Trust." *Academy of Management Review* 20 (3): 709–34.

Mbembe, Achille. 2001. *On the Postcolony*. Berkeley: University of California Press.

McIntosh, Janet. 2001. "Tradition and Threat: Women's Obscenity in Giriama Funerary Rituals." In *Gender in Cross-Cultural Perspective*, edited by Caroline Brettell and
Carolyn Sargent, 409–22. Upper Saddle River, NJ: Prentice Hall.

Meagher, Kate. 2010. *Identity Economics*. London: James Currey.

Meiu, George. 2017. *Ethno-erotic Economies: Sexuality, Money, and Belonging in Kenya*.
Chicago: University of Chicago Press.

Microsave. 2017. *Where Credit Is Due: Customer Experience of Digital Credit in Kenya*.
Nairobi: Microsave.

———. 2019. *Making Digital Credit Truly Responsible: Insight from Analysis of Digital
Credit in Kenya*. Nairobi: Microsave and the Smart Foundation.

Morange, Marianne. 2015. "Street Trade, Neoliberalization, and the Control of Space:
Nairobi's Central Business District in the Era of Entrepreneurial Urbanism." *Journal
of East African Studies* 9 (2): 247–69.

Morawczynski, Olga. 2009. "Exploring the Usage and Impact of 'Transformational' Mobile Financial Services: The Case of M-PESA in Kenya." *Journal of Eastern African
Studies* 3 (December 2012): 509–25.

Morduch, Daniel, and Vaclav Jaros. 2019. "Free-Fare Policy as a Tool for Sustainable
Development of Public Transport Services." *Human Geographies: Journal of Studies
and Research in Human Geography* 13 (1): 45–59.

Morduch, Jonathan. 2017. "Economics and the Social Meaning of Money." In *Money
Talks: Explaining How Money Really Works*, edited by Nina Bandelj, Frederick
Wherry, and Viviana Zelizer, 25–38. Princeton, NJ: Princeton University Press.

Morduch, Jonathan, and Rachel Schneider. 2017. *The Financial Diaries*. Princeton, NJ: Princeton University Press.

Mukhulu, Anne-Maria. 2017. "The Debt Imperium: Relations of Owing after Apartheid." In *The Political Economy of Everyday Life in Africa: Beyond the Margins*, edited by Wale Adebanwi, 216–38. London: Boydell and Brewer.

Mullainathan, Sendhil, and Eldar Shafir. 2013. *Scarcity: Why Having Too Little Means So Much*. New York: Henry Holt.

Muniesa, Fabian, Yuval Millo, and Michel Callon. 2007. "An Introduction to Market Devices." Supplement, *Sociological Review* 2, no. S2: S1–12.

Mureithi, Muriuki. 2017. "The Internet Journey for Kenya: The Interplay of Disruptive Innovation and Entrepreneurship in Fueling Rapid Growth." In *Digital Kenya: An Entrepreneurial Revolution in the Making*, edited by Bitange Ndemo and Tim Weiss, 27–43. London: Palgrave Macmillan.

Muthiora, Brian. 2015. "Enabling Mobile Money Policies in Kenya: Fostering a Digital Financial Revolution." Mobile Money for the Unbanked Programme, GSMA. https://www.gsma.com/mobilefordevelopment/resources/enabling-mobile-money-policies-in-kenya-fostering-a-digital-financial-revolution/. London: GSMA.

Nangendo, Steven. 1998. "The Heartbeat and Rhythm of Life: The Cardinal Points in the Socio-Cultural Construction of Bukusu Personhood." *Nordic Journal of African Studies* 7 (2): 39–62.

Ndambuki, Berida, and Claire Robertson. 2000. *We Only Come Here to Struggle: Stories from Berida's Life*. Bloomington: Indiana University Press.

Ndemo, Bitange. 2017. "The Paradigm Shift: Disruption, Creativity, and Innovation in Kenya." In *Digital Kenya: An Entrepreneurial Revolution in the Making*, edited by Bitange Ndemo and Tim Weiss, 1–12. London: Palgrave Macmillan.

Ndemo, Bitange, and Tim Weiss. 2017. *Digital Kenya: An Entrepreneurial Revolution in the Making*. London: Palgrave Macmillan.

Nelms, Taylor C., Bill Maurer, Lana Swartz, and Scott Mainwaring. 2018. "Social Payments: Innovation, Trust, Bitcoin, and the Sharing Economy." *Theory, Culture, and Society* 35 (3): 13–33.

Neumark, Tom. 2017. "'A Good Neighbor Is Not One That Gives': Detachment, Ethics, and the Relational Self in Kenya." *Journal of the Royal Anthropological Institute* 23 (4): 748–64.

Oboler, Regina Smith. 1994. "The House Property Complex and African Social Organization." *Africa* 64 (3): 342–58.

———. 1996. "Whose Cows Are They, Anyway?: Ideology and Behavior in Nandi Cattle 'Ownership' and Control." *Human Ecology* 24 (2): 255–72.5Ogawa, Sayaka. 2006. "Earning among Friends: Business Practices and Creed among Petty Traders in Tanzania." *African Studies Quarterly* 9 (1): 23–38.

Ojong, Nathanael. 2020. *The Everyday Life of the Poor in Cameroon: The Role of Social Networks in Meeting Needs*. New York: Routledge.

Oka, Rahul. 2011. "Unlikely Cities in the Desert: The Informal Economy as Causal Agent for Permanent Urban Sustainability in Kakuma Refugee Camp, Kenya." *Urban*

Anthropology and Studies of Cultural Systems and World Economic Development 40 (3/4): 223–62.

Omwansa, Tony, and Nicholas Sullivan. 2012. *Money, Real Quick*. London: Guardian Books.

Oranye, Nnamdi. 2017. *Taking on Silicon Valley: How Africa's Innovators Will Shape Its Future*. Self-published.

Okoudjou, Dare. 2019. "The Mobile Money Landscape in Africa. In *Digital Finance in Africa's Future: Innovations and Implications*, edited by J. Sharp, L. Gronbach, and R. de Villiers, 18–20. Pretoria, South Africa: Human Economy Research Programme, University of Pretoria.

Owen, Joy. 2015. *Congolese Social Networks: Living on the Margins in Muizenberg, Cape Town*. Lanham, MD: Lexington Books.Pallaver, Karin. 2015. "'The African Native Has No Pocket': Monetary Practices and Currency Transitions in Early Colonial Uganda." *International Journal of African Historical Studies* 48 (3): 471–99.

Park, Emma, and Kevin P. Donovan. 2016. "Between the Nation and the State." *Limn* 7. https://limn.it/between-the-nation-and-the-state/.

Parry, Jonathan, and Maurice Bloch. 1989. "Introduction: Money and the Morality of Exchange." In *Money and the Morality of Exchange*, edited by Jonathan Parry and Maurice Bloch, 1–32. Cambridge, UK: Cambridge University Press.

Paulus, Trena M., and Katherine R. Roberts. 2017. "Crowdfunding a 'Real-Life Super-hero': The Construction of Worthy Bodies in Medical Campaign Narratives." *Discourse, Context, and Media* 21:64–72.

Penwill, D. J. 1951. *Kamba Customary Law*. London: East African Literature Bureau, Macmillan.

Poggiali, Lisa. 2016. "Seeing (from) Digital Peripheries: Technology and Transparency in Kenya's Silicon Savannah." *Cultural Anthropology* 31 (3): 387–411.

Portes, Alejandro. 1998. "Social Capital: Its Origins and Applications in Modern Sociology." *Annual Review of Sociology* 24 (1): 1–24.

Prahalad, C. K. 2005. *The Fortune at the Bottom of the Pyramid*. Upper Saddle River, NJ: Wharton School Publishing.

Pritchard, E. E. 1940. *The Nuer: A Description of the Modes of Livelihood and Political Institutions of a Nilotic People*. New York: Oxford University Press.

Radcliffe-Brown, A. R. 1940. "On Joking Relationships." *Africa* 13:195–210.

———. 1952. "On Social Structure." In *Structure and Function in Primitive Society*, edited by E. Evans-Pritchard and F. Eggan, 188–204. London: Cohen and West.

Ramisch, Joshua J. 2015. "'Never at Ease': Cellphones, Multilocational Households, and the Metabolic Rift in Western Kenya." *Agriculture and Human Values* 33 (4): 979–95.

Rhyne, Elizabeth, and Sonja Kelly. 2018. "Financial Inclusion: Hype versus Reality." Washington, DC: Center for Financial Inclusion.

Riley, Thyra A., and Anoma Kulathunga. 2015. *Bringing E-Money to the Poor: Successes and Failures*. Washington, DC: World Bank Group.

Robertson, Claire. 1997. *Trouble Showed the Way: Women, Men, and Trade in the Nairobi Area, 1890–1990*. Bloomington: Indiana University Press.

Rodima-Taylor, Daivi. 2013. "Gathering Up Mutual Help: Relational Freedoms of Tanzanian Market-Women." *Social Analysis* 57 (3): 76–94.

Rodima-Taylor, Daivi, and Erik Bähre. 2014. "Introduction: Mutual Help in an Era of Uncertainty." *Africa* 84 (04): 507–9.

Roessler, Philip. 2018. "The Mobile Phone Revolution and Digital Inequality: Scope, Determinants, and Consequences." Prosperity Commission Background Paper Series. Oxford, UK: Pathways for Prosperity Commission.

Roodman, David. 2011. *Due Diligence: An Impertinent Inquiry into Microfinance.* Washington, DC: Center for Global Development.

Ross, Marc, and Thomas Weisner. 1977. "The Rural-Urban Migrant Network in Kenya: Some General Implications." *American Ethnologist* 4 (2): 359–75.

Roy, Ananya. 2010. *Poverty Capital.* London: Routledge.

Sahlins, Marshall D. 1965. "On the Sociology of Primitive Exchange." In *The Relevance of Models for Social Anthropology*, edited by Michael Banton, ASA Monographs 1, 139–236. London: Tavistock Publishers.

Schmidt, Mario. 2017a. "'Disordered Surroundings': Money and Socio-Economic Exclusion in Western Kenya." *Africa* 87 (2): 278–99.

———. 2017b. "'Money Is Life': Quantity, Social Freedom, and Combinatory Practices in Western Kenya." *Social Analysis* 61 (4): 66–80.

Schneider, Harold. 1968. "People as Wealth in Turu Society." *Southwestern Journal of Anthropology* 24 (4): 375–95.

———. 1981. "Livestock as Food and Money." In *The Future of Pastoral Peoples: Proceedings of a Conference Held in Nairobi, Kenya, 4–8 August 1980*, edited by John G. Galaty, Dan Aronson, Philip Carl Salzman, and Amy Chouinard, 210–23. Ottawa, Canada: International Development Research Centre.

Schuster, Carolyn. 2014. "The Social Unit of Debt: Gender and Creditworthiness in Paraguayan Microfinance." *American Ethnologist* 41 (3): 563–78.

———. 2015. *Social Collateral: Microfinance in Paraguay's Smuggling Economy.* Berkeley: University of California Press.

Schwittay, Anke. 2011. "The Financial Inclusion Assemblage: Subjects, Technics, Rationalities." *Critique of Anthropology* 31 (4): 381–401.

———. 2014. "Designing Development: Humanitarian Design in the Financial Inclusion Assemblage." *Political and Legal Anthropology* 37 (1): 29–47.

———. 2015. *New Media and International Development: Representation and Affect in Microfinance.* Oxford: Routledge.

Scully, R. T. K. 1974. "Two Accounts of the Chetambe War of 1895." *International Journal of African Historical Studies* 7 (3): 480–92.

Seamster, Louise, and Raphael Charron-Chenier. 2017. "Predatory Inclusion and Education Debt: Rethinking the Racial Wealth Gap." *Social Currents* 4 (3): 199–207.

Sen, Amartya. 2010. "The Mobile and the World." *Information Technologies and International Development* 6 (Special Edition): 1–3.

Senders, Stefan, and Allison Truitt. 2007. Introduction to *Money: Ethnographic Encounters*, 1–14. New York: Berg Publishers.

Servon, Lisa. 2017. *The Unbanking of America: How the New Middle Class Survives*. Reprint. New York: Mariner Books.

Shipton, Parker. 1989. *Bitter Money: Cultural Economy and Some African Meanings of Forbidden Commodities*. Washington, DC: American Anthropological Association.

———. 2007. *The Nature of Entrustment: Intimacy, Exchange, and the Sacred in Africa*. New Haven, CT: Yale University Press.

———. 2010. *Credit between Cultures*. New Haven, CT: Yale University Press.

Simone, Abdoumaliq. 2004. "People as Infrastructure: Intersecting Fragments in Johannesburg." *Public Culture* 16 (3): 407–29.

Smart Campaign. 2017. "Tiny Loans, Big Questions: Consumer Loans in Mobile Credit." Washington, DC: Smart Campaign.

Smith, Daniel Jordan. 2004. "Burials and Belonging in Nigeria: Rural-Urban Relations and Social Inequality in a Contemporary African Ritual." *American Anthropologist* 106 (3): 569–79.

———. 2017. *To Be a Man Is Not a One-Day Job: Masculinity, Money, and Intimacy in Nigeria*. Chicago: University of Chicago Press.

Smith, Stephen, and Jessica Kulynych. 2002. "It May Be Social, but Why Is It Capital? The Social Construction of Social Capital and the Politics of Language." *Politics and Society* 30 (1): 149–86.

Somé, Batamaka. 2013. "'Hot Money': Gender and the Politics of Negotiation and Control over Income in West African Smallholder Households." *Africa* 83 (2): 251–69.

Srinivasan, Janaki, and Jenna Burrell. 2015. "On the Importance of Price Information to Fishers and Economists: Revisiting Mobile Phone Use among Fishers in Kerala." *Information Technologies and International Development* 11 (1): 57–70.

The Standard. 2017. "End of the Road for Mobile Money Defaulters." June 23, 2017.

Stoll, David. 2012. *El Norte or Bust: How Migration Fever and Microcredit Produced a Financial Crash in a Latin American Town*. New York: Rowman and Littlefield.

Stovel, Katherine, and Lynette Shaw. 2012. "Brokerage." *Annual Review of Sociology* 38 (1): 139–58.

Strathern, Marilyn. 2000. "The Tyranny of Transparency." *British Educational Research Journal* 26 (3): 309–21.

Sunderland, Patricia, and Rita Denny. 2016. "Introduction to Section II: Boundaries Breached and Blurred." In *Handbook of Anthropology in Business*, edited by Patricia Sunderland and Rita Denny, 159–66. London: Routledge.

Suri, Tavneet, and William Jack. 2016. "The Long-Run Poverty and Gender Impacts of Mobile Money." *Science* 354 (6317): 1288–92.

Thaler, Richard H. 2015. "Unless You Are Spock, Irrelevant Things Matter in Economic Behavior." *New York Times*, May 8, 2015.

Thaler, Richard H., and Cass R. Sunstein. 2009. *Nudge: Improving Decisions about Health, Wealth, and Happiness*. New York: Penguin.

ThinkPlace. 2016. "User Insights Brief on Initial Research with M-Changa." Nairobi: ThinkPlace.

Tilley, Helen. 2011. *Africa as a Living Laboratory: Empire, Development, and the Problem of Scientific Knowledge, 1870–1950*. Chicago: University of Chicago Press.

Tooker, Lauren, and Chris Clarke. 2018. "Experiments in Relational Finance: Harnessing the Social in Everyday Debt and Credit." *Theory, Culture, and Society* 35 (3): 57–76.

Torkelson, Erin. 2020. "Collateral Damages: Cash Transfer and Debt Transfer in South Africa." *World Development* 126:104711.

Toyama, Kentaro. 2015. *Geek Heresy: Rescuing Social Change from the Cult of Technology*. New York: Public Affairs.

Tronto, Joan. 1993. *Moral Boundaries: A Political Argument for an Ethics of Care*. New York: Routledge.

Tuwei, David Kiplagat. 2018. "Communication Technology, Capabilities, and Livelihoods: The Role of Mobile Money in Facilitating Financial Inclusion and Development in Rural Kenya." Ph.D. diss., University of Iowa.

Waelbers, Katinka. 2009. "Technological Delegation: Responsibility for the Unintended." *Science and Engineering Ethics* 15:51–68.

Wagner, Gunter. 1949. *The Bantu of North Kavirondo*. Vol. 1. Oxford: Oxford University Press.

———. 1975. *The Bantu of North Kavirondo*. Vols. 1 and 2. London: Oxford University Press for the International African Institute.

Waigi, Munyutu. 2017. "Towards Digitizing Information for the Benefit of the Many Rather than the Few." In *Digital Kenya: An Entrepreneurial Revolution in the Making*, edited by Bitange Ndemo and Tim Weiss, 219–23. London: Palgrave Macmillan.

Walsh, Carl E. 1983. "Saving in Primitive Economies." *American Anthropologist* 85 (3): 643–49.

Wandibba, Simiyu. 1985. "Some Aspects of Pre-Colonial Architecture." In *History and Culture in Western Kenya: The People of Bungoma District through Time*, edited by Simiyu Wandibba, 34–41. Nairobi: Gideon Were Press.

———. 1997. "Changing Roles in the Bukusu Family." In *African Families and the Crisis of Social Change*, edited by T. S. Wiesner, C. Bradley, and Philip Kilbride, 332–40. Westport, CT: Bergen and Garvey.

Weisner, Thomas S., Candice Bradley, and Philip L. Kilbride. 1997. *African Families and the Crisis of Social Change*. Westport, CT: Bergin and Garvey.

Weiss, Tim. 2017. "Entrepreneuring for Society: What Is Next for Kenya?" In *Digital Kenya: An Entrepreneurial Revolution in the Making*, edited by Bitange Ndemo and Tim Weiss, 461–85. London: Palgrave Macmillan.

Wherry, Frederick F. 2012. "Performance Circuits in the Marketplace." *Politics and Society* 40 (2): 203–21.

Wherry, Frederick F., Kristin S. Seefeldt, and Anthony S. Alvarez. 2018. "To Lend or Not to Lend to Friends and Kin: Awkwardness, Obfuscation, and Negative Reciprocity." *Social Forces* 98 (2): 753–75.

———. 2019. *Credit Where It's Due: Rethinking Financial Citizenship*. New York: Russell Sage Foundation.

White, Luise. 1990. *The Comforts of Home: Prostitution in Colonial Nairobi*. Chicago: University of Chicago Press.

Whyte, Michael A. 1997. "The Social and Cultural Contexts of Food Production in Uganda and Kenya." In *African Families and the Crisis of Social Change*, edited by Thomas S. Weisner, Candice Bradley, and Philip L. Kilbride, 125–34. Westport, CT: Bergin and Garvey.

Whyte, Susan Reynolds, and Priscilla Wanjiru Kariuki. 1997. "Malnutrition and Gender Relations in Western Kenya." In *African Families and the Crisis of Social Change*, edited by Thomas S. Weisner, Candice Bradley, and Philip L. Kilbride, 135–56. Westport, CT: Bergin and Garvey.

Williams, Brett. 2005. *Debt for Sale: A Social History of the Credit Trap*. Philadelphia: University of Pennsylvania Press.

Woldmariam, Mesfin, Gheorghita Ghinea, Solomon Atnafu, and Tor-Morten Groenli. 2016. "Monetary Practices of Traditional Rural Communities in Ethiopia: Implications for New Financial Technology Design." *Human-Computer Interaction* 31 (6).

Wu, Timothy. 2018. "The Tyranny of Convenience." *New York Times*, February 16, 2018.

Wyche, Susan, and Jennifer Olson. 2018. "Kenyan Women's Realities, Mobile Internet Access, and 'Africa Rising.'" *Information Technologies and International Development* 14:33–47.

Wynne-Jones, Stephanie, and Jeffrey Fleisher. 2012. "Coins in Context: Local Economy, Value, and Practice on the East African Coast." *Cambridge Archaeological Journal* 22 (1): 19–36.

Zelizer, Viviana A. 2000. "Fine-tuning the Zelizer View." *Economy and Society* 29 (3): 383–89.

———. 2005. *The Purchase of Intimacy*. Princeton, NJ: Princeton University Press.

———. 2012. "How I Became a Relational Economic Sociologist and What Does That Mean?" *Politics and Society* 40 (2): 145–74.

———. 2017. *The Social Meaning of Money*. Princeton, NJ: Princeton University Press.

Index

Page numbers in italic indicate material in figures or tables.

Culture and Economic Life

Diverse sets of actors create meaning in markets: consumers and socially engaged actors from below; producers, suppliers, and distributors from above; and the gatekeepers and intermediaries that span these levels. Scholars have studied the interactions of people, objects, and technology; charted networks of innovation and diffusion among producers and consumers; and explored the categories that constrain and enable economic action. This series captures the many angles from which these phenomena have been investigated and serves as a high-profile forum for discussing the evolution, creation, and consequences of commerce and culture.

Black Privilege: Modern Middle-Class Blacks with Credentials and Cash to Spend
Cassi Pittman Claytor
2020

Global Borderlands: Fantasy, Violence, and Empire in Subic Bay, Philippines
Victoria Reyes
2019

The Costs of Connection: How Data Is Colonizing Human Life and Appropriating It for Capitalism
Nick Couldry and Ulises A. Mejias
2019

The Moral Power of Money: Morality and Economy in the Life of the Poor
Ariel Wilkis
2018

The Work of Art: Value in Creative Careers
Alison Gerber
2017